FREE BANKING AND MONETARY REFORM

FREE BANKING
AND
MONETARY REFORM

DAVID GLASNER

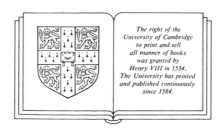

The right of the
University of Cambridge
to print and sell
all manner of books
was granted by
Henry VIII in 1534.
The University has printed
and published continuously
since 1584.

CAMBRIDGE UNIVERSITY PRESS

Cambridge
New York   New Rochelle   Melbourne   Sydney

Published by the Press Syndicate of the University of Cambridge
The Pitt Building, Trumpington Street, Cambridge CB2 1RP
32 East 57th Street, New York, NY 10022, USA
10 Stamford Road, Oakleigh, Melbourne 3166, Australia

First published 1989

Printed in the United States of America

Library of Congress Cataloging-in-Publication Data
Glasner, David.
Free banking and monetary reform / David Glasner.
p.   cm.
Bibliography: p.
ISBN 0-521-36175-3
1. Money supply.   2. Monetary policy.   3. Banks and banking.
1. Title.
HG226.3.G57   1989
332.4'6 — dc19   88–20408
                                                  CIP

British Library Cataloguing in Publication Data
Glasner, David
Free banking and monetary reform.
1. International monetary system. Reform
1. Title
332.4'5

ISBN 0 521 36175 3

For Tovi and Chaya Miriam

Contents

vii

Preface

My aim in writing this book has been to change some deeply entrenched attitudes about monetary institutions and monetary policy. Few tasks of the sovereign state are less controversial than its supposedly exclusive control over the monetary system within its territory. According to a well-established tradition in monetary economics, the provision of money, unlike that of most other goods and services, is somehow incompatible with the operation of competitive forces on which we ordinarily rely. The central theme on which I shall be elaborating in what follows is that monetary theory and monetary policy have mistakenly ignored the crucial role competition could (and to a surprising extent already does) have in modern monetary systems – a role scarcely different from the role it has in the supply of most other goods and services.

Until recently, this notion would have seemed almost bizarre because most economists, whatever their theoretical orientation, insisted on treating the money supply as something over which the government had virtually total control. Although everyone recognized that the private banking system was a creator of money, the behavior of banks was viewed as mechanical, not competitive. The banking system was therefore presumed to be totally subject to the manipulation of government policy makers. Moreover, competitive forces, so much admired by economists in other spheres of economic activity, were viewed by most economists as disruptive of a stable monetary system and, unless systematically extirpated, a source of potentially limitless inflation. (Thus Don Patinkin [1961/1972, p. 33] spoke of "the War of Amalek between economists against bankers with which we feel it our duty to indoctrinate our beginning students.")

Yet hostility to competition in the supply of money was not always the characteristic attitude of economists. Indeed, the ultimate authority figure in economics, Adam Smith, strongly supported free competition in the supply of money. And he was not alone. Most economists in the first half of the nineteenth century took the same position. In fact, both the British and the American monetary systems at the time allowed substantial competition. Although much of the stock of money then consisted of coin minted by the state, private banks were creating banknotes and deposits – with few, if any, restrictions. Trying to describe and analyze that monetary system, Smith and his successors in the classical school went a considerable distance toward working out a monetary theory that was relevant to a system in which money was privately produced under competition.

Yet there were always those economists who, taking their lead from Smith's best friend, David Hume (a monetary theorist of considerable reputation), regarded banks as engines of inflation that had to be rigidly controlled. Since, completely apart from concern about inflation and monetary stability, there are compelling political reasons, which I shall discuss in Chapter 2, for the state to control the monetary system, the British Parliament in 1844 tried to suppress competition in the supply of money. Although the legislation calculated to do this, Peel's Bank Charter Act, restricted the role of private banks in supplying notes, the dominant laissez-faire liberal philosophy of the nineteenth century precluded any restrictions on the creation of deposits. Thus, during the latter part of the nineteenth and the beginning of the twentieth centuries, the dominant monetary theory – the quantity theory of money – did not correspond well to the prevailing monetary institutions. For despite some important restrictions on competition, the supply of money was still largely determined by competitive forces. Meanwhile, economists were adopting a monetary theory that not only ignored the competitive forces still operating but suggested that competition in the supply of money was actually dangerous.

The Great Depression of 1929–33 may have caused a revolution in economic theory, but it only reinforced the antipathy of economists toward competition in the supply of money. Moreover, that cataclysm provided the political impetus for suppressing competition in the supply of bank deposits that, notwithstanding the implications of the quantity theory, had previously been tolerated.

However, this suppression was only temporary. For after gaining absolute control over their monetary systems, governments exploited that control to generate increasing inflation. But high inflation, which raised the cost of holding government-supplied currency or government-regulated deposits, unleashed a competitive response that has overwhelmed the regulatory barriers erected to suppress competition in the supply of money.

Willy-nilly, then, we are again moving toward a world of competitive banking in which the supply of money is competitively determined. Intelligent conjectures about the future evolution of our monetary system must be rooted in an understanding of the forces that determined its past evolution, so in Chapters 1 and 2 I begin by discussing the roles of the market and of the state in the evolution of monetary institutions. Chapter 1 focuses on the market forces that economize on the costs of holding and supplying money. Since market forces alone, without any special role for the state, would suffice to provide the public with a stable medium of exchange, it is my task in Chapter 2 to explain why the state has almost always endeavored to keep control over the suppy of money.

Our understanding of the emerging competitive monetary system will be enhanced if we reconsider the views of Adam Smith and the other classical economists who supported competition in the supply of money, as well as the objections that were then raised against competitive banking. So in Chapter 3 I present the main features of what I call the classical theory of a competitive supply of money, and in Chapter 4 I discuss the alternative theory, the quantity theory, which took a decidedly less optimistic view of competition in monetary affairs. For most of the nineteenth century, it was the quantity theory that inspired most attempts at monetary reform. And it was the misunderstanding of how a competitive monetary system operates that was responsible for the indifferent success of nineteenth-century attempts at monetary reform.

Of course, the key difference between the monetary system we have now and that of the nineteenth century is that ours is not tied to gold or to any real commodity. Chapter 5 describes how the gold standard operated during its heyday between 1879 and 1914 as a truly international monetary system. In Chapter 6 I argue that it was the link to gold, rather than the excesses of competition, that helped cause the Great Depression and the financial collapse that went along with it. The problem with the monetary system of the nineteenth century, which the world tried to resurrect in the 1920s after its collapse in World War I, was that the link to gold exposed the purchasing power of money to fluctuations emanating from changes in the value of gold.

In Chapter 7 I discuss the Keynesian revolution as a response to the Great Depression. Unfortunately, I argue, Keynes learned the wrong lesson from the depression. Instead of confirming him in his previous attachment to price-level stabilization as the goal of monetary policy, the depression led Keynes, in *The General Theory*, to make an unnecessary attack on all aspects of received economic theory. Yet in one respect Keynes continued to follow the trend of economic thinking of his time. For a key element of the new Keynesian theory was the explicit assumption that the nominal quantity of money was a policy instrument under the complete control of the monetary authority. Even when a Monetarist counterrevolution later challenged the new Keynesian orthodoxy, however, it only reinforced the consensus that the monetary system and the nominal quantity of money had to be kept under the strict control of the government.

But as I show in Chapter 8, not only is financial innovation making the monetary system more competitive, but modern monetary theory is finally recognizing the possibility that determination of the supply of money could be safely left to competitive forces. The final three chapters explain how to reform an increasingly competitive monetary and financial system to protect against the danger of banking panics and financial collapse and to ensure macroeconomic stability by stabilizing the price level.

Chapter 9 focuses on the danger that competition would drive banks to adopt unduly risky strategies that might undermine the stability of the banking system and eventually trigger a banking panic. It contends that financial innovation has now created the possibility of a perfectly stable monetary system. But standing in the way is federal deposit insurance, which, instead of safeguarding the banking system, has become the principal threat to its stability.

The other danger we face as we move toward a competitive monetary system is that the monetary authorities may lose control over the price level under the existing fiat monetary standard. Since the largely competitive monetary system of the nineteenth century was undermined (and finally destroyed in the Great Depression of 1929–33) by the instability of the price level under the gold standard, a stable price level is the key requirement for ensuring the success of the emerging competitive system. Ensuring price-level stability, it turns out, is the one exception to my general argument in favor of competition in the supply of money. But the exception, though significant, is a narrow one, analogous to the role of the government in defining weights and measures. And just as the role of the government in defining weights and measures is no argument for it to produce – and certainly not to monopolize the supply of – scales or yardsticks, the role of the government in defining a stable monetary unit is no argument for the government to monopolize the supply of money.

So in Chapter 11 I propose a modified form of currency convertibility that would stabilize the average wage level in the economy and in effect create a kind of labor standard. Free banking under a labor standard would be immune to the threat of financial collapse and avoid the instabilities to which the nineteenth-century gold standard was susceptible while also eliminating the dangers inherent in an unconstrained monetary policy. Such a combination would, I am convinced, provide us with a monetary system far superior to any we have ever had before.

Yet what I hope to achieve in writing this book is not so much a specific set of monetary reforms as a change in attitudes about monetary theory, policy, and institutions. If I do no more than move the discussion of options for monetary policy toward a fuller recognition of the role of competition in the supply of money and of the dangers besetting any monetary system that fails to guarantee the future purchasing power of money, my hopes will have been realized.

Because this book rests on ideas that are both simple and important, I have tried to make it accessible to the largest possible readership. I believe economists and even specialists in monetary and banking theory will find many of the arguments, interpretations, and policy recommendations I am presenting both novel and interesting. But I have been at pains not to write a book that was comprehensible only to other economists. So the book is unencumbered by any mathematical notation and contains only a very few diagrams. Where I have had to enter into technical discussions, I have done my best to explain all technical concepts to those who have the benefit of no previous training in economics. Yet though I have striven always for the utmost clarity of expression, I suspect that few will want to read the book simply for the quality of its prose. On the other hand, anyone interested in the history, evolution, and future development of money and monetary institutions, in the conduct of monetary policy, and in the prospects for monetary reform will, I trust, find this book worth reading.

Virtually all of the book was written before I joined the Federal Trade Commission. The views and opinions expressed here do not necessarily reflect the views of the commission or the individual commissioners.

Acknowledgments

My interest in the notion of a competitive supply of money, which is the unifying idea of this book, was first aroused by Benjamin Klein when I began my graduate studies at UCLA. In 1970 the idea seemed almost heretical. But the notion that the analysis of the supply of money should be carried out within the same theoretical framework that we use to analyze the supply of other goods was a compelling one. And at a time when the search for the microfoundations of macroeconomics was just starting, a suggestion for extending that search from the supply of labor to the supply of money was a hard one to resist.

I soon found out that another young member of the UCLA faculty, Earl Thompson, was, like Klein, working on the idea of a competitive money supply. Although their basic approaches, which had been conceived independently, were similar, they emphasized very different issues. Klein, whose primary interest was in industrial organization, worked out the theory of a competitive money supply within the framework of partial equilibrium analysis. Thompson, however, worked out the theory within a general equilibrium model and showed how crucial the money-supply process is for a variety of macroeconomic issues. And he also suggested what for me has become a central point: the importance of a competitive paradigm in the work of many of the classical economists.

Thus my two greatest intellectual debts in writing this book are owed to Ben Klein and, especially, to Earl Thompson. Indeed, much of this book can be viewed as my attempt to work out for myself ideas that were first suggested to me by Thompson, the most creative economist I have ever met. Most of the important ideas in this book – the national defense rationale for the state monopoly over money, the reinterpretation of classical monetary theory, the explanation of the Great Depression, and the proposal for monetary reform based on a labor standard – were suggested to me by Thompson. My gratitude to him for his inspiration and encouragement since my days as a graduate student is more than I can express.

My interest in the notion of a competitive money supply was further stimulated by F. A. Hayek when he began writing about the possibility of competing currencies in the mid-1970s. Although I now believe that Hayek erred in asserting that completely free banking would lead private producers to introduce their own new stable monetary units, I remain indebted to him for his daring and ingenious exploration of that possibility and for helping to make currency competition a respectable notion among monetary economists. And I still recall with pleasure the lively conversations about classical monetary theory, competing currencies, and other topics that I was fortunate enough to have had with Professor Hayek in the summer of 1977 when we were both visiting the Institute for Humane Studies in Menlo Park, California.

Axel Leijonhufvud taught me much of what I know about monetary theory and macroeconomics. His important work on the costs of inflation and the concept and role of a monetary regime was particularly valuable to me in writing Chapters 10 and 11.

I am also indebted to many others who assisted me while I wrote this book. David Laidler has for years been a welcome and unfailing source of advice, encouragement, and friendly criticism. His comments on early drafts of Chapters 3, 4, 5, and 6 were extremely helpful. Anna Schwartz has been a similarly helpful and friendly critic, and her comments on the entire manuscript aided me greatly as I revised it. An extended correspondence with Charles Goodhart helped me think through the analysis of how a competitive monetary system would work. And the paper he wrote (Goodhart 1987b) for the Manhattan Institute/Liberty Fund Conference I organized in March 1986 inspired my proposal in Chapter 9 for eliminating deposit insurance. Harvey Segal, who spent a year at the Manhattan Institute while I was writing the book, read at least one and often two drafts of every chapter. His enthusiasm for the project never flagged and his advice and suggestions were uniformly worthwhile.

Arthur Bloomfield, Phil Cagan, and Larry White read drafts of several chapters and provided me with detailed comments on them for which I am grateful. Kevin Dowd and George Selgin read the entire manuscript and offered numerous helpful comments and suggestions. They kindly allowed me to read the manuscripts of their own new books, which also explore the theory of free banking and (I am pleased to report) reach broadly similar conclusions (Selgin 1988; Dowd 1989). Two anonymous reviewers also provided helpful comments and criticisms for which I am most grateful. Janis Bolster provided me with her very skillful and astute editorial services, and I thank her for helping me to say what I wanted to as clearly as possible.

Acknowledgments

As a fellow of the Lehrman Institute in 1985–86, I gave seminars in April and May of 1986 on drafts of Chapters 5, 6, and 8 and an early draft of what grew into Chapters 9, 10, and 11. I should like to thank Nick Rizopoulos, director of the Lehrman Institute, for organizing the seminars, and Annabel Alafriz for taking copious notes of the discussions. Thanks are also due to Larry White and Dick Zecher, who served as chairmen for the seminars, and to all the other participants, including Fischer Black, Phil Cagan, Barry Eichengreen, Heywood Fleisig, Robert Greenfield, Tom Huertas, Jim Lothian, Mark Miles, Robert Mundell, Anna Schwartz, and Harvey Segal. I also thank the Lehrman Institute for supporting my research.

In January 1988, I discussed Chapter 9 at a seminar held at the Federal Reserve Bank of Cleveland. The discussion was extremely helpful to me in making the final revisions of that chapter. I thank all those who attended the seminar for their stimulating comments.

It goes without saying, however, that responsibility for any errors that remain in this volume is mine alone.

Most of the book was written while I was a senior fellow at the Manhattan Institute. I am most grateful to the Institute and particularly to Bill Hammett, its President, for seeing the importance of the book and providing me the opportunity to devote myself to writing it. I also thank Larry Mone and Wally Olson for their assistance to me while at the Institute. My fellowship was partially underwritten by a grant from the Earhart Foundation for which I am greatly indebted.

"The last is most dear." My most special thanks go to Tovi and Chaya Miriam, to whom this book is dedicated, for making it all worthwhile.

PART I

A theory of monetary institutions

I

The evolution of money and banking

> One of the chief things which monetary theory ought to explain is the evolution of money. If we can reduce the main lines of that evolution to a logical pattern, we shall not only have thrown light upon history, we shall have deepened our understanding of money, even modern money, itself.
>
> J. R. Hicks, *A Theory of Economic History*

Money – general purchasing power over goods – is surely among the most remarkable products of human civilization. Without it, the incredibly complex division of labor that provides us with the highest standard of living in human history would be unthinkable. I propose in this book to make the workings of the increasingly sophisticated and complex monetary system that is an integral part of our modern economy somewhat more comprehensible. That task can be made a bit less daunting if we follow J. R. Hicks's advice and begin by trying to understand the forces that determined the early evolution of money and banking. Once we understand those forces, we shall have gone a long way toward understanding more recent monetary developments.

From the earliest times, thinkers have been perplexed by this peculiar artifact of civilization. Although no one doubts the usefulness of money, why people began using money in the first instance is not at all obvious.

For an object – be it a coin, a banknote, a check, or government currency – to be a medium of exchange, people must find it acceptable in exchange. They must accept the object even though it has no use of its own except to be passed on to someone else in exchange for a commodity that does have a real use of its own.

Why do people accept money if it has no intrinsic use except to be exchanged again? Obviously because we all expect that we shall later be able to use the money to buy something else we want more urgently than we want whatever we are giving up now.

3

But here is the problem. Since no one would expect to be able to use money in exchange unless everyone else was already accepting it, what made people start accepting it in the first place? How does money differ from a gigantic chain letter?

The most popular solution to this puzzle, going back to ancient times, has been to say that money was instituted by a sovereign authority who could force his subjects to accept whatever he designated as money. Plato and Aristotle both taught that money was instituted by the will of the sovereign lawgiver.[1] Other ancient and medieval philosophers and legal authorities followed their teaching that money was the creation of the sovereign.[2] The explanation was changed somewhat in form, but not really in substance, by Rousseau, who attributed all human institutions to a social contract individuals entered into when they abandoned a state of nature for a civil society. And at the beginning of the twentieth century, the German economist G. F. Knapp, adorning this explanation with the trappings of Hegelian philosophy, elaborated on it at excessive length in an unjustly famous book, *The State Theory of Money* (1905/1924).

These traditional accounts of the origins of money are refuted by both economic theory and historical research. Money was not deliberately invented by anyone, nor did it originate in a collective agreement that committed everyone to accept it in exchange for real goods. In fact, money emerged gradually and spontaneously. No one foresaw its beneficial effects for society. Rather, it emerged simply as an unintended consequence of the self-interested behavior of countless individuals.

But what about the paradox we just encountered? Why would people accept something that provides them no direct benefit in exchange for intrinsically useful commodities unless a prior agreement or edict assured them that everyone else would also accept the object in exchange?

The answer was first provided by the nineteenth-century economist Carl Menger (1892; 1871/1981, chap. 8). Menger's explanation follows directly from the insight that even in a premonetary economy with no single generally accepted medium of exchange, some commodities would still be more easily marketable than others.

---

1 Plato called money a "token for purposes of exchange" (*Republic* II.371). Aristotle held that money originated by convention, not by nature but by law (*Nichomachean Ethics* V.1133a.29–32). And in his *Politics* (i.9.1257a.36–40) he said that "men agreed to employ in their dealings with each other something . . . for example iron, silver, and the like," and proposed this as an explanation of the origin of money.

2 The Roman jurist Paulus wrote that to overcome the difficulties of barter, "a substance was selected whose *public* evaluation exempted it from the fluctuations of the other commodities, thus giving it an always stable external (nominal) value. A mark (of its external value) was stamped upon this substance by society. Hence its exchange value is based, not upon the substance itself, but upon its nominal value" (quoted in Menger 1871/1981, p. 316). Nicole Oresme, Bernardo Davanzatti, and numerous other medieval writers reiterated the classical position.

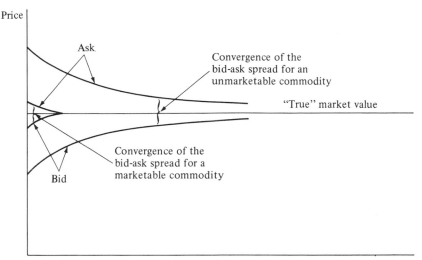

Figure 1. Convergence of the bid-ask spread

What do I mean by saying that some commodities are more market-able than others? All commodities are marketable in some degree, since one can always buy or sell a commodity in an instant if one will pay a high enough, or take a low enough, price for it. "Marketability" there-fore refers to the spread between the prices at which any commodity can be bought or sold at any moment. That gap is known as the "bid-ask spread." Ordinarily, a seller will obtain a higher price and a buyer will find a lower price by waiting or searching for additional offers rather than agreeing to the first offer made. The longer one waits or searches, the better one's chance of trading at the best possible price. Thus the bid-ask spread for any commodity converges over time to its "true" or "equi-librium" market value.

For some commodities, though, the bid-ask spread is narrower, and converges to the equilibrium value faster, than for others (see Figure 1). The bid-ask spread for a thousand bushels of winter wheat on the Chi-cago Board of Trade is obviously narrower and converges faster (both absolutely and as a percentage of the true market value) than the bid-ask spread for, say, the Empire State Building. No one, I daresay, would deny that a thousand bushels of wheat are more marketable than the Empire State Building.

What characteristics make one commodity more marketable than an-other? Obviously, marketability is related to the number of potential buyers and sellers of a commodity and to how easily they can communicate with each other. The better communication is between the potential buyers

5

and sellers of a given commodity, the more marketable that commodity is. Similarly, the more potential suppliers and demanders there are, the cheaper transportability and storability are, and the easier divisibility is, the greater the marketability of a commodity will be.

Think of what a premonetary economy must have been like. With no commodity generally used as money, trading was costly and time-consuming. In those circumstances, some alert people realized that they could benefit by holding greater stocks of the most marketable commodities than they had immediate use for. Thus they would accept highly marketable commodities in exchange even when they really wanted something else, because marketable commodities could be exchanged quickly on reasonable terms for what they did want. Extra stocks of highly marketable goods increased the chances of acquiring desired goods on favorable terms.

When some people began to realize the advantages of holding extra stocks of easily marketable commodities, two consequences followed. First, observing the success of their more alert and innovative neighbors, others began adding to their stocks of these commodities. Second, as more people began trading them, the commodities became even more marketable, so that the incentive to increase holdings of them kept growing.

We can now begin to see how one or, at most, a very few commodities would gradually and spontaneously emerge as money in any economy in which there is trade. A fascinating account of this process was given by R. A. Radford (1945), who described how cigarettes emerged as a medium of exchange in a POW camp in World War II. Moreover, the process reinforces itself because it constantly adds to the marketability of the most marketable commodities.

Money, therefore, did not originate in a deliberate decision taken at a particular moment by a single individual or by an entire community. It emerged as the unintended consequence of a multitude of individual decisions. What concerned people was the relative marketability of various commodities, the relative costs of trading them, and the relative costs of holding inventories of those commodities.

In primitive societies passing from a nomadic economy to agriculture, domestic animals seem to have served as money. They had a variety of uses, were demanded by almost everyone, were not too expensive to transport, were durable stores of value, and so long as cattle could be kept out of doors and land was freely available, were not too costly to hold. Even after precious metals displaced cattle as money, a remnant of earlier moneys was often preserved by stamping the image of an animal on minted coins. The origins of money are also evidenced in our language: The word "pecuniary" is derived from the Latin *pecu*, which means "cattle."

The evolution of money and banking

Whenever it became less costly to use and hold one potential medium of exchange than the others, the desire to minimize costs led to a switch in the commodity serving as money. When ancient societies began engaging in handicraft as well as simple agriculture, the increasing complexity of economic activity caused metals to replace cattle as media of exchange. The growing number of transactions increased the importance of divisibility as an attribute of money, enhancing incentives for people to use metals in exchange. Since holding cattle was more costly for city dwellers than for those in the country, the emergence of cities and towns greatly reduced the suitability of cattle as money. And as city dwellers began using metals as media of exchange, country folk gradually did too.

Copper and brass may have been the first of the metals to be used as media of exchange, but in the Mediterranean and most other areas, silver quickly became the most widely exchanged metal. Indeed, "silver" and "money" are denoted by the same word in several languages, such as French (*argent*), Greek (*argurion*), and Hebrew (*keseph*).

Only after precious metals had already emerged as media of exchange did coins begin to circulate. Coinage was a successful innovation because it reduced or eliminated costs borne when people traded uncoined metals. The costs were of two types. One was the cost of assaying the metal being exchanged to determine its purity and fineness. The other was that of weighing the metal and dividing it into a weight corresponding to the price agreed on. Because coined metal eliminated or reduced these costs, traders preferred coins to uncoined metal of equal weight and fineness. The role of the mint was, thus, to provide some assurance that the metal being traded was of a prescribed weight and fineness, so that the costs of determining its weight and fineness would not be incurred in each transaction. The premium that minted coin could command over unminted metal of equal fineness reflected this saving.

What gave rise to coinage was not the desire for a more efficient monetary system. It was simply the pursuit of the profit to be earned from the premium coins could command in the market. Nor did coinage arise immediately after precious metals came into use as money; it was only the last of a series of innovations calculated to lower the costs of weighing and identifying pieces of metal used in exchange.

At first, small globs of metal circulated as money. After assaying and weighing them, some merchants would affix markings indicating their weight and fineness. A merchant, seeing his own mark, or that of another merchant he knew, on a piece of copper or silver offered in exchange, avoided the cost of weighing and assaying pieces with no recognizable marking. From these markings followed more formal forms of stamping or "punching." That is when specialized mints began making coins in something like their modern form, a practice which provided some, but

7

scarcely total, safeguard against clipping and sweating (Burns 1927/1969, Selgin and White 1987).

There is a strong reason to suspect that private entrepreneurs began operating mints before governments did. The reason for state involvement was not to improve the monetary system but to raise revenue at a time when the power to tax was not at all well developed.

The role for law or the state in monetary affairs emerges only with the appearance of coinage. But ever since then, the state has sought to control coinage and the monetary system in general (Hicks 1969, pp. 65–66).[3] Why this has been so and how it has influenced the evolution of monetary institutions are questions I address in the next chapter. For now, let me just note that the potential revenue the operator of a mint could collect was such that a private operator could finance a take-over of the primitive state. So it is likely either that private mint owners took over sovereignty themselves or that the incumbent sovereign took over minting in self-defense (Burns 1927/1969, pp. 82–83).

But to show that a special state role, beyond enforcing property rights and contracts, is not essential to the emergence or the functioning of a monetary system, I shall proceed here without considering the role of the state. Coinage was a service that provided a better, more useful money with which people could conduct their business. It required that some agency in whose integrity people had confidence certify that pieces of metal had the stipulated weight and fineness.

Although the desire for profit would have induced private individuals to mint coins of assured weight and fineness, the state might still have had an advantage over private mints in circulating coins. The assurance of the sovereign that his coins were of a stipulated weight and fineness may have been more credible than the promises of private mints. On the other hand, the ban on private mints is itself evidence that they could have competed successfully – perhaps too successfully – with governments had they not been barred from the market.

THE EMERGENCE OF BANKING

Economic development always increases the number and variety of transactions. The greater the number of transactions, the stronger the incentives for reducing the cost of transacting by incurring the start-up costs for various arrangements that facilitate trade. Economic development is thus a major stimulus to monetary innovation. But causation runs in

---

3 See Kraay (1964). Kraay argued that it was because the state insisted that taxes be paid in coin from its own mint that state-operated mints became dominant. This is an idea which will become important for us in later chapters.

both directions here, for monetary innovation is a major factor in economic development (Cameron et al. 1967).

Banking was a successful monetary innovation because it reduced the cost of using and holding money by substituting abstract claims to the concrete physical objects that had previously served as money for the physical objects themselves. As these abstract claims became more widely used, they became money in their own right. This substitution, which continues even now, went along with the evolution of banking – an evolution that can, in fact, be described as a continuing substitution of claims to the primary money for the primary money itself. The substitution allows payments to be made by bookkeeping entries within or between banks instead of between the transactors themselves.

Just when and how banking got started is something we don't know for sure. There is evidence that banks held deposits in ancient Greece and Rome, but we know little about them. Whether they were actually creating deposits or just holding coins and other valuables for safekeeping is still in doubt.[4] But when economic activity in Western Europe and the Mediterranean contracted after the fall of Rome and the Islamic conquests, banking of any kind probably ceased. Eventually, toward the end of the twelfth century, as the Mediterranean trade recovered, banking began to reemerge in Italy, which was then the most economically advanced part of Europe (de Roover 1948, pp. 247–48).[5]

Historians agree that medieval banking grew out of money changing. The word "bank" is itself derived from *bancum* or *bancherium*, both of which mean "table" – a reference to the table behind which money changers used to do business. Many of the Italian city-states, such as Venice, Genoa, and Florence, operated their own mints, and people in one city would frequently receive payment in the coins of another.

Dealing with more than one currency was not the only problem people had to cope with. The currencies were often incoherent mixtures of gold, silver, and copper coins. The disparate coins making up a currency were generally defined in terms of an abstract money of account – a ghost money that legally the various coins were different denominations of (Einaudi 1953). If the market exchange rate between gold and silver was

---

4 Will Durant (1939, p. 590; 1942, pp. 331–32) suggests that banking in both Greece and Rome was highly developed, that banks were sources of credit, paid interest on deposits, had introduced checks, and were making payments on behalf of their customers via book entries. M. I. Finley (1973, pp. 141–42), on the other hand, denies that banks were doing anything other than acting as bailees for their customers.
5 Concrete evidence that deposit banking was being carried on in Italy before 1200 is presented in Reynolds (1938). Reynolds showed that it was customary for merchants to have bank accounts, that they could borrow from bankers by overdrawing their accounts, that credit on the books of banks was transferable, and that there were interbank arrangements that allowed payments to be effected by the transfer of credits between banks.

near the ratio implied by their legal definition, there was no problem. But the market rate usually diverged from the legal rate so that either gold or silver coins were overvalued. "Overvalued" means that the legal value of a coin in discharging an obligation denominated in the money of account exceeded the market value of the metal contained in the coin. In that case, people would seek to pay their obligations in overvalued coins and to hoard undervalued coins. The undervalued coins would tend to disappear from circulation. This tendency is commonly known as "Gresham's Law."

Many people found it convenient to change any coins they received into the particular currency or accounting unit in which they kept their records. This the money changer could do for them. But rather than receive actual coins of that unit, the customer would often prefer to receive a credit for an equal number of currency units on the money changer's books. Since they dealt with many customers, money changers could often discharge payments between customers by transferring credits on their books from the account of one to that of another. Moreover, transfer by book credit saved the time and effort required to inspect and count all the coins required to settle a given transaction.[6] Besides saving the cost of inspecting and counting coins – and, when they were of more than one denomination, agreeing on their value – banks also allowed customers to save the costs of transporting coin or specie, including the cost of safeguarding against robbery or theft.

Once they began accepting, or creating, deposits, it was natural for money changers to begin extending credit also. At first, a money changer might have done no more than create a deposit in, say, ducats, in exchange for florins, even though he did not actually have an equal number of ducats on hand. But, believing that his stock of ducats would enable him to withstand any likely demand by depositors for ducats, the money changer probably perceived little risk in creating the ducat deposit. And the money changer would probably not have felt it risky to allow his best customers occasionally to overdraw their accounts.

6 De Roover (1948, p. 250) aptly describes the difficulties of cash transactions in the Middle Ages: "Mediaeval trade would have been greatly hampered if it had been necessary for all payments to be made in cash. The Venetian Senator Tommaso Contarini goes even so far as to say that trade would have been well-nigh impossible. Because of the great variety of coins in circulation, it was not practical to pay out or to receive large sums without expert advice. If a money-changer were called in for consultation, he would charge a fee for his services. It should also not be forgotten that there existed no bank-notes of large denominations in the Middle Ages. As a result, money-telling, when large sums were involved, represented a considerable waste of time. The businessmen of yesterday, as well as those of today, were pressed for time and were therefore glad to take advantage of the book-transfer system devised by the money-changers. . . . Moreover, the books of the money-changers were public records and there was no need to give acquittance, to have witnesses, or to draw up legal instruments. This facility was great, indeed, and it is not surprising that it was extensively used."

The evolution of money and banking

So money changers gradually developed the business of creating deposits that were not held strictly for safekeeping but were general obligations to pay depositors, or those they designated, on demand. Recognizing that all depositors would not make such demands simultaneously, bankers created deposit entries on their books that exceeded in value the cash reserves they held to redeem them.

The benefits of holding deposits that could be used to make payments obviously increased along with the number of people holding bank deposits and making payments by transfer of bank credits. The more often payments were made in bank by book transfer, the easier it became for people to avoid holding substantial amounts of coin for transactions with people who did not have bank accounts.

At first, such transfers could not be executed unless both parties to the transaction were clients of the same banker. The transfers also had to be made orally in the presence of both parties and the banker (Usher 1943, pp. 6–8). One might have thought that this constraint on the transferability of deposits would have been a serious obstacle to developing a system of payment based on the transfer of book entries in banks and, hence, to the usefulness of bank deposits as a medium of exchange. However, the early banks stood ready to create accounts for the recipients of their clients' payments. Those recipients could then use the new accounts to make payments or withdraw cash until their accounts were exhausted (Usher, pp. 184–85).

As their numbers increased, banks began opening accounts with each other. By doing so, they not only facilitated the mutual clearing of liabilities, they gave each other access to their reserves in times of financial stress (Usher pp. 185–86). Even before the negotiability of bank checks and banknotes was recognized, correspondent accounts enabled banks to clear mutual liabilities and helped to create a system of payment transfers among banks.

Without negotiability, when say Lorenzo di Medici wrote a check to the order of Leonardo da Vinci, only Leonardo, but not Leonardo's bank, could collect from the Medici bank. Direct interbank clearing was not possible. But if Leonardo's bank, say, the Pazzi bank, and the Medici bank held correspondent accounts with each other, the same result could be achieved through a more roundabout process. Lorenzo the Magnificent and Leonardo would appear at the Medici bank and, at Lorenzo's direction, the bank would debit his account to a newly created account in Leonardo's name. Then Leonardo, in the presence of a representative of the Pazzi bank, would direct the Medici bank to debit his newly opened account and credit the Pazzi bank's correspondent account at the Medici bank. On its own books, the Pazzi bank would then debit the Medici bank's correspondent account with it and credit Leonardo's account (de

Roover 1948, pp. 273–76). Although cumbersome, such transactions were not too inconvenient in medieval cities, since the money changers and bankers were all located near one another.

Like the transformation of a highly marketable commodity into money, the development of banking was self-reinforcing. The greater the number of people utilizing banking services, the more useful are bank deposits, and hence the more acceptable they become in exchange. In the fourteenth century it seems that more than 30 percent of the population in some urban areas, including most of the middle classes, held bank accounts (de Roover 1948, pp. 250–56).

We should reflect a moment on the significance of the change I have just described. No longer was the creation of money dependent on the physical costs of producing or mining the commodity serving as the medium of exchange. The transformation of money changers, who merely held deposits in safekeeping, into banks that produced money by creating deposits with the stroke of a pen marked a basic change in the technology of supplying money. Nor, since banking required far more business skill than did operating a mint, was the technology susceptible, like minting, of being copied and taken over by the state.

In creating money without holding an equivalent amount of cash in reserve, banks provided two enormously important services: reducing the social costs of creating money and intermediating between ultimate borrowers and lenders. If banks had merely kept deposits as idle cash in safekeeping, the cost of supplying bank money would have equaled the cost of creating an equivalent amount of cash reserves. In that case, there might have been some gain in convenience, but there would have been no saving in the resources devoted by society to the creation of money. By creating money without holding equivalent cash reserves, banks freed for more valuable uses the capital tied up in holding and producing money.

To whom were those resources made available? To the borrowers whose willingness to borrow at interest made lending more attractive to bankers than holding idle cash reserves. Banks thus became specialists in evaluating borrowers and the investment projects for which they were seeking financing – something they were by no means infallible at doing, but something they were certainly better at than the typical holder of cash.

Before banks appeared on the scene, people who wanted to save either had to hoard their cash or, to earn any interest, had to risk lending it to someone else. Since most savers are not very good at evaluating the likelihood of repayment by the borrower, people usually preferred hoarding money unless an exceptionally high return was promised. With loans available only at high interest rates, investment projects would be undertaken only by those who had extremely profitable opportunities or those who could finance the projects from their own savings.

The evolution of money and banking

Like all middlemen, bankers provided more attractive terms to the ultimate transactors between whom they mediated than those transactors could have obtained otherwise. By distinguishing between good and bad risks and pooling the good ones, banks bore less risk than ultimate lenders would have by lending directly to ultimate borrowers. In so doing, they increased total lending and reduced interest rates to borrowers. And by offering a low-risk way for savers to earn a return on their funds, banks attracted funds that would otherwise have lain idle. Banks thus increased the amount and, above all, the quality of saving and investment, thereby speeding up economic development (Cameron et al. 1967). It is no exaggeration to say that banks converted the holder of money from a miser who diverted costly resources from competing uses to a supplier of the capital that fueled economic growth.

Had banks accepted and maintained only deposits against which they held an equivalent amount of coin or specie in reserve, creating deposits would have been prohibitively costly. Unless cash is appreciating, holding cash reserves is as much a cost of doing business as renting space and paying wages. Exchanging non-interest-bearing cash reserves for interest-bearing assets reduces a bank's costs and allows (or, if banks are competing, forces) it to reduce its charges to customers. Customers respond by increasing their holdings of deposits, a step which enables banks to undertake additional lending.

For reasons I have already mentioned, and for others that will become clear in due course, the operating costs of banks fall as their scale of operations expands. To some extent this is true of a single bank, but it is even more true of the banking system in general. Because economies of scale in banking can only be realized when the demand to hold deposits is increasing, a fall in the cost of holding deposits, which induces people to increase their deposit holdings, makes further reduction in banks' costs possible. Here is another example of the self-reinforcing processes that drive the evolution of monetary institutions.

Having described in a general way how primitive banks evolved, I should now like to go through a simple example to show how a bank would operate in a competitive environment. The example will clarify some key concepts which we shall be coming back to repeatedly in the coming chapters.

A MODEL OF A COMPETITIVE BANK IN A COMPETITIVE BANKING SYSTEM

Let us follow for a while the fortunes of the Bank of Barchester, which has recently opened for business. Suppose the Earl De Guest comes to the bank and asks for a loan of £1,000. (To stay in the spirit of the example, I shall assume that all transactions are carried out in pounds sterling rather than in dollars.) After sizing up the earl, the manager of the bank decides that the earl is a good credit risk and informs his lordship how pleased the bank will be to lend him £1,000 for one year at 10 percent interest. The earl signs a note of indebtedness to the Bank of Barchester, and in exchange he is credited with a £1,000 deposit on which he may draw at will. In other words, the Bank of Barchester is exchanging its IOU (the deposit) for the earl's IOU of £1,100 falling due in one year. The difference between the two IOUs is that the bank's IOU is instantly redeemable and is generally recognized as such, while the earl's IOU cannot be converted into cash for a year. Thus, despite the earl's exalted social status, his IOU lacks the wide acceptability of the bank's IOU.

What is going on will become clear if we look at balance sheets for the bank and for the earl reflecting their financial positions before and after the loan (see Table 1).

Presumably, the earl borrowed from the bank because he wanted funds to make some purchase. The earl's balance sheet shows that although he has a lot of assets, he has little ready cash, so rather than liquidate any of his real or personal property he chooses to take out a loan. It might be that, not having decided exactly what or from whom he wants to buy, the earl wants merely to hold the deposit to have ready funds so that he can make an immediate purchase should he so desire. But for simplicity, let us assume that he immediately spends the £1,000 of Bank of Barchester money by giving the Duke of Omnium a check for £1,000 as payment for ten head of cattle.

What does the Duke of Omnium do with the Bank of Barchester money he receives from the Earl De Guest?

From the bank's point of view, there are two possibilities. Either the Duke of Omnium wants to hold Bank of Barchester money or he doesn't. If he does – that is, if he deposits the check in a new or existing account at the Bank of Barchester – there is no problem for the bank. The bank's balance sheet does not change on the asset side, but on the liability side, the £1,000 it had owed the earl is now owed the duke. However, if his grace does not want, even temporarily, to hold Bank of Barchester money, but prefers to convert it either into the money of another bank (say, the Bank of Allington, at which he already has an account) or into hard cash, things get more complicated for the Bank of Barchester.[7] Either way, the

---

7 If the duke has or opens an account at the Bank of Barchester, but then spends the same amount himself drawing on the Bank of Barchester account, the identical possibilities arise in connection with whomever he is making a payment to. Either that person – say, his agent, Mr. Fothergill – will keep a deposit at the Bank of Barchester or he will not. If he does, the money the bank created continues to be held and the bank need not relinquish any of its interest-earning assets or incur any additional liabilities. If he chooses,

Table 1. *Balance sheets for the Bank of Barchester and the*
Earl De Guest

	Assets (£)		Liabilities (£)	
A. Before loan				
Earl De Guest	Guestwick estate	20,000	Mortgage on	
	Livestock	2,500	Guestwick estate	10,000
	Personal effects	1,000	Owed to local	
	UK bonds	1,000	merchants	500
	Deposit at Bank		Net worth	14,250
	of Barchester	250	Total	24,750
	Total	24,750		
Bank of Barchester	UK bonds	1,000	Deposits	10,000
	Discounted bills	8,000	Paid-in capital	1,000
	Personal loans	2,000	Total	11,000
	Total	11,000		
B. After loan				
Earl De Guest	Guestwick estate	20,000	Mortgage on	
	Livestock	2,500	Guestwick estate	10,000
	Personal effects	1,000	Owed to local	
	UK bonds	1,000	merchants	500
	Deposit at Bank		IOU to Bank	
	of Barchester*	1,250	of Barchester*	1,000
	Total	25,750	Net worth	14,250
			Total	25,750
Bank of Barchester	UK bonds	1,000	Deposits*	11,000
	Discounted bills	8,000	Paid-in capital	1,000
	Personal loans*	3,000	Total	12,000
	Total	12,000		

* Change from status before loan.

Bank of Barchester will have to redeem its IOU when the earl's check is presented either by the duke himself or by the Bank of Allington.

What does the Bank of Barchester do now? If it has been as prudent and as conservative as it has encouraged its customers to think, the bank will be holding cash reserves for just such a contingency. If so, the bank can redeem its obligations without difficulty. But having depleted its cash reserves somewhat, the bank may decide to replenish, at least in part, the cash it has just surrendered. The bank, for example, may liquidate some

instead, to hold the money of another bank, the Bank of Barchester will have to give up an interest-bearing asset or incur additional liabilities. If Mr. Fothergill spends the money, the same question will be raised with respect to someone else. The ultimate question is, therefore, how much Bank of Barchester money the public, on average, will hold.

of its assets, such as IOUs obtained from the public in exchange for its own IOUs. A riskier alternative would be to borrow cash reserves without selling off any assets. Either way, the Bank of Barchester will lose the interest income accruing from the Earl De Guest's IOU (unless the bank can borrow at a lower interest rate than the rate on its loan to the earl).

Of course, the Bank of Barchester may not have been behaving as prudently and conservatively as it wants people to think. In that case, the bank will not have enough cash to redeem its IOUs. To avoid default, the bank will immediately have to borrow or to sell assets to raise enough cash to meet its obligations.

Thus, if no one wants to continue holding the money the bank creates when it lends to the earl, the bank loses all or part of the interest accruing from the loan. And if its cash reserves are inadequate, lending increases the risk of default. So additional lending will not add to a bank's profits unless the public is willing to hold the additional money it creates in making those loans. In other words, the capacity of a bank to lend and, in so doing, to increase the quantity of its outstanding liabilities is strictly constrained by the willingness of the public to hold the money it creates or to provide it capital in some other way, such as buying newly issued stock or long-term bonds.[8] The point is that as an intermediary, the bank can only lend capital that the public is willing in some form to provide to the bank.

What is somewhat special about banks is that they can raise capital by creating a liability that they promise to redeem instantly. This promise allows the liability to function as a medium of exchange. But it is still a liability of the issuing bank, and it cannot provide a safe basis for additional lending by the bank unless the public really wants to hold additional amounts of the bank's instantaneously redeemable liabilities.

It is important to distinguish here between the capacity of a bank to create more money by lending and the profitability of doing so. Obviously, it is the latter, not the former, which determines how far a bank will expand. So let us consider explicitly how profitable the Bank of Barchester is. Suppose that, over a year, the bank can maintain, on average, £10,000 in deposits or, put differently, that the bank can induce the public to hold, on average, £10,000 of deposits at the bank. If it can lend at an interest rate of 10 percent, its revenue over the year will be £1,000.[9]

---

8 Of course, if the bank is very efficient at lending, but does not have the capacity to induce the public to hold its deposits, the bank could increase its lending by raising capital directly from the public by issuing stock or long-term debt or by selling new loans to other banks that are able to induce the public to hold deposits represented by those loans.

9 One might wonder how the bank earns revenue on deposits that were created by a deposit of cash with the bank, not by a loan. But any deposit that is created enables the bank to acquire interest-bearing assets of equal amount. A bank can be thought of as

The evolution of money and banking

Aside from holding non-interest-bearing reserves, what other costs does a bank incur? Primarily wages. Banking is a labor-using activity and, before computers, was even more so. The other principal costs are the rental of space in which to do business and the purchase of materials.

But for now, I shall assume that the Bank of Barchester operates with none of these costs. Although unrealistic, this assumption will focus our attention on the key characteristics of competition in banking. Costless creation of deposits means that the bank holds no non-interest-bearing reserves and that it costs the bank nothing to make loans – either in evaluating borrowers' credit worthiness or in collecting repayment of loans.[10]

However, we cannot assume that everyone is capable of evaluating borrowers and collecting loans at zero cost. If everyone could, there would be no reason for people to prefer payment in bank liabilities to payment in the IOUs of some ordinary individual. Only because evaluating IOUs is costly for most people do they generally prefer the IOUs of a reputable bank to those of just anyone with whom they may be making a transaction.

If the Bank of Barchester operates costlessly, it appears that, since profit equals revenue minus cost, the bank's profit equals its revenue of £1,000 a year. However, such a situation would be unstable for both the Bank of Barchester and the banking system as a whole. Why? Because in the situation I have just described the Bank of Barchester would have an immediate incentive to increase the amount of deposits it is creating. For every £10 of additional deposits the Bank of Barchester can maintain outstanding through lending, it will increase its annual revenue by £1. In other words, the marginal revenue accruing to the bank from creating an additional £1 is £.10 (or, under the ancient system, 1 shilling and 4 pence). Since it costs the bank nothing to create additional deposits, the bank

---

selling deposits to the public. It sells them for an equivalent amount of cash, an equivalent amount of another bank's deposits, or an interest-bearing IOU. Thus the interest that accrues from the creation of a deposit is properly regarded as the revenue generated by that deposit.

But what about the non-interest-bearing cash reserves the bank holds to protect itself against unforeseen withdrawals or demands for redemption? If the bank holds non-interest-bearing reserves, are all its deposits really generating revenue? The holding of reserves is properly viewed as a decision that the bank makes independently of the act of creating the deposit. It is a decision the bank makes about how best to diversify its assets. Thus the holding of such reserves can be regarded as a cost the bank incurs in selling deposits to the public just as easily as it can be regarded as a deduction from the bank's revenue.

10 An alternative, more realistic assumption is that although there are some costs of creating deposits, these are all sunk or fixed costs, so that the marginal cost of creating deposits is zero. In such a case, an optimal pricing policy would impose a certain fixed charge on depositors to cover the fixed costs and would pay depositors competitive interest rates.

will obviously want to create more than the £10,000 of deposits it has outstanding. Indeed, it will want to expand its lending and creation of deposits without limit.

If other banks can also create deposits costlessly, they have exactly the same incentive to expand their deposits. Moreover, since profit for all banks is obviously positive, there would seem to be an incentive for new banks to keep entering the market. So on the face of it, my example suggests an indefinite expansion of banking and deposit creation with nothing to hold it in check. Would a competitive banking system keep expanding without limit? And if it did, would not the consequent increase in the quantity of money send prices skyrocketing?

That is a charge that as we shall see in later chapters, has repeatedly been made against competition in banking. The charge that competition in banking might drive the value of money to zero seems to be based on the simple proposition that firms stop expanding production only when the marginal revenue from additional output no longer exceeds marginal cost. As long as marginal revenue is greater than marginal cost, firms increase their profit by increasing output. If the marginal cost of creating money were truly zero, the incentive to create more money would be eliminated only when the marginal revenue from creating more money equaled zero. But, supposedly, that would only happen when the value of money went to zero. Thus, the argument goes, competition drives the value of money down to the marginal cost of creating it. And that cost in a modern banking system is surely not far from zero.

However, the argument overlooks a simple point. Realizing the incentive for unconstrained banks to create money without limit, the public would simply not accept the money of any bank that did not commit itself to convert its money at a stipulated rate into an asset whose value the bank could not control.[11] That commitment is what gives a bank's money value in the first place. So long as the public's confidence in the solvency of the bank is unshaken, the commitment allows the bank's money to be worth just as much as the asset into which it is convertible. Thus, when a bank's marginal revenue is greater than marginal cost, simply creating more money by making more loans does not allow it to expand and increase its profit. Unless the bank can induce the public to hold more of its money, creating additional money to support further lending only causes the bank to lose assets through adverse clearings with other banks. The point, again, is that if a bank tries to lend money that hasn't, in some way, been provided to it by ultimate savers, some other part of its balance sheet will have to adjust to compensate. Either it will

---

11 This argument for convertibility can be read into the works of Adam Smith and other classical economists. I am indebted to Earl Thompson for having made it clear to me.

have to borrow to raise additional capital or it will have to restrict some other form of lending. As a financial intermediary, a competitive bank is no less limited in the amount of lending it can undertake than any other financial intermediary.

But if the gap between marginal revenue and marginal cost is not closed by a fall in the value of money, what is the mechanism that would lead the Bank of Barchester and the rest of the banking system to an equilibrium in which marginal revenue equaled marginal cost and in which new banks were not continually being formed to share in a seemingly inexhaustible flow of assured profits.

I have just shown that for the bank to be able to expand by additional lending, the new lending must be matched by an increase in the amount of the bank's money the public wishes to hold or, more generally, by an increase in the amount of capital the public supplies to the bank. If the bank lent by creating more of its money than the public wished to hold, it would undergo a drain on its reserves that would, unless curtailed quickly, drive the bank into insolvency. Simply reducing the interest rate it charges borrowers would not enable the Bank of Barchester to induce the public to hold any more of its money.

To achieve that goal, the bank would have to create additional incentives for the public to hold its money. The simplest way to create those incentives is by offering to pay interest to holders of its money. Thus the essential feature of competition among banks is the payment of interest on the moneys they create. They may compete in other ways also – say, by providing various services and conveniences that customers may want, as any competitive firm tries to do. But no bank will survive in a competitive environment if it offers its depositors an interest rate substantially lower than the rate its competitors offer. It is by trying to expand their deposits, not by reducing the interest rate they charge borrowers, that banks seek to enlarge their market share.

If, as I have assumed, banks can produce money costlessly, competition would oblige them to pay the same interest to holders of their moneys that (adjusted for default risk) they were charging their borrowers. When the rate paid on deposits is less than the rate charged on loans, banks have an incentive to expand their operations. They do that by raising the rate they offer depositors, which attracts the capital needed to increase their lending.

As rates paid on deposits rise, the marginal revenue from creating £1, which corresponds to the difference between the interest rate charged on loans and the rate paid on deposits, declines to the zero marginal cost of producing £1. This means that holding deposits will be costless, since it will entail no sacrifice of interest in comparison to any other financial asset of comparable risk. Thus, in our example, competition in banking operates not to reduce the value of money to zero but to reduce the implicit rental price of holding money down to zero.

Let me again emphasize that my assumption that banks can create money costlessly is just a device for bringing into focus the competitive mechanism that determines the rate paid on deposits. Nothing essential would change if I assumed that banks do incur costs when making loans and creating deposits. Suppose, for example, that it costs the Bank of Barchester £.02 to maintain and service a £1 deposit for one year. If the bank could charge 10 percent annual interest on loans, a £1 deposit would generate £.10 a year in gross revenue to the bank. The margin of £.08 would be the most the bank would willingly offer depositors for holding £1 of their money a year. If other banks had similar costs, competition for additional deposits would drive them relentlessly to raise the rate they offered depositors to 8 percent.

To take another example: If the interest rate on loans were only 5 percent, the yearly gross revenue from a £1 deposit would be £.05. If it cost the bank £.02 a year to maintain £1 in circulation, then since the margin on a deposit would be 3 percent, competition would require banks to pay 3 percent to depositors.[12]

To sum up: Competition obliges each bank in a competitive banking system to make its money as attractive to depositors as it can by paying the highest possible interest rate on deposits while still covering costs. How much money a bank can create depends on, and is constrained by, the amount of that bank's money that the public wishes to hold. If a bank could supply money to the public at a lower cost than its competitors, it would induce people to switch from its competitors' money to its own by paying higher interest on its money than the competitors paid on theirs. But if it sought to take advantage of its cost advantage by reducing the interest it charged on loans, it would give the public no incentive to hold more of its money or otherwise supply the additional savings it required to finance additional lending. The increase in lending at reduced rates would simply cause a drain on the bank's reserves as depositors, those to whom they made payments, or their banks demanded redemption of the bank's liabilities.

Because the point is frequently misunderstood, it is important to emphasize again that in a competitive banking system – indeed, in any banking

---

12 Insofar as the bank incurs costs by holding non-interest-bearing reserves against deposits, a reduction in interest rates would also reduce the cost of creating those deposits. For example, if a bank chooses to increase its holdings of non-interest-bearing cash by £.10 when it increases its deposits in circulation by £1, the marginal cost in forgone interest of a £1 deposit is £.01 when the interest rate is 10 percent and £.005 when the interest is only 5 percent. I ignore this complication in the text.

system – the money banks create is their own IOU. Although a bank promises to redeem its IOU on demand for a stipulated amount of another asset, it is the IOU – not the asset, whether currency, gold, or silver – that is the money that the bank is creating.[13] It is not a prior deposit of money that allows the bank to create a deposit, and it is wrong to conceive of any fixed mechanical relationship between the cash reserves of the bank and its ability to create deposits.[14]

It may be useful to try to think of a bank as offering to sell or to rent the deposits it creates. The bank sells its money to customers in exchange for assets that the bank regards as equally valuable. Sometimes it sells its money for another producer's money – that of another bank, perhaps, gold coin, or government currency. But a bank also sells its deposits for valuable assets that aren't money. If someone borrows money from a bank by issuing an IOU against himself, the exchange is not of one brand of money for another but of money for something that isn't money. In this case the bank exchanges its money, which yields a competitive rate of interest, for the IOU of the borrower, which yields an equal rate of interest adjusted for default risk. As long as the borrower holds the bank's money, the interest the money earns offsets the interest accruing on his IOU to the bank. So, in effect, he is renting the bank's money for free. Only if he does not hold the money, but spends it, does he bear the burden of the accrued interest on his IOU to the bank.

When one brand of money is sold for another brand of money, the total stock of money in existence does not change. But when a bank sells its money for an IOU, the total stock of money in existence does increase. That doesn't mean that the bank can increase the quantity of its money by an unlimited amount. Money is created only through an exchange of equal values, so there is no net addition to the total stock of assets in existence. But the stock of assets has been changed into a more desired configuration than it was in before.

The way of looking at an individual bank and a banking system that I have suggested here is different from conventional textbook interpretations of how banks and the banking system operate. Conventional interpretations view banks as mechanical entities whose behavior is not grounded in the profit-maximization condition (i.e., marginal revenue equals marginal cost) that underlies the economic analysis of the ordinary business firm. The creation of money by banks, in this view, comes about purely as a by-product of their lending and is mechanically deter-

13 The distinction made in the literature is between outside money, which is not the liability of anyone, and inside money, which is the liability of its issuer.
14 See White (1984) for a model describing the determinants of a competitive bank's demand for cash reserves. The model has been further amplified by Selgin (1988).

mined by the volume of the cash reserves that has been produced by the gold mines or that has been provided to them by the government or the central bank.

For all its simplicity, the model of a single bank and of a banking system that I have outlined is perfectly general and follows directly from the assumption of profit maximization. It enables us to identify and analyze the competitive forces that have driven the evolution of banking since its origins in the Middle Ages and that continue to do so even now. That is why this approach will continue to be helpful to us in later chapters as we seek to analyze more recent monetary developments within this theoretical framework.

THE DEVELOPMENT OF BANKING IN THE LATE MIDDLE AGES

As I mentioned in discussing the early evolution of money, the competitive forces that reduced the costs of banking and of creating money were mutually reinforcing. Reductions in the cost of banking and of creating money allowed banks to improve the terms on which they offered their moneys. As the cost of holding bank money fell, more and more people began holding, and transacting with, bank money. As more people began using bank money, its growing acceptability led to further increases in the demand to hold bank money. On the other hand, the increasing acceptability of bank money enabled banks to enjoy savings that no single bank could realize but that accrued to all banks when the entire banking system expanded. These savings resulted from the rapid growth of transactions carried out by banks which enabled banks to settle transactions by clearance rather than individually.[15]

Falling costs came from other sources as well. One was the invention of improved accounting techniques by the Italian bankers in the thirteenth, fourteenth, and fifteenth centuries. By the end of the fourteenth century, Italian merchant bankers had developed double-entry bookkeeping, with credits and debits recorded on both sides of the ledger. The presence of Italian bankers in most of Western Europe speeded the transmission of these principles to bankers and merchants outside Italy (de Roover 1956/1976).

Nevertheless, banking in the Middle Ages had to overcome some formidable obstacles that made costs and risks higher than they would have been otherwise. Bankers adopted a variety of techniques to overcome these hurdles. I explained earlier how they dealt with the lack of negotiability of checks, but other obstacles will also bear some attention. Most

---

15 "The development of banking can be described as a progressive centralization of clearance" (Usher 1943, p. 4).

of the obstacles arose owing to religious and temporal prohibitions against charging interest. These prohibitions added to the costs of the very activity that made creating money profitable, namely, lending the money they created at interest.

Some banking was undertaken by pawnbrokers, usually Jews or Lombards, who had legal dispensation to charge interest (de Roover 1948, pp. 99–108). But local deposit banking was largely carried out by money changers who were subject to the usury prohibitions. The money changers lent mostly by allowing depositors overdraft privileges. Unable to charge explicit interest, they often recovered interest covertly by raising their fees for money changing to depositors with debit balances. Another way of recovering interest was to acquire direct shares in the businesses of their customers. Since church doctrine did not condemn profits, the latter arrangement was considered legitimate (de Roover 1948, pp. 293–322).

There were also merchant bankers who had offices and correspondents in several major trading cities. They combined lending with exchange transactions by accepting bills of exchange in one location for payment in another. Bills of exchange were ostensibly just contracts entitling exporters to receive immediate payment in their local currency for goods they were shipping elsewhere. But the time elapsed between payment in one currency and repayment in another introduced the interest rate into the transaction. How banks used bills of exchange to earn implicit interest is worth a brief explanation to show the ingenuity of traders – no less apparent now than in the Middle Ages – in evolving instruments to circumvent prohibitions on the transactions that they want to make.

In the Middle Ages, exchange rates between different currencies varied systematically between different locations to reflect the implicit interest that accrued from the time (usually from ten days to a month) when a bill of exchange was accepted until it fell due. Let us suppose that the Medici bank in Venice accepted a bill of exchange for payment in Florence, falling due in one month. Say the exchange rate between ducats and florins quoted in Venice was 5 ducats a florin. The bank would then pay 100 ducats immediately to the issuer of the bill (say, an exporter), and its agent or its branch in Florence would receive 20 florins in one month (presumably, from the importer). In Florence, however, the ducat-florin exchange rate might have been 5.1 ducats a florin. If the funds paid in Florence when the bill fell due were used to buy a bill on Venice, the offsetting exchange transaction would, with no change in the exchange rate, entail the repayment, two months after the initial transaction, of 102 ducats to the Medici bank. The bank would have earned 2 percent on a loan of two months or 12.6 percent a year (de Roover 1944/1976). In general, the church did not object to such disguised payments of interest when the bills were drawn to finance a real commercial transaction and the interest itself was not explicitly contracted for. The churchmen tolerated the implicit payment of interest in these contracts because the acceptor of a bill of exchange risked an adverse change in the exchange rate that might reduce or even wipe out the interest he anticipated.

In our example, the ducat might have appreciated against the florin before the second half of the transaction was completed. The ducat-florin exchange rate in Venice might have gone from 5 to 4.9 ducats a florin and in Florence from 5.1 to 5 ducats a florin. The Venetian bank would then get back only 100 ducats. If the ducat had appreciated any more than that, the bank would have sustained a loss on the transaction. Since the receipt of interest was uncertain, though on average certainly positive, such transactions avoided the church's strictures (de Roover 1944/1976).

Although bills of exchange arose to help finance international trade and usually were drawn to facilitate an international commercial transaction, medieval banks routinely used bills of exchange either to borrow or to lend independently of any commercial transaction. The market in bills of exchange was the closest thing the medieval economy had to an organized money market.

The trade in bills of exchange without a corresponding flow of real commodities was known in medieval times as "dry exchange." Since lending at interest was the obvious purpose of dry exchange some Scholastic authorities held it to be a violation of the usury prohibition. Nevertheless, the riskiness of the transaction was a wide-enough loophole to allow bankers to engage in it freely. However, specifying the exchange rate on the return bill rather than allowing it to be determined at the expiration of the first bill – a practice known as "fictitious exchange" – was definitely prohibited, because the absence of exchange risk made the receipt of interest certain and hence, in the eyes of the church, illicit (de Roover 1944/1976).

Beside allowing banks to acquire short-term, interest-bearing assets, bills of exchange economized tremendously on the costly use of gold and silver in international trade. Rather than ship specie to settle international debts, transactors could settle them by using bills of exchange. At most, specie was used in settling trade imbalances among different areas. But even trade imbalances did not always have to be settled by a shipment of specie, because bills of exchange permitted a transfer of capital to offset the imbalance.

England and the Low Countries, for example, consistently ran balance-of-trade deficits with Italy. The deficits were partly financed by exporting specie. But they were also financed in part by Italian lending. The lending mostly took the form of deposits held by Italian banks in their branches in London, Bruges, and other locations in northern Europe. Those deposits allowed the branches to acquire the bills of exchange that financed northern Europe's trade deficit with Italy (de Roover 1944/1976, 1963). Even while hampered by the restrictions and prohibitions of the Middle Ages, the early European banking system functioned as an international financial intermediary channeling the savings of highly developed Italy to the underdeveloped northern European countries and financing the growth of international trade and the European economy.

Yet by making banks riskier and more likely to default, the usury prohibition prevented bank money from gaining as wide a circulation as it would have had if banks had been safer. Moreover, the lack of organized markets for short-term funds, which was another consequence of the usury prohibition, made it harder for banks to weather a crisis than if they could have borrowed funds readily in an organized market. To cope with the riskiness and illiquidity of most of their assets, banks had to hold an excessive fraction of their assets as non-interest-bearing reserves. Evidence from medieval bank records suggests that reserve ratios were often as high as 30 percent (de Roover 1948).

The usury prohibition was also an obstacle to paying interest openly on deposits. But just as banks could evade the prohibition on lending at interest, they could also evade the prohibition on paying interest on deposits. The most frequent method of paying interest on deposits was to pay a bonus, *discrezione,* to depositors at year's end in amounts depending on the bank's profits over the year. Restrictions never succeeded in suppressing the underlying economic incentives.

DEVELOPMENTS IN ENGLAND

Both of the obstacles to the progress of banking that I have mentioned – the prohibition of usury and the lack of negotiability of checks – were first removed in England. English banking had lagged behind banking on the Continent during the Middle Ages; in the thirteenth, fourteenth, and fifteenth centuries, banking in England was carried out almost exclusively by Italian merchant bankers with branches in London. By the sixteenth century, London goldsmiths began accepting deposits of coin and specie for safekeeping – a business that soon evolved into full-fledged banking. That change was helped along by a statute (enacted in 1571 after Henry VIII broke with the Roman Catholic church) that permitted interest rates up to 10 percent. In 1620 goldsmiths began discounting inland bills (Richards 1929/1965, p. 30; de Roover 1963, p. 109). Thus, unlike banking on the continent, which was based on money changing and foreign exchange, banking in England was based on discounting.

The principle of negotiability had begun to be recognized in the Low Countries in the sixteenth century, but only in relation to bills of exchange. Checks were considered personal orders of payment and hence not negotiable. In England, however, common law courts treated checks as a special type of bill of exchange and hence as negotiable (Richards 1929/1965, pp. 44–47; de Roover 1963, p. 109). Besides promoting the use of checks, and thus increasing the fraction of payments cleared through the banking system, the doctrine of negotiability also contributed to another great milestone in monetary evolution, the invention of the banknote (Usher 1943, pp. 108–09).

CONCLUSION

The point of this chapter has been to show how some of the chief elements of our monetary system evolved in consequence of competitive forces aimed at reducing the costs of trading and of holding money. Money emerged because trading was less costly with money than without it. Metals replaced cattle as media of exchange when, as primitive economies became more sophisticated, complex, and urbanized, metals became less costly than cattle to hold and to exchange. Coinage was adopted because it reduced the costs of trading with metals. And banking emerged because holding and transferring money within banks was often less costly than holding and exchanging cash.

Banks achieved these economies by substituting abstract claims to cash for the cash itself. They did so by exchanging their own instantly redeemable IOUs for hard cash or for the IOUs of members of the public. Because of the public's confidence that banks would redeem their IOUs when asked to do so, and because the IOUs could be transferred from one person to another, the IOUs themselves could be used as money.

The creation of these liabilities was limited by the willingness of the public to hold them, not by the amount of cash actually deposited in the banks. Thus banks provided a medium of exchange that was more flexible and responsive to the public's demand for money than a pure commodity monetary system could be. This flexibility and responsiveness, as we shall later see, has important implications for the performance of modern monetary systems.

2

Money and the state

What you should tell the governor of the Bank and the board is that they should inscribe these words in letters of gold in their meeting place: "What is the object of the Bank of France? To discount the credits of all French commercial houses at four percent."

Napoleon Bonaparte

In describing the evolution of money and banking in the previous chapter, I deliberately slighted the role of the state. I wanted to show that money is not a mere creature of the state, so it was necessary to show how money and the institutions that supply it could have emerged without state intervention. But let there be no misunderstanding. Just because money could have evolved without a special role for the state does not mean that the state ought not to have a special role in monetary affairs. It simply means that we need to think about why the state has played such a dominant role in the supply of money. Once we answer that question, we then can ask what role the state ought to play in an efficiently operating monetary system. The latter question will occupy our attention in Part III. But for now, it is the former question that concerns us.

Why did the state play so important a role in the evolution of money? What is so special about money that has led governments of all types to try to control its production and supply? Innumerable goods and services have, from time to time, been monopolized by the state, but no other has been so universally monopolized by the state as has money.

To account for the ubiquitous state role in monetary affairs, some economists have suggested that the production of money is a natural monopoly, that is, a monopoly brought about by a technology of production (i.e., economies of scale) that makes it cheaper for just one firm to produce all output than for two or more firms to do so.

Why a single supplier of money would have lower costs than two or more suppliers is not at all clear. One might say that quoting prices in, and transacting with, a single money eliminates some formidable accounting and transaction costs. Think how complicated life would be if your salary were paid in dollars while you had to pay rent in pounds, pay off your car loan in francs, buy your clothing with marks, and buy groceries with pesos. If exchange rates between the different moneys were constantly fluctuating, your difficulties would become overwhelming. You would lose the advantages of transacting with money and, in effect, would be reverting toward a barter economy. A single supplier of money automatically ensures that the monetary system does not degenerate into a barterlike hodgepodge of different monetary units.

But just to avoid the inconvenience of multiple monetary units, money does not have to be supplied monopolistically. If many suppliers of money were making their moneys convertible into the same asset, all the moneys would be exchangeable at a one-for-one rate. The benefits of a single monetary unit could be secured without monopoly.

Today, in the United States, for example, the government defines the dollar as the monetary unit, and the Federal Reserve System is, indeed, the sole supplier of currency. Nevertheless, thousands of private banks produce their own brands of dollars by creating deposits convertible into Federal Reserve dollars. And if allowed to, many banks would also issue their own currencies, which, like deposits, would be convertible into Federal Reserve dollars. All privately produced dollars are exchangeable at par. The natural monopoly argument for a state monopoly over money is thus not easy to understand, or even take seriously.

Now there may be a role for the state in selecting or defining the asset into which all money producers make their moneys convertible. I shall have a good deal more to say about such a role in Part III. But that role is more akin to defining weights and measures than to being the sole producer of money.

Other economists have maintained that competition in the supply of money is inherently self-destructive and must drive the value down to its cost of production, which is zero. Even Milton Friedman (1960, p. 7), not ordinarily hostile to competitive markets, warned of the consequences of allowing free competition in the supply of money:

This analysis, then, leads to the conclusion that some external limit must be placed on the volume of currency in order to maintain its value. Competition does not provide an effective limit, since the value of the promise to pay, if the currency is to remain fiduciary, must be kept higher than the cost of producing additional units. The production of a fiduciary currency is, as it were, a technical monopoly, and hence, there is no such presumption in favor of the private market as there is when competition is feasible.

I showed in the previous chapter, however, that competition in supplying money reduces not the value of money but the cost of holding it. The value of money is maintained because banks commit themselves contractually to redeem their moneys into an asset whose value they cannot control. The value of money, therefore, is identical to the independently determined value of the asset into which it is convertible.

But even if the argument that money can't be supplied efficiently by competing producers were correct, that still would not explain the dominant role of the state in monetary affairs. Governments, after all, have not been quick to follow the policy prescriptions of economists in other instances. All economists favor free international trade, yet no government will tolerate it. Economists propose regulating some products and deregulating others, yet governments often regulate the products economists want deregulated and deregulate the ones economists want regulated. So why suppose that governments have been taking the advice of economists in this one instance? When the state first began to control the monetary system over two millennia before anyone ever heard of an economist, was it because the state foresaw what economists would later say on the subject?

One might argue that governments were responding not to economists but to the inability of the market to supply money and that economists have merely tried to explain why the market failed to supply money. But the history of government debasement and mismanagement of the currency lends only ambiguous support to the hypothesis that the state intervened in monetary affairs to make the monetary system more efficient. So we had better turn elsewhere to find an explanation for the role of the state in monetary affairs.

A RATIONALE FOR THE STATE MONOPOLY OVER MONEY

The question remains: What makes money special? I alluded briefly to the answer earlier when I observed that private mints posed a threat to ancient sovereigns. Lacking effective taxing power, an ancient ruler was vulnerable to an insurrection led by a private individual with a great deal of money to spend. The owner of a mint would be just such a person. To amass the required funds, the owner might issue debased or fraudulent coins, violating his guarantee of their weight and fineness. But if successful, the owner would, as the new sovereign, not be troubled by the legal sanctions normally imposed on those who flagrantly violated their contractual obligations. And if unsuccessful, his violation of those obligations would be the least of his worries. The importance of controlling the mint in the ancient world had little to do with the monetary system and everything to do with the struggle for political power.

The oldest known coins, dating from about the seventh century B.C., are from Lydia. Lydians used electrum, a naturally occurring alloy of gold and silver, as their money. Because it was an alloy, traders had to assay the metal to ascertain the proportions of gold and silver in each exchange. The benefits from certifying those proportions explain why it was that coinage originated in Lydia. Interestingly, the names on those coins are not those of any known Lydian sovereign, so we can safely conclude that they were privately minted (Burns 1927/1969, p. 75).

But it was not only coinage that originated in Lydia; tyranny also started there. Gyges, the Lydian king to whom the term "tyrant" was first applied (Durant 1939, p. 122), is reputed to have "completed the evolution of coinage by making it the prerogative of the state after he had first used it to obtain supreme power" (Ure 1922, p. 143). The wealth of Lydian kings, such as Croesus, was renowned in the ancient world and immortalized by Herodotus. Their practice of coinage undoubtedly invited imitation. By the sixth century B.C., coinage had spread to Greece, where it was monopolized locally by individual city-states. But Sparta, the most antityrannical state in Greece, never had a real coinage (Ure, p. 14).

The Greeks recognized that allowing private mints meant permitting competition for sovereignty. The city-states strengthened their local monopolies by requiring taxes to be paid in coins issued by their own mints (Kraay 1964). But ancient governments were constrained in exploiting their monopolies. For if they raised mint charges too high, or debased the coinage too recklessly, people could switch from coins to unminted precious metals.

As the primitive state enhanced its power to tax, the urgency of a monopoly over coinage that restrained competition for sovereignty should have diminished. Yet the ancient state became no more tolerant of private mints as it found new revenue sources. Besides the attraction any revenue source has for a sovereign, the monopoly over coinage had a particular advantage the ancient state was loath to relinquish. Because the monopoly over coinage could be exploited quickly in an emergency, it was a welcome source of funds in wartime when other revenue sources could not generate additional funds as quickly. Providing the sovereign with security against both internal and external threats, the monopoly over coinage became the acknowledged prerogative of the sovereign.[1]

The first use of the monopoly over coinage for wartime revenue was undertaken by the Greeks. In the fourth century B.C., Timotheus of Ath-

---

1 This hypothesis of the origin of the state monopoly over money was suggested to me by Earl Thompson, who has stressed (1974b, 1979) national defense considerations in explaining a variety of governmental institutions.

ens, when fighting the Olinthians, used a forced token coinage, which he promised would be redeemed, to pay his soldiers (Burns 1927/1969, pp. 365–66).

Dionysius of Syracuse, trying to stave off the Carthaginians, used both depreciation and debasement of the currency to raise funds. The distinction between depreciation and debasement is that the former openly reduces the weight of coinage while preserving its fineness, whereas the latter surreptitiously reduces its fineness while maintaining its weight.[2] After conquering Rhegium, Dionysius called in all coins for counterstamping. He reduced the standard by half and reissued the coins at double their nominal value. Half the coins remained as profit. Dionysius used the profit to pay off his debts, whose real value the subsequent inflation reduced by 50 percent. He thereby obtained half the value of outstanding coins and reneged on half the real value of his obligations to creditors. Later he debased the currency by passing off tin-plated bronze coins as silver. Although his tactics have been deplored, Dionysius did prevent the Carthaginians from sacking Syracuse as they did other Sicilian cities (Burns, pp. 368–69).

In 217 B.C., under attack by Hannibal, and unable to pay its soldiers, the Roman Republic enacted the Lex Flaminia, formally depreciating the bronze *as* by half and the silver *denarius* by 14 percent. To extract additional revenue, the republic also issued some silver-plated copper coins among the silver *denarii* (Burns pp. 392–97).

This brief survey of the ancient use of the state monopoly over money as an instrument of wartime finance should at least establish the plausibility of my contention that this monopoly was founded on security considerations. Not only is there no evidence that the state established a monopoly over coinage to improve the efficiency of the monetary system, ascribing that monopoly to the desire for monetary efficiency cannot explain why control of the monetary system has been so generally presumed to be an attribute of sovereignty. That feeling, engendered by centuries of historical experience, must stem from a real, if only historical, connection between control over money and the protection of sovereignty. That connection would also explain the otherwise surprising fact that counterfeiting was a treasonable offense under English law (Blackstone 1773/1979, IV, p. 84; Maitland 1908, p. 266).

Just how strong that feeling still is was vividly illustrated not so long ago. Trying to halt runaway inflation, the Israeli finance minister, Yoram Aridor, proposed in 1983 to make the shekel fully convertible into the dollar at a fixed parity and to make all contractual obligations, including

---

2 Depreciation presumably causes a more or less immediate adjustment in prices, while debasement does so only gradually as the public learns of the reduced metallic content of the coins.

tax liabilities, payable in dollars. Despite an extensive de facto dollarization of the Israeli economy that had already occurred, all segments of the Israeli public united in denouncing the plan. A typical response was the comment of a right-wing politician that if the plan were implemented, Israel might as well start flying the American flag and singing the "Star-Spangled Banner."

BANKING AND THE MONOPOLY OVER MONEY

The rise of banking was (and is) a threat to the state monopoly over money. Bank customers could avoid the costs and risks of holding and transferring precious metals and coins by switching from those forms of money to deposits. Of course banks had to hold coins and specie, too. But since banks held less coin and specie than the amount of deposits they created, they reduced the net demand for coins.

Moreover, banks also engaged in the questionable practice of picking and culling the coins they received in exchange for deposits. When called upon to redeem deposits, they paid out light coins, exporting the full-weight coins and thereby reducing the quality of the coinage. And at least some banks also clipped and sweated coins (de Roover 1948, pp. 350–51).

These practices enabled banks to appropriate some of the profit from currency debasement that would otherwise have accrued to governments and their mints. Because many of their assets were equity shares in businesses they lent to, banks also gained from any devaluation or debasement of the currency. Debasement reduced the real value of their fixed nominal liabilities but not the real value of their equity assets. So with ample reason not to be enamored of bankers, medieval rulers sometimes took measures to restrict or even suppress the business of banking.

Late in the fourteenth century, for example, the Duke of Burgundy prohibited money changers from conducting exchange transactions by crediting accounts rather than paying out coin or specie. Since medieval banking grew out of exchange transactions, this was an extremely restrictive prohibition. Further edicts in the fifteenth century apparently suppressed private banking in the Low Countries altogether, for we find no mention of private banks operating there in the sixteenth century (de Roover 1948, pp. 350–51).

In Catalonia similar complaints were voiced against private bankers. The Barcelonan authorities did not try to suppress private banking; they just established a municipal Bank of Deposit. However, because the municipal Bank of Deposit could not induce many depositors to switch from the private bankers, who provided superior service, the city granted monopolistic privileges to the Bank of Deposit. The authorities required all escrow accounts, all deposits held in trust for a beneficiary, and all deposits subject to any legal dispute to be held in the municipal bank (Usher 1943, pp. 269–74).

Since it did not serve ordinary customers very well, the Bank of Deposit might have concentrated on becoming a central bank for the private banks. The private banks could have made it a vehicle for clearing mutual liabilities by opening up their own accounts with the municipal bank. But in what antitrust experts would now call a predatory refusal to deal, the authorities foolishly prohibited private banks from holding accounts with the Bank of Deposit. A more profitable strategy would have been to require banks to hold minimum accounts with the Bank of Deposit. Even so, the prohibition was probably evaded rather easily because banks could hold accounts opened in the names of private individuals (Usher 1943, pp. 309–10).

When these privileges failed to curtail private banking, the city finally required all banks to be licensed. Only a few banks received licenses, and the rest went out of business.

The suppression of banking in the Low Countries was a major handicap to merchants.[3] The loss of banking facilities greatly increased the costs of making and collecting payments. Merchants tried to function without banking facilities by endorsing bills of exchange and accepting endorsed bills instead of money – a practice merchants continued for centuries. To provide payments services without private banks, the city of Amsterdam eventually founded a *giro* or transfer bank that was supposed to be a pure depository holding reserves equal to deposits. But the obligation of holding cash equal to deposits prevented the Bank of Amsterdam from acting as a financial intermediary and added to its operating costs.

Unlike minting, banking requires considerably more business acumen than governments typically possess. It was not difficult for governments to set up their own mints and exclude competing ones. But they could not so easily set up their own banks and exclude competing ones without also forgoing the benefits of banking and financial intermediation. Only a few governments have been willing to go that far just to protect their monopoly over money. Instead, most governments have preferred allowing banks to operate and exploiting them as a source of credit to suppressing them or to operating banks of their own.

In the sixteenth and seventeenth centuries, for example, Venice used its private, but tightly regulated, banking system as a source of funds in

---

3 The difficulties arising from the absence of banking facilities were well described by de Roover (1948, p. 250): in the passage quoted in n. 6 of the previous chapter.

several wartime financial emergencies. On one of those occasions, in 1520, the Venetian banks helped finance a war by creating deposits against government debt. Spending and the corresponding creation of deposits were so great that the banks had to suspend the convertibility of deposits into coin. Bank money continued to circulate, but it depreciated against coin – perhaps the first instance of an inflationary increase of bank credit to finance deficit spending by the state (Lane 1937, p. 205; de Roover 1954/1976, p. 215).

But the most telling example of the use by the state of its control over banking to meet the exigencies of wartime finance is the establishment of the Bank of England in 1694.

THE ESTABLISHMENT OF THE BANK OF ENGLAND

Obtaining funds was always a difficult problem for English monarchs and never more so than in the seventeenth century. Conflicts between the Stuart kings and Parliament led to the Civil War and Cromwell's accession to power. After the Restoration, Charles II was unable to obtain sufficient revenues to cover his spending plans and became heavily indebted to the London goldsmiths. Unable to repay his debts, he repudiated them in 1672, undermining his own credit and that of his successors for several decades (Dowd 1989, chap. 5).

The Glorious Revolution of 1688 overthrew the last Stuart monarch, James II, and forced him into exile in France, where he sought and received the protection of another Catholic, Louis XIV. The French monarch committed himself to support James's efforts to recover his throne from the Protestant usurper, William of Orange, whose army had driven James from England. Even after quelling loyalist resistance in Ireland and Scotland in 1690–91, William still faced a Jacobite resistance supported by French arms. Moreover, William, a staunch Protestant, was committed to fighting French expansion on the Continent. Strongly opposed by elements of the Tory aristocracy and the Church of England, William could not persuade Parliament to appropriate the funds he needed to pursue his military objectives. And with the memory of what Charles II did to his creditors still fresh, William could only borrow at exorbitant interest rates.

Unable to muster parliamentary support for William, some of his Whig supporters devised a plan to charter a bank that would come to the aid of the crown. Under their plan Parliament would charter a joint-stock bank on condition that the stockholders buy £1,200,000 of government bonds yielding 8 percent annual interest. Although few would lend to the king directly at 8 percent interest, there were many who, anticipating its future profits, were willing to acquire stock in what would be, until 1826, the only joint-stock bank in England.

"Here," wrote Sir Arthur Feavearyear (1963, p. 127), referring to the Bank of England,

was where William III had the advantage of Charles II. Charles's credit in 1672 was utterly bad. His paper orders were payable, not on demand, but eighteen months hence. He could not have issued notes payable on demand even if people would have accepted them, for he had no reserve. William and his government were themselves in no better position. But the Bank was an institution newly floated in triumph in the face of all opposition. At least half the City of London believed in it. The king's "pay" was bad; but where his tallies would no longer go he could place with ease the Bank's "bills," sealed with the common seal of the corporation, and engraved with the figure of Britannia seated upon a bank of money. Thus the king's immediate difficulties were surmounted by an inflation of credit of the simplest order.

And in his *History of England,* Macaulay (1914, pp. 2438–39) vividly described the close connection among the government, the crown, the Whig Party, and the Bank of England in the years following the establishment of the bank:

It soon appeared that Montague had, by skillfully availing himself of the financial difficulties of the country, rendered an inestimable service to his party. During several generations the Bank of England was emphatically a Whig body. It was Whig not accidentally, but necessarily. It must have instantly stopped payment if it had ceased to receive the interest which it had advanced the government; and of that interest James would not have paid one farthing. Seventeen years after the passing of the Tonnage Bill, Addison in one of his most ingenious and graceful little allegories, described the situation of the great Company through which the immense wealth of London was constantly circulating. He saw Public Credit on her throne in Grocers' Hall, the Great Charter over her head, the Act of Settlement full in her view. Her touch turned everything to gold. Behind her seat, bags filled with coin were piled to the ceiling. On her right and on her left the floor was hidden by pyramids of guineas. On a sudden the door flies open. The Pretender rushes in, a sponge in one hand, in the other a sword which he shakes at the Act of Settlement. The beautiful Queen sinks down fainting. The spell by which she turned all things around her into treasure is broken. The money bags shrink like pricked bladders. The piles of gold pieces are turned into bundles of rags or faggots of wooden tallies. The truth which this parable was meant to convey was constantly present to the minds of the rulers of the Bank. So closely was their interest bound up in the interest of the government that the greater the public danger the more ready were they to come to the rescue. In old times when the Treasury was empty, when the taxes came in slowly, and when the pay of the soldiers and sailors was in arrear, it had been necessary for the Chancellor of the Exchequer to go hat in hand, up and down Cheapside and Cronhill, attended by the Lord Mayor and by the Alderman, and to make up a sum by borrowing a hundred pounds from this hosier, and two hundred pounds from that ironmonger. Those times were over.

The government, instead of laboriously scooping up supplies from numerous petty sources, could now draw whatever it required from an immense reservoir, which all those petty sources kept constantly replenished.

How fully the monopoly of the Bank of England was incorporated into the general state monopoly over money is evidenced by an act of Parliament that in 1773 made counterfeiting Bank of England notes a capital offense, just as counterfeiting the coin of the realm had always been.

WAR FINANCE AND THE STATE MONOPOLY OVER MONEY

It is not difficult to find other instances in which wartime financial distress drove the state to extend its monopoly over coinage to a degree of control over banking. American history provides a clear example.

The Constitution left authority over banking to the states. Both early attempts by nationalist politicians to charter a national bank were resisted as unconstitutional. Campaigning against big government and big finance, states' rights Democrats twice succeeded in terminating the national banks. Enjoying complete authority over banking before the Civil War, many states permitted free entry into banking and allowed banks to issue notes that circulated as hand-to-hand currency. When the war came, the Union helped finance it by issuing inconvertible Greenbacks and chartering national banks that issued notes backed by government bonds. To increase the demand for Greenbacks and national banknotes, Congress imposed a 10 percent tax on the notes of state-chartered banks, driving them out of circulation. After the war, with its dominance over the states secure, the federal government did not surrender its newly acquired monopoly over banknotes.

If I am correct in attributing the state monopoly over money to the interest of the state in defending its sovereignty, then the governments most likely to relinquish control over the creation of money are ones with no defense responsibilities. That was the American experience. The states, which under the constitution had legal authority over banking but minimal defense responsibilities, often allowed free entry into banking and let banks issue their own notes. However, when some states challenged the political and military supremacy of the federal government, the federal government preempted state control over banking.

A similar legal situation led to the other major instance of unregulated banking. In the eighteenth and the first half of the nineteenth centuries, Scotland, unlike the rest of Great Britain, allowed free entry by joint-stock and private banks and did not restrict their right to issue notes. Scotland enjoyed this privilege because existing Scottish law was not altered by the Act of Union of 1707 that unified England and Scotland. Between the accession of James I to the English throne upon the death of Elizabeth I and passage of the Act of Union, Scotland and England were united under a single monarch but retained separate legal systems and parliaments. With no defense responsibilities, the Scottish Parliament imposed no restrictions on banking. Since enactments of the English Parliament had no force in Scotland before the Act of Union, the monopoly of the Bank of England did not extend to Scotland. Even after the Act of Union abolished the Scottish Parliament, the local attachment of Scots to their own banking system made it politically difficult for the English Parliament to change the status quo in Scotland (Checkland 1975; White 1984).

Neither the American nor the Scottish episode of free banking was ended because of local dissatisfaction with it. In Scotland local opinion ran heavily against the Bank Charter Act of 1844 and the follow-up Act of 1845 restricting the right of Scottish banks to issue notes (Fetter 1965). Although the free-banking era in the United States has a bad reputation in American historiography, recent historical investigations show that the system actually worked well (Rockoff 1975; Rolnick and Weber 1983, 1984, 1988). Nor is there evidence that public dissatisfaction with the banks prompted Congress to terminate the competitive note issues of state banks. The National Bank Act of 1864 that taxed those notes out of existence was motivated by the exigencies of wartime finance, and it would never have been passed had the Southern states not seceded and Southern senators and representatives, who had resisted all extensions of federal power, not resigned their seats.

Canada, which was protected by Britain in the nineteenth century and shared unfortified borders with the United States, had no central bank and allowed private note issue, but not free entry into banking, until 1935 (Shearer and Clark 1984). Before Germany and Italy became unified national states, note issue, although regulated, was left in the hands of private banks. One of Bismarck's first achievements was to unify the currency under a monopolistic central bank of issue dominated by the government (Goodhart 1987a). In Italy the note-issuing privileges of several private banks were only gradually circumscribed. Not until 1926, after Mussolini came to power, did the Bank of Italy gain an exclusive monopoly of issue (Fratianni and Spinelli 1984).

Other governments that have forgone monopolistic control of their money supplies are the administration in Hong Kong, which has no defense role, and Panama, which, owing to the Panama Canal, has always been under the military protection of the United States. Moreover, Eurodollars – dollar-denominated deposits created in banks domiciled outside the United States – are mostly created in Western Europe and the Caribbean Islands, which are partial free riders on American defense expenditures. Since no government has reason to protect the monopoly of another government over its currency, governments often allow banks freedom from regulatory interference in creating Eurodollar deposits that they would not allow banks in creating deposits denominated in their own currencies.

HOW TO EXPLOIT THE MONOPOLY OVER MONEY

If, as I maintain, the state monopoly over money emerged not to increase the efficiency of the monetary system but to help the state protect its sovereignty, what can we infer about how governments have managed their monopolies over money? What considerations would have governed the state's exploitation of its monopoly over money?

To answer these questions, we must distinguish between two methods of exploiting the monopoly over money. One is to generate a flow of seignorage either by imposing charges at the mint or, when issuing a fiat currency, by monetary expansion that generates predictable inflation. Under certain conditions, the government could choose a rate of inflation to be maintained indefinitely that would generate a maximum flow of seignorage.[4] The other is for the government to extract wealth from holders of its money and its debt by unexpectedly devaluing or debasing the currency or by sudden monetary expansion that causes unanticipated inflation. This generates a large immediate return. But it falls off quickly.

Whether the stream of revenue generated by the second method is greater or lesser than that generated by the first depends on the rate at which we discount the two streams. But in a wartime situation, when the discount rate may be extraordinarily high, the second method is sure to be the preferred one. Since the second method can be implemented at short notice, generates a lot of revenue in a hurry, and may evade parliamentary restrictions on the imposition of explicit taxes, it is obviously superior to the first as a means of financing wartime expenditures.

But the second method can be effective only if it takes the public by surprise. If people anticipate currency debasement or inflation, they reduce their holdings of money and lend only at interest rates high enough to compensate for the anticipated loss in the purchasing power of money. So to exploit its monopoly over money in an emergency, the state must

4 There is a substantial literature that has developed on this question since early discussions by Friedman (1953a) and Bailey (1956). An important contribution to this literature was a paper by Auernheimer (1974). My discussion in the next section was also influenced by Barro (1983).

avoid currency debasement or inflation at other times. Unfortunately, the better a government's reputation for monetary rectitude, the greater the payoff for springing a surprise inflation.

This point is crucial for understanding how our monetary institutions evolved and is borne out by the view that English law took of the right of the sovereign to debase the coinage. According to both Sir William Blackstone (1773/1979, I, p. 268) and Frederic Maitland (1908, p. 260), it was part of the royal prerogative to debase the coinage. Nevertheless, it was considered reprehensible for him to exercise that prerogative. I interpret that to mean that the monarch had a moral obligation not to tamper with the currency except in an emergency in which the safety of the realm was in jeopardy.

THE NEED FOR CONSTRAINTS ON THE STATE MONOPOLY OVER MONEY

The national defense rationale for the state monopoly over money implies that governments optimally exploit the monopoly by avoiding inflation in peacetime. If they don't avoid inflation, they risk being left defenseless in wartime. Governments that invest in the monopoly over money by not inflating in peacetime therefore improve their chances of surviving in military competition with other governments. So it would seem that there is a tendency for governments that create inflation in peacetime to be weeded out.

Two objections immediately come to mind. First, the inference is not borne out empirically, rapid inflations and currency devaluations having occurred in peacetime as well as in wartime. Second, one wonders what would motivate a government to forgo the current benefits it can derive from inflating now in return for the contingent future benefits of not doing so.

However, the second problem partially takes care of the first. There are obvious reasons for governments to exploit the monopoly over money in peacetime even though that makes the monopoly less useful in wartime. One disincentive to investing in the monopoly over money in peacetime is that government decision makers have a limited tenure in office and have no transferable property rights in the assets they create while in office.

To understand the problem, think of a private business. The owner has strong incentives to make any investment that generates future earnings large enough to increase the present discounted value of the firm's current and future cash flow. Even if the investment does not add to the firm's cash flow until far into the future, the owner will still make the investment if the discounted value of the increased cash flow exceeds the current cost of the investment. He will do so because the market for shares capitalizes those future additions to cash flow in the current value of the firm. Because there are transferable property rights in the firm, the increase in the value of the firm redounds immediately to the owner's benefit.

That expected future additions to cash flow really are reflected in the current value of firms is evident in the wide variations in price-earning ratios among firms listed on the stock exchanges. Firms with high price-earning ratios are those which the market expects to show increasing earnings in the future; firms with low price-earning ratios are those which the market expects to show declining earnings in the future.

Without ownership of, or marketable shares in, the state, the incentives to undertake investments that redound to the future benefit of the state are much weaker than those to invest in privately owned enterprises.

The lack of transferable property rights in the state suggests that government decision makers have an inflationary bias. Under an absolute and hereditary monarchy, the bias would be reduced, though not eliminated. On the other hand, hereditary monarchies have an inordinately high probability of producing incompetent rulers who are unable or unwilling to follow policies in their own, and the state's, long-term interest. Thus a small, homogeneous ruling elite, such as the aristocracy of a city-state like the Venetian Republic, would seem to be the form of government most likely to invest in the monopoly over money in peacetime.

There is a related incentive to exploit the monopoly over money in peacetime instead of saving it for wartime. To stay in power, any government requires the support of some coalition of interests. Competitors for power within the state often make commitments that would entail expenditures exceeding its revenues. One way to cover the deficit is to exploit the monopoly over money. But then competition for power within the state must dissipate the value of the monopoly over money in peacetime instead of maintaining it for use in wartime. A stable and secure ruling elite would seem to be less prone to such competitive dissipation.

Roman history provides us with an extreme example of this process. The Roman emperor was an absolute, but nonhereditary, monarch. By the third century A.D. the army had become the most powerful interest group in the empire. Selection of an emperor after the (often premature) demise of his predecessor degenerated into a bidding war for the army's support.[5] The direct revenues of the state could not pay what emperors

---

5 The nature of the process of succession is nicely captured in a passage from Gibbon's great work (chap. 11): "Encompassed by his declared or concealed enemies, he soon,

promised the army, so the difference had to be made up by currency debasement. Perhaps one reason for the absence of inflation in Byzantium was the adoption of the principle of hereditary succession.[6]

Before the eighteenth century, hereditary monarchies and aristocracies controlled most European states securely enough to prevent the unlimited exploitation of the monopoly over money in peacetime. But the democratization that began in the eighteenth century, and accelerated in the nineteenth, reduced the willingness of government decision makers to resist this exploitation.

However, during the eighteenth and nineteenth centuries, the ascendant political attitudes, at least in English-speaking countries, were hostile to the arbitrary exercise of government power. Consequently, the monopoly over money was circumscribed by both law and custom. For example, at the insistence of the more doctrinaire Whigs, the Tonnage Bill that helped establish the Bank of England prohibited the bank from advancing funds to the crown without authority of Parliament (Macaulay 1914, p. 2435). Throughout the eighteenth and nineteenth centuries, a body of rules – some enacted explicitly and others unwritten, but regarded as morally and politically binding – sharply limited official discretion over the money supply. The Bank Charter Act of 1844, while granting a monopoly over the creation of banknotes to the Bank of England, also prescribed explicit rules governing its use. But the fundamental constraint on that monopoly was the obligation to maintain convertibility of currency into gold at a fixed parity.

The role of the gold standard in the evolution of our monetary system now comes into view. When Parliament formally adopted a gold standard in 1816, the pound had never before been legally defined by Parliament as a prescribed weight of gold, silver, or anything. It was the prerogative of the king to set mint prices, although, as I pointed out before, he was thought to be morally obligated not to debase the coinage except

amidst the nocturnal tumult, received a mortal dart from an uncertain hand. Before he expired, a patriotic sentiment rising in the mind of Gallienus induced him to name a deserving successor, and it was his last request that the Imperial ornaments should be delivered to Claudius, who then commanded a detached army in the neighbourhood of Pavia. The report at least was diligently propagated, and the order cheerfully obeyed by the conspirators, who had already agreed to place Claudius on the throne. On the first news of the emperor's death the troops expressed some suspicion and resentment, till the one was removed and the other assuaged by a donative of twenty pieces of gold to each soldier. They then ratified the election and acknowledged the merit of their new sovereign."

6 However, de Cecco (1985, pp. 812–13) quotes Mommsen (1860) to suggest that Roman currency debasement had created so much mistrust of coinage that coins in Byzantine times were accepted only by weight. Without a nominal or face value, it was impossible to engage in currency debasement or devaluations that would produce inflation.

in an emergency. But in the nineteenth century, power was passing from the king and a narrow circle of peers and influential commoners to the mass of people represented in Parliament. To prevent the improper use of the monopoly over money, which was greatly feared in the nineteenth century, a legal definition of the pound as a fixed weight of gold attained an almost constitutional status (Fetter 1965).

Subsequently, a suspension of the gold standard would have been almost inconceivable in Britain except under the most extraordinary circumstances. Indeed, the mystique of the gold standard was such that in World War I, the British refused even to acknowledge that the gold standard and convertibility of the pound into gold had been suspended.

That a country could create confidence in its currency by adopting the gold standard and that this confidence would help it to finance wartime expenditures was a familiar point in the nineteenth century. Austrian and Russian proponents of the gold standard relied on it heavily when Austria-Hungary and Russia were considering whether to adopt the gold standard in the 1890s (Yeager 1984). This view of the gold standard points to a more favorable interpretation of Britain's decision in 1925 to go back on gold at the prewar parity than the one now generally accepted.

BRITAIN'S RETURN TO GOLD IN 1925

Britain's decision to rejoin the gold standard was characteristic of British attachment to tradition and precedent. A century earlier, after having suspended convertibility of the pound during the Napoleonic Wars, Britain had restored convertibility at the old parity of £3 17s 10.5d. Besides the force of precedent, the decision also reflected a nostalgic desire, after the horrors of the First World War, to restore the prewar state of affairs, a feeling of moral obligation to repay British war debts in pounds of full value, and a patriotic wish for "the pound to be able to look the dollar in the face."

Economists ever since have not dealt kindly with the decision to restore convertibility at the prewar parity. Yet the seemingly insubstantial reasons on which the decision rested were expressions of an eminently practical consideration: If Britain ever again had to finance a war by borrowing and printing money, doing so would be easier if people believed in the long-run stability of the value of the pound. Restoring the pound to its prewar parity was a way of fostering that belief and was thus an investment in Britain's national security. For the British people and their statesmen to have been willing to bear the costs of that investment may have been a misjudgment, but it was hardly an irrational decision. Nor is the surmise that the decision rested on national security considerations belied by the fact that the chancellor of the Exchequer who oversaw the restoration of the gold standard was a former, and future, first lord of the Admiralty named Winston Churchill.

My approach to explaining the state monopoly over money would imply that similar restorations of the standard after wartime inflations or debasements have not been uncommon. Such restorations are not easily explained on other grounds, since there are few benefits to be extracted from deliberate deflation. Yet Sir Arthur Feavearyear (1963, p. 12), in his history of the pound sterling, records that between 1100 and 1300 there were at least seven recoinages, designed to eliminate the worn, clipped, and counterfeit coins whose share of the circulation inevitably increased between recoinages. Those recoinages all maintained the same legal standard, but each one, therefore, increased the de facto standard by eliminating underweight coins.

It was the uniform commitment of early English monarchs to always maintaining the purity, and usually maintaining the weight, of the silver pound sterling that made "sterling" an adjective for anything of the highest standard or quality. It was that confidence built up over centuries which enabled Henry VIII, when foreign troops were fighting on British soil, to raise the funds needed to defend his throne with a massive debasement of the currency.

The French experience in the late Middle Ages in which repeated devaluations were always followed by restorations of the old standard is also instructive. However, the devaluations were so frequent that despite the restorations, they eventually did not generate substantial revenues (Miskimin 1984; Bordo 1986).

THE WEAKENING CONSTRAINTS ON THE MONOPOLY OVER MONEY

In the event, the attempt to restore to the gold standard after World War I proved, as I shall show in Chapter 5, disastrously unsuccessful. And after World War II the world, recalling what had happened twenty-five years earlier, adopted the Bretton Woods System, which retained a few of the forms, but almost none of the substance, of the gold standard. Partially freed from those constraints, governments assumed for the first time an obligation to maintain full employment by controlling the monetary and fiscal instruments at their disposal. Despite the weakening constraints on exploitation of the monopoly over money, a residual commitment to price stability and balanced budgets seems to have restrained that exploitation for about two decades after World War II.

But after the collapse of the Bretton Woods System in 1971 a general worldwide acceleration of inflation ensued. The blame for that inflation should not necessarily be assigned to the abandonment of the Bretton Woods System. It was not abandoned out of any misunderstanding. It was abandoned because its provisions proved incompatible with the discretionary monetary policy it allowed national governments to exercise. The tendency toward increased exploitation by governments of their monopolies over national money supplies eventually had to undermine the fixed parities of the Bretton Woods System. The only possible outcome was a system of floating exchange rates.

Thus my argument so far implies that despite recent reductions in inflation, the scope for government exploitation of its monopoly power over money is growing. If so, unless this monopoly power is somehow constrained, we seem to be headed for even more rapid inflation, perhaps with some cyclical deviations from the long-term trend, than we suffered from not so long ago.

FINANCIAL INNOVATION AND THE EROSION OF THE MONOPOLY OVER MONEY

The evolution of our monetary system over the last three millennia reflects a tension between two conflicting forces. One is the competitive search for lower-cost media of exchange; the other is the desire of the state to monopolize the supply of money. The tension between them became more acute with the emergence of banking. On the one hand, banking substantially reduced the cost of providing money; on the other, the state could not monopolize banking as effectively as it could monopolize coinage.

When prices were stable or even falling, as they usually were under the gold standard, there were only modest incentives to seek, or to offer, alternatives to holding government currency. But as democratic governments gradually shed the constraints on exploiting the monopoly over money, the incentives also increased for banks and other financial intermediaries to offer less costly alternatives to government currency and regulated deposits. Moreover, this competitive response coincided with, and was accelerated by, revolutionary technological advances in data storage, data processing, and telecommunications that sharply cut the costs of providing monetary and financial services.

How great the shift from regulated to unregulated monetary assets has been shows up in the shrinkage of the real value of the non-interest-bearing reserves held by financial institutions. Without these reserves, held as either currency or non-interest-bearing deposits with the Federal Reserve System, the government would earn no seignorage from the creation of deposits by financial institutions. Adjusted for inflation, the amount of reserves fell by nearly half between 1972 and 1984 – from just over $70 billion[7] in 1972 to just over $35 billion in 1984 (measured in 1982 dollars). Even the substantial increase in the holding of currency caused by the rise of the underground economy did not prevent the real value of the monetary base – the sum of currency held by the public and the reserves held by the banking system – from falling in the same period.

This erosion of the monopoly over money has had at least three major effects. First, it has reduced the maximum one-time wealth transfer the government could extract by further exploitation of the monopoly over money. Second, it has reduced the maximum steady flow of seignorage that the monopoly can generate. And finally, for reasons G. P. Dwyer and T. R. Savings (1986) and I (Glasner 1986) have explained elsewhere, it has reduced the rate of inflation that would yield that maximum seignorage revenue.

The final conclusion suggests that although relaxing the constraints on the monopoly over money has given governments license to indulge their inflationary appetites, the inflationary binge may be curtailed by a new kind of constraint – competition. If governments don't curtail inflation, they risk losing control over the supply of money, as private financial institutions undercut the government by supplying less costly monetary instruments and payments services than the government provides.

A final observation comes to mind. The erosion of the monopoly over money also coincides with what may be a reduced national security role for that monopoly when enormous expenditures are continually required to maintain a military establishment at an ostensibly high state of readiness. The monopoly may, therefore, no longer be necessary to finance small-scale conflicts. And since the weapons to be used in a nuclear conflict must be prepared in advance, the monopoly is not well suited for paying for those weapons either.

So the erosion of the monopoly over money might be viewed as a response to the declining importance of the national security rationale for the monopoly. If so, governments may have less interest in reducing inflation just to try to preserve the value of a monopoly over money that is losing importance anyway. High inflation may be a strategy of disinvestment in a state monopoly whose social justification no longer exists.

MONETARY POLICY IN A COMPETITIVE MONETARY SYSTEM

Although the emergence of a competitive monetary system may offer us the possibility of eventually creating a less inflationary monetary environment than the one we have grown accustomed to, if we don't improve

---

7 Throughout, values in billions are in U.S. billions.

our understanding of monetary policy, we could still face an unpleasant period of fluctuating inflation and extreme monetary instability. What policies can we adopt and implement to avoid the latter prospect? The answer to that question has grown more uncertain as the increasingly competitive nature of the monetary system has cast doubt on the continuing ability of the monetary authorities to conduct monetary policy in the conventional way. If the monetary authorities are losing control over the supply of money, how can they follow the policy advocated by Milton Friedman and other Monetarist economists of maintaining a steady rate of growth in the money stock? Others ask whether it is possible any longer for governments to peg exchange rates or control interest rates – the other levers by which governments have traditionally sought to operate monetary policy.

In Part III of this book, I am going to argue that although the emerging competitive monetary system has curtailed the ability of governments to conduct monetary policy in the ways they have been accustomed to since the demise of the gold standard, they can still ensure price stability, and hence overall economic stability, through a modified commitment to convertibility. But to understand the rationale for that kind of system, we have to look at some of the early sources of monetary theory.

So in Part II, I am going to explain how monetary theory developed in the nineteenth century and how that development affected, and in turn was affected by, numerous attempts to reform the monetary system in the nineteenth century. Unfortunately, change did not always, as we shall see, mean progress, either in monetary theory or in monetary reform.

The uncertain progress of monetary theory and monetary reform

3

The classical theory of money

The conventional explanation for suppressing competition in the supply of money is that competition increases the supply and reduces the price of whatever competitors are supplying. For most goods this a great benefit. But unlike the physical services generated by, say, a refrigerator, which do not depend on how much, or how little, the refrigerator is worth, monetary services would vanish if money lost its value. Cheapening an ordinary good does not destroy the physical attributes that make it desirable. But money, as such, has no physical attributes that people desire. What they want from it is the convenience it offers as a medium of exchange, not any physical services. Thus cheapening money subverts its usefulness as a medium of exchange.

In the conventional view, private money suppliers would, if allowed to compete, increase the quantity of their moneys until those moneys lost all value. The state, therefore, must restrain competition to keep the monetary system from self-destruction.

Opposing the conventional view, I argued earlier that competing suppliers of money would be foolish to allow the value of their moneys to fall. Instead, they would compete to reduce the cost of holding their moneys. To ensure against depreciation, they would make their moneys convertible, at a stipulated conversion rate, into a real asset whose value they could not control, such as gold or silver. And as a further inducement for people to hold their moneys, they would pay competitive interest. Thus a competitive monetary system is not inclined toward self-destruction because the price of money that competition drives down is the cost of holding money, not its exchange value.

I also argued that the state almost always assumed a dominant role in defining the monetary unit and in coining and issuing money, not because that role was essential for a monetary system to function, but because that role was vital to the defense of its sovereignty. Far from wishing to protect the public from a debased currency, the state barred competition in the supply of money precisely to eliminate any alternative moneys to which the public might switch when it chose to debase the currency for its own purposes. Those purposes, I hasten to add, may have been wholly legitimate, and my intention is not to challenge them. I merely want to make clear what the motives of the state were in restricting competition in the supply of money.

At the end of the last chapter, I conjectured that the national defense rationale for a monopoly over money may be losing importance for the modern state and that the benefits from allowing competition are growing. If I am correct, then the recent trend toward deregulation of banking and financial markets marks a fundamental shift from a state-dominated to a competitive monetary system.

What does this shift hold in store for us? My argument suggests that it will eventually mean reduced inflation (Dwyer and Saving 1986; Glasner 1986). But that inference pertains only to average inflation; it says nothing about the variability of inflation. To make inferences about how a competitive monetary system may affect the variability of inflation and macroeconomic performance, we need a monetary theory of inflation and of macroeconomic performance. But following the conventional view of the role of the state in the monetary system, monetary theory for over a century has ignored the role of competition in that system. So conventional monetary theory, whether Keynesian or Monetarist, has little to tell us about what current developments mean.

A new approach to monetary theory might therefore seem to be in order. My earlier discussion of how money would be supplied competitively suggests what such an approach to monetary theory might be like. Yet this approach is not entirely new; it can be traced back to some of the most illustrious figures in the history of economics. Most of its basic elements, for example, are plainly discernible in Adam Smith's *Wealth of Nations*. Unfortunately, lacking the analytical tools to develop it, he left the theory in a somewhat primitive form.

That is no criticism of Smith. His greatness lay in an intuitive grasp of the forces shaping the economic life of humankind that far outran his purely analytical skills. In most branches of economics, his exposition of fundamental principles was the foundation for later advances. And for about seventy-five years after *The Wealth of Nations* was published, many of Smith's successors developed the monetary theory that he was the first to articulate. It is this imperfectly developed theory of a competitively supplied money that I call the classical theory of money.

But scientific progress does not always proceed along a straight path. Although the outlines of a theory of a competitive money supply took shape in the classical period, the quantity theory of money was also being developed at that time. The theories took shape simultaneously because the rapidly changing monetary conditions of the late eighteenth and early nineteenth centuries called for a theory of a competitively supplied money and for a theory of a monopolistically supplied money. The parallel development of two different approaches to monetary theory relevant to different institutional setups did not have to cause confusion. But it did. The confusion arose, in part, because correct inferences about how the quantity of a monopolistically supplied money affects prices were incorrectly applied to circumstances in which money was supplied competitively. By the end of the nineteenth century, most economists either ignored or rejected what to Smith had been a crucial distinction: whether a money was supplied monopolistically by the government or competitively by private banks.

But I am getting slightly ahead of myself. The story of how the quantity theory displaced the classical theory is one I shall tell in the next chapter. First we need to get a better grasp of what the strengths and weaknesses of the classical theory of money were.[1] Where better to start than with Adam Smith?

ADAM SMITH ON THE QUANTITY AND VALUE OF MONEY

The overwhelming importance of Adam Smith's contribution to economics is beyond dispute. So it is more than just a curiosity that Smith has not been highly regarded as a monetary economist by later – particularly twentieth-century – commentators.[2] This low esteem demands some ex-

---

1 The theoretical argument of this and the following chapter rests on a seminal article by Earl Thompson (1974a). For a more complete development of the argument see Thompson's article and two of my own (Glasner 1985a, 1989).
2 Jacob Viner (1937a/1965, p. 87), one of the leading historians of monetary theory, was particularly critical of Smith for ignoring the price-specie-flow mechanism David Hume had formulated to explain the international adjustment of prices and gold flows. And Joseph Schumpeter (1954, p. 367), perhaps the preeminent historian of economics, com-

planation. The obvious one, of course, is that the quality of Chapter 2 of Book 2 of *The Wealth of Nations* – the chapter on money – is inferior to the rest of that masterpiece. But this explanation raises all sorts of embarrassing questions about why Smith should have written such a poor chapter when he was well acquainted with the monetary writings of his close friend David Hume, which Smith's critics regard as superior to anything Smith had to say.

So we ought to consider the possibility that the bad reviews Smith's monetary theory has received tell us more about his critics than about his theory. That they have rated Hume – the quantity theorist par excellence – so far above Smith suggests that they share Hume's quantity-theoretic presumptions so completely that they do not even realize that Smith was offering a theory fundamentally different from Hume's. His failure to incorporate Hume's monetary analysis into *The Wealth of Nations* has therefore been a continuing source of puzzlement and controversy (Viner 1937/1965, p. 87). And until very recently, that failure has been regarded as a major shortcoming, though from a different perspective it is surely a strength.[3]

At the close of the nineteenth century, there were few economists who still were using the classical model Smith originated. Since Smith paid little attention to the quantity theory and instead concentrated on explaining how a competitive banking system would operate, it is not surprising that twentieth-century commentators, writing after the competitive approach had long since fallen out of favor, found "comparatively little of theoretical interest" (Hayek 1939/1969, p. 37). Despite the eminence of its source, that judgment was, as I shall now show, thoroughly misguided.

Smith grounded his monetary theory in the proposition that the value of metallic money equals that of the metals it contains, while the value of convertible paper money equals that of the metallic money into which it is convertible. Since convertibility pins it down, the value of money is independent of how much money the banking system creates. If banks create more money than the public is willing to hold, the result is not a depreciation of money, which is impossible under convertibility, but a drain on the banks that forces the withdrawal of excess money.

What determines the values of gold and of silver? Precisely the same forces that determine the values of all other commodities. In Smith's words (1776/1937, pp. 312–13):

pares Smith's monetary performance unfavorably with Hume's. Another historian, Lloyd Mints (1945), castigates Smith as the inventor of the fallacious real-bills doctrine.

3 A trend toward a more favorable reassessment of Smith's work has begun to emerge. See, for example, Girton and Roper (1978), Humphrey (1981), Laidler (1981), and Glasner (1985a, 1989).

The classical theory of money

A paper currency which [because of doubtful convertibility] falls below the value of gold and silver coin, does not thereby sink the value of those metals, or occasion equal quantities of them to exchange for a smaller quantity of goods of any other kind. The proportion between the value of gold and silver and that of goods of any other kind, depends in all cases, not upon the nature and quantity of any particular paper money, which may be current in any particular country, but on the richness or poverty of the mines, which happen at any particular time to supply the great market of the commercial world with those metals. It depends upon the proportion between the quantity of labour which is necessary in order to bring a certain quantity of gold and silver to market, and that which is necessary in order to bring thither a certain quantity of goods.

This passage shows Smith's keen understanding of the relationship between the value of paper money and the value of precious metals. Competitively issued paper money has value only insofar as it is convertible into a valuable asset such as gold or silver. Uncertainty about convertibility would correspondingly reduce the value of paper money, causing it to circulate at a discount in relation to the precious metals.

The passage also shows that, contrary to conventional assessments, Smith's monetary theory was better than his theory of relative prices. On most points, his monetary theory can stand independently of his theory of relative prices. But on some crucial issues, the weakness of his theory of relative prices, based on some sort of cost-of-production or labor theory of value, led him and his followers into confusion and error.

Where his value theory went wrong was in asserting that the causal relationship between cost and price runs from cost to price. He thought that if an ounce of gold is worth five hundred times more than an ounce of lead, it is *because* it takes five hundred times more resources to produce an ounce of gold than to produce an ounce of lead. But it is more nearly correct to reverse the direction of causation. People will devote five hundred times more resources to producing an ounce of gold than they will to producing an ounce of lead only because an ounce of gold is worth five hundred times more than an ounce of lead.

The point is not just semantic. Costs of production are not fixed once and for all. How much it costs to produce something depends on how much of it is being produced. Producing more allows certain economies to be realized by making better use of otherwise only partially used resources; but beyond some rate of production, producing more in a given length of time puts pressure on resources that drives up costs. So the reason that price usually approximates the cost of production is that the cost changes along with the rate of output. A high price elicits a higher rate of output and a higher cost of production than a low price. But that is an insight neither Smith nor any of his immediate successors were aware of — at least not sufficiently to be able to deploy it in their theory of the relative values of commodities.

As I just noted, Smith not only developed a theory of the value of money, he also worked out at least the outlines of a theory of what determines the quantity of money in existence. In doing so, he drew on his familiarity with the emergence of the Scottish banking system (Checkland 1976). That banking system (the most advanced of the eighteenth century) obviously impressed him with its efficiency in substituting a less costly medium of exchange (paper notes or checks drawn against deposits) for a more costly one (coins or bullion consisting of precious metals).

In contrast, David Hume (1752a/1955, 1752b/1955), Smith's close friend and fellow Scotsman, took a decidedly hostile view of banks. That hostility may have been occasioned by Hume's lengthy stay in France, where he witnessed firsthand the unhappy French experience with banks in the eighteenth century. Hume thought banks would inevitably debase the currency because they would always try to substitute cheap paper for precious metals. Substituting a lot of cheap paper for a smaller amount of precious metals would cause inflation and a loss of precious metals to foreign countries. "I scarcely know," wrote Hume (1752b/1955, pp. 67–68),

any method of sinking money below its level, but those institutions of banks, funds, and paper-credit which are so much practiced in this kingdom. These render paper equivalent to money, circulate it throughout the whole state, make it supply the place of gold and silver, raise proportionately the price of labour and commodities, and by that means either banish a great part of those precious metals, or prevent their farther encrease.

Smith strongly disagreed. He denied that banks, while committed to converting notes into gold or silver on demand, would issue too much money. The banknotes issued by the banks merely displaced an equal amount of specie, so that neither the total quantity of money in circulation nor the general level of prices would be affected. Without mentioning him by name, Smith (pp. 308–09) directly addressed Hume's argument:

The increase of paper money, it has been said, by augmenting the quantity, and diminishing the value of the whole currency, necessarily augments the money price of commodities. But as the quantity of gold and silver, which is taken from the currency, is always equal to the quantity of paper which is added to it, paper money does not necessarily increase the quantity of the whole currency.

Although essentially correct, this passage is subject to two qualifications. First, in asserting that banknotes would displace an equal amount of gold (it will be less tedious if I leave silver out of the discussion, since in this context everything said about one applies to the other) from circulation, Smith implicitly assumed that people would want to hold exactly the same amount of banknotes they had been holding in gold. In fact, they would probably want to hold a larger amount of banknotes than they were holding in gold; so less gold would be displaced than the amount of banknotes issued by the banks.[4] But that still doesn't mean that the introduction of banknotes would raise prices. It just means that a competitive banking system is so sensitive to the demand for banknotes that it would supply as many notes as the public demanded in place of specie and coin. A generous reading of Smith confirms that this is how he believed a competitive banking system works.

The second qualification is necessary to fill in a gap left by Smith's faulty theory of relative prices. Using the theory to determine the relative value of gold, he failed to note that the gold displaced by banknotes reflected a reduction in the total world demand for gold, which would depress its value in relation to commodities and raise all prices measured in gold. This effect of the creation of bank money is to be distinguished from the one Hume worried about, since it would arise only insofar as the creation of banknotes reduced the demand for gold enough to affect its value.

Hume contended that prices would rise only in the country in which the notes were issued. But a decline in the value of gold would affect equally prices in every country whose currency was defined in terms of gold, not just the one in which banknotes had displaced gold. Unfortunately, because he thought that only the cost of production of, not the demand for, gold determined its value, Smith ignored the possibility that banknotes could affect the demand for, and hence the value of, gold.

Let me now summarize the basic elements of the classical theory of money. The value of money equals the value of the amount of gold into which it is convertible. In the classical theory, that value corresponds to the cost of producing gold. But in the modern version of the classical theory, the value of gold depends on the demand for gold and the existing stock at any moment. Either way, for a small country on the gold standard, the value of gold is invariant.

The quantity of money, however, is not fixed. The banking system supplies whatever quantity of money the public demands, either in notes or in deposits. Under convertibility, therefore, the price level doesn't depend on how much money the banking system produces; it depends on the value of gold. But the value of gold, at least under the small-country assumption, is independent of the amount of money produced by the banking system.[5]

---

4 But the point was not made explicitly until 1802, when Henry Thornton (1802/1969, pp. 95–96), perhaps the greatest of all classical monetary economists, made just this criticism of Smith, but without falling into the opposite mistake of David Hume.

5 I am overlooking the possibility that the changes in the demand for money could affect the demand for gold. Certainly this assumption could be defended for a single country which constituted only a small part of the international market for gold. I discuss the

Most classical economists believed that competition among banks would ensure their good behavior. A bank could not issue more notes or create more deposits than the public wished to hold at the prevailing price level, because doing so would mean accumulating too many debits at the clearinghouse at which the mutual claims of banks were settled. An adverse balance would require the expanding bank to settle its balance with other banks in gold or some other acceptable form of payment. The unacceptable alternative to demanding redemption would be for the banks to allow the expanding bank to increase its market share at their expense. Unless all the banks in the banking system colluded to expand in concert, a bank would expand on its own only if it believed that its notes and deposits would be held willingly by the public after they were issued. But for all banks to expand in concert would mean that banks were not competing with each other, a circumstance contrary to a fundamental assumption of classical theory.[6]

THE ROLE OF COMPETITION IN CLASSICAL MONETARY THEORY

The desirability of competition in the supply of money was a basic premise of the classical theory. The premise was always a controversial one, which is why Adam Smith devoted special attention to criticizing David Hume's arguments against competition in the supply of money. Although Smith's position received widespread support for a while, the weight of opinion swung decisively over to Hume's side in the second half of the nineteenth century.

Because the anticompetitive view became so predominant in monetary theory, the very notion of competition in the supply of money may still seem eccentric if not outlandish. So a bit more explanation of the classical position may be useful. The central question at issue in the debate over competition in the supply of money is whether such competition necessarily induces the banking system to overexpand. Why should competition lead to overexpansion? Early opponents of competition in banking, such as Longfield (1840) and McCulloch (1831), believed that banks would compete for market share by increasing their lending, creating additional notes and deposits. The response of other banks, they assumed, would be to increase their lending as well.

point in "The weak link in classical theory," later in this chapter. In Chapters 4 and 5 we shall see that monetary disturbances that affected the value of gold caused many of the worst fluctuations in the international economy in the nineteenth and twentieth centuries.

6 See Selgin (1988) for a more complete discussion of the mechanisms that would thwart an expansion by all banks in concert.

The classical theory of money

It is not difficult to see that, formulated in this way, the argument that competing banks create more notes and deposits than the public wants to hold presumes that some banks will passively allow others to expand at their expense. That is not a very plausible assumption about how banks behave. It seems more likely that, instead, they would seek to acquire the liabilities of the expanding bank and demand their redemption, forcing the expanding bank to shrink to its original size. Nevertheless, the modern money-multiplier analysis, which for two generations has been taught in all economics textbooks, embodies this untenable assumption. Let me explain how it does so.

The money-multiplier analysis (which is usually carried out only for deposits but could be carried out for banknotes equally well or poorly) begins by assuming a stable relationship between the reserves banks hold and the amount of deposits they are willing or legally allowed to create on the basis of those reserves. This relationship is expressed as a required reserve ratio. If the ratio is 20 percent, the banking system can create five times the amount of deposits that it holds in reserves. If reserves are $1,000, the banking system can create $5,000 in deposits.

Now suppose that one morning Mr. Jones deposits $100 of government currency (or, if you prefer, gold coin) into Security Bank. Since currency can be counted as reserves, the reserves of Security Bank and of the entire banking system have just increased by $100. Security Bank needs to hold only $20 of the $100 deposited as reserves against that amount. So with $80 of excess reserves, Security wants to increase its lending by $80, because even if the proceeds of the loan are deposited in another bank, it will have the reserves it needs to meet a demand for payment.

Let's say that Security lends to Mr. Smith by crediting him with a deposit of $80. Presumably, Mr. Smith borrowed to finance a purchase. So he writes a check for $80 to, say, Mr. Wilson as payment. What does Mr. Wilson do with the $80 check he receives? Suppose he deposits it in Safety Bank. After receiving the deposit, Safety Bank gets $80 of reserves transferred to it from Security Bank. But Safety needs only $16 more as reserves for the new deposit, so it feels free to increase its lending by $64. A similar round of lending, deposit creation, and spending would transfer the deposit to Stability Bank and enable it to increase its lending by creating $51.20 in new deposits. We have followed this story far enough to learn all it has to teach us. But if we let it go on further, we could verify that $400 of deposits had been created in addition to the initial deposit of $100 in currency. The deposits of the entire system would be raised to $5,500. And presumably, if there were no legal reserve requirement, the banking system might expand to infinity.

But the whole story is based on a misconception. It presumes that banks don't compete for deposits. Each successive deposit allows a bank to expand lending and increase its profits. Banks, therefore, are always primed to expand and have to be restrained from doing so. The question that arises, then, is why banks don't compete to attract those profitable deposits instead of just waiting passively to receive them willy-nilly as the loans made by other banks are spent and as other banks expand at their expense. If they did compete, they would pay interest on those deposits commensurate with the interest they were charging on the loans they made. But if it were paying competitive interest on deposits, a bank whose reserves increased would not automatically be induced to increase its lending, and there would be no tendency to expand that had to be restrained (Tobin 1963).

In the conventional view, convertibility is a constraint imposed by law on the expansionary tendencies of the banking system. But it is not, in that view, a very good constraint. The constraint becomes effective only after expansion has gone on long enough to cause a drain on the reserves of the banking system. A serious drain would threaten convertibility, thereby forcing banks to contract sharply to avoid having to suspend convertibility.

But in the classical view, since a bank, unlike the state, cannot force the public to hold its money, it must offer its customers sufficiently attractive terms to induce them to hold its money voluntarily. So convertibility is not a constraint imposed by law;[7] it is the means by which banks ensure the general acceptability of their money, without which acceptability they could not stay in business. Its function is not somehow to prevent banks from expanding as much as they otherwise would want to; it is the means by which they can guarantee the purchasing power of the money they create and the interest payments they promise. By providing such a guarantee, competing banks can achieve a competitive equilibrium in which they provide the public with just the amount of money – and no more – that the public wants to hold on the competitive terms they offer.

7 However, Smith did argue (1776/1937, pp. 309–10, 313) that the law should require that redemption be made on demand and that banks should not be allowed to invoke, as Scottish banks had occasionally, an "optional clause" that would allow them to convert at a later date with interest. See Dowd (1987, 1989) for a defense of the option clause. While Smith was not dogmatic in his support of competitive banking, and he did allow perhaps more scope for government intervention in banking than in other areas, he certainly was committed to the general principle of competition in banking.

The classical theory of money

In the economy the classical theorists envisioned, the monetary sector could not, barring a change in the value of gold, be a source of instability. A disturbance could only arise in the nonmonetary or real sector (including the market for gold).

What renders the classical economy immune from monetary disturbances? To give an answer, I must first explain how the monetary sector could conceivably disturb the rest of the economy. The best way to do that is to think of an economy, let us call it Eldorado, in which only gold is used as money. Suppose that, after years of stability, Eldoradons stumble onto an enormous new deposit of gold.

What interests us here is how Eldoradans respond to the new gold they have found. As the new gold is extracted, the Eldoradans who acquire it don't just want to hold it; they try to exchange at least some of it for other goods. But the additional gold does not get used up through exchange because whatever someone gives up someone else acquires. Those who acquire it next probably don't want to continue holding the gold either, at any rate, not all of it, and will try to exchange it for other goods. But the community as a whole in a closed economy like Eldorado cannot trade its gold away for other goods.

Since the community is stuck with the gold it extracts, there is only one way for the growing stock of gold in Eldorado to be held willingly: the value of gold must decline. This means that all prices quoted in gold must rise. As gold loses value, people will want to use more of it for its various nonmonetary purposes, and they will also want to increase the amount of it they hold for monetary purposes in proportion to the general rise in prices.

Gold in this economy is a hot potato. Somebody has to hold it even though it is too hot (too valuable) to hang onto. So it gets passed from hand to hand until it cools down (loses value). When it is very hot (valuable), people cannot (are not willing to) hold it. But by trying to get rid of it (exchange it for something else), people cool it off (drive its value down). Eventually, it becomes cool (cheap) enough for people to be able (willing) to hold it.

The point of this example has been to show how an economy responds to a particular monetary disturbance – an increase in the stock of money in the absence of a change in demand for it. But it was the real economy that had to adjust to the increase in the stock of money. As people tried to get rid of their excess holdings of gold, they demanded more goods and services than before. Not only did it cause prices in general to rise, but the increased demand for goods and services would stimulate — not permanently, but for a while at any rate — more production and employment.

That is one kind of monetary disturbance; three others could also occur in our model economy. One is a reduction in the public's demand for gold, say, because merchants begin extending credit to their customers, enabling people to hold less gold than they did before. The response to this disturbance would be the same as the response to an increase in the gold stock. If the community is holding more gold than it wants to and if there is no one outside the community with whom to exchange it, the only possible adjustment is for gold to depreciate.

The other two monetary disturbances are a loss of gold[8] and an increase in the public's demand to hold gold. Either one would cause the public to seek to add to its holdings of gold. Just as the community as a whole cannot reduce its holdings of gold, neither can it increase its holdings — at least not by more than the current output of the mines. But as people try to increase their holdings of gold, the total supply of gold offered in exchange declines and gold becomes more valuable. As it does, the community economizes on gold for nonmonetary uses and reduces its holdings for monetary uses in proportion to the fall in prices. When prices fall enough, the community will find that it is no longer holding less gold than it wants to.

But the economy of Eldorado is not the one classical theorists envisioned. They were not interested in an economy in which the only money was gold; they were concerned with one in which the money was largely supplied by the banking system. As we just saw, if there is no banking system, the community can respond to a monetary disturbance only by altering its expenditures on real goods and services. In that case, it is the real economy that must adjust to any divergence between the community's desired and its actual holdings of money.

However, classical theorists believed that the banking system always adjusts to provide the public with as much money as it wants to hold. That adjustment keeps a monetary disturbance from obliging the public to alter its rate of expenditure and thus also avoids any disturbance in the real economy that would have been caused by a change in the rate of expenditure.

This explains why classical economists believed that there was an analytical dichotomy between the monetary and the nonmonetary sectors of an economy.[9] Under the classical dichotomy, the relative price ratios

---

8 In this closed economy, a loss of gold could occur only through some natural disaster.
9 The notion that there was a dichotomy in classical theory between the forces that determined the relative prices of goods and the forces that determined the absolute level of their prices quoted in money is one that has been explored extensively in the litera-

between real commodities are determined exclusively in the nonmonetary sector, and the price level and the real quantity of money are determined exclusively in the monetary sector. Since money bears competitive interest, no one incurs a cost of holding money. So there is no reason for people to adjust their holdings of money by altering their rate of expenditure. The rate of expenditure depends on the demand for real commodities, which, in turn, depends only on the relative prices of commodities, not on the quantity of money.

Say's Law

Although their intuition was excellent, the classical economists did not fully explain how the profit-maximizing behavior of competing banks guaranteed that the public would be supplied with as much money as it demanded. Their attempts to provide such an explanation are now known as Say's Law and the Law of Reflux. The former addresses the possibility that there might be too little money in the economy, so that the public would not spend enough (at current prices) to buy up all the goods being produced. The latter addresses the possibility that there might be too much money in the economy, so that the public would spend more than was needed (at current prices) to buy up all the goods being produced.

Say's Law takes its name from a French economist of the early nineteenth century, Jean Baptiste Say, whose *Treatise on Political Economy* was the next great general work in economics after *The Wealth of Nations*. The industrial revolution was getting started, and the more advanced European countries were beginning to undergo the fluctuations of the business cycle. There were those who contended that depressions were occurring because productive capacity was increasing more rapidly than purchasing power. That imbalance supposedly caused a general glut of unsold products in the market, leading to bankruptcies and unemployment.

Say advanced his law of the markets to explain these depressions. He argued that since people produce goods only to earn enough to be able to buy other goods, it was not possible for too much of everything to be produced. It was possible that too much of some things might be produced; but in that case, too little would have been produced of other things. The cure for depressions was to redeploy resources from the pro-

ture. The *locus classicus* for all these discussions is Patinkin (1965). The classical theorists certainly distinguished between real and monetary analysis for expository purposes, but whether they believed that is how the world actually worked has been disputed. The general consensus that has emerged from Patinkin's work is that insofar as they did dichotomize the real and the monetary sectors, they were mistaken. I follow Thompson (1974a) in arguing that they did dichotomize between the real and monetary sectors and that they were correct to do so given their belief in a competitive banking system.

duction of things that were not wanted to the production of things that were. No general glut of all things was possible. Or, as Say's Law is sometimes paraphrased, supply creates its own demands.[10]

Modern economists, misunderstanding the classical theory, now argue that Say's Law is valid only for a barter economy in which goods are exchanged directly for goods and not for money (Patinkin 1965, chap. 8). The reason they insist on limiting Say's Law to a barter economy is that if the public wanted to increase its holdings of money, it seems obvious that it could do so only by curtailing spending. If people had to cut back their spending to increase their holdings of money, then as our earlier discussion showed, there would be excess supplies of all real goods on the market until prices fell enough to raise the value of the public's money balances to the desired level. Thus Say's Law, in the strict sense of denying the possibility of a general glut of all real commodities on the market seems invalid. Or, lacking a theory of a competitive supply of money, so most modern economists seem to think.

But in the world of classical monetary theory, it is the banking system, not the real economy, that adjusts to a divergence between the public's actual and desired holdings of money. Thus no glut of real goods is possible without offsetting shortages of other real goods. Say (1880/1971, p. 134) himself explicitly denied that too little money could be the cause of a general oversupply of goods:

Sales cannot be said to be dull because money is scarce but because other products are so. There is always money enough to conduct the circulation and mutual interchange of other values, when those values really exist. Should the increase of traffic require more money to facilitate it, the want is easily supplied and is a strong indication of prosperity. . . . In such cases, merchants know well enough how to find substitutes for the product serving as a medium of exchange or money (by bills at sight, or after date, bank notes, running credits, write-offs, etc. as at London and Amsterdam) and money itself soon pours in for this reason, that all produce naturally gravitates to that place where it is most in demand.

Say recognized that the banking system would increase the quantity of banknotes (at the time he wrote, deposits were not commonly used in France) to meet any unsatisfied demand of the public to hold money.[11]

---

10 Say's Law, to be sure, has been interpreted in various ways, not all of which are consistent with my interpretation here. But my interpretation does, I believe, conform to the most widely accepted interpretations (Lange 1942; Patinkin 1965), though I strongly disagree with their assessment of its validity and significance. See Sowell (1972) for a comprehensive rundown of possible interpretations.

11 In his testimony before a parliamentary commission investigating the resumption of the gold standard in 1819, David Ricardo (1952a p. 386), who was, if anything, a more devoted adherent of Say's Law than Say himself, also considered the possibility that the desire of the public to add to its holdings of money could cause a general glut:

Q. When merchants have a want of confidence in each other, which dis-

The classical theory of money

In his usage, only coin or specie was actual money; banknotes and other credit instruments that performed as media of exchange he called money substitutes. But semantic differences do not alter his basic point that a competitive banking system would never allow an unsatisfied demand for money to turn into a general oversupply of all real goods.

A second error modern interpreters of classical monetary theory and Say's Law commit is to argue that an economy in which Say's Law held would have an indeterminate price level. Here is another inappropriate application of quantity-theoretic reasoning. For in classical theory, the price level is determined by the convertibility of money into gold. According to the quantity theory the price level is determined by the demand to hold, and the existing stock of, money. When people want to hold more money than there is in existence, the price level falls as people reduce spending on real goods. If demand is less than supply, the same reasoning implies that the price level rises. Since Say's Law says that the quantity of money, not the price level, adjusts to any difference between desired and actual holdings of money, it rules out a quantity-theoretic explanation of the price level. The conclusion modern economists – most notably Patinkin (1965) – have drawn is that if Say's Law did obtain, the price level could wander about in any direction because Say's Law rules out the very mechanism that forces it to settle down at a particular value.

But this criticism of Say's Law overlooks the possibility that convertibility is what pins the price level down. Given the value of gold, the price level is fully determined by that value and the conversion rate of money into gold. To see why, consider an economy with three real commodities, gold, wheat, and wool. Suppose the relative price of wheat in terms of gold is one-half ounce a bushel and the relative price of wool in terms of gold is one-quarter ounce a yard. Let the conversion rate of money into gold be $10 an ounce. Then the money prices of wheat and wool will be $5 a bushel and $2.50 a yard. Nothing that happens to the demand for, or the supply of, money need change any of those relative prices. So even though Say's Law could still hold, the price level is indeed determined.

inclines them to deal on credit, is there not a greater demand for money?
A. Undoubtedly.
Q. Then if this is a period when there is a greater demand for money on account of a want of confidence, does it not follow that it would be an inconvenient period for reducing the means of accommodation?
A. It appears to me that that very circumstance would make a smaller reduction efficacious for that purpose; a demand for currency in consequence of a want of confidence, I should think a legitimate demand; it would enable the bank to keep their circulation at a higher level than they would be able to do, if there had not been a demand from such a cause.

The Law of Reflux

Although implicit in Adam Smith's discussion of banking, the Law of Reflux was not explicitly formulated until 1844, when the English monetary theorist John Fullarton, perhaps the most underrated monetary economist of the nineteenth century, advanced it to refute the now-familiar contention (the reverse of the one Say had addressed) that the banking system might issue too much money and that, trying to reduce its excess holdings of money, the public would increase spending, driving up prices and undermining the gold standard.[12]

This was the argument made by supporters of Peel's Bank Charter Act of 1844, which I shall have more to say about in the next chapter. They held that a persistent overissue of banknotes by the Bank of England and, particularly, by the country banks had driven prices up in, and gold out of, England. Fullarton, an opponent of the act, maintained that an excess issue of banknotes was impossible because any unwanted notes would be returned to the banks rather than generating additional spending that would raise prices. He made this point more directly and more clearly than Say had made the corresponding one in the opposite case. Distinguishing between irredeemable paper money issued by the government and convertible bank money, Fullarton (1845/1969 p. 64) wrote:

Still more decidedly have the conventional issues of governments all the characteristics of a forced currency. . . . [E]ven after the notes have become depreciated, the law compels the private creditor to accept them in satisfaction of his claim; and the government having no better money to offer, the only alternative left to its creditors and dependents is to take this or none. Bank-notes, on the other hand, are never issued but on the demand of the recipient parties. New gold coin and new conventional notes are introduced into the market by being made the medium of payments. Bank-notes, on the contrary are never issued but on *loan*, and an equal amount of notes must be returned whenever the loan comes due. Bank-notes never, therefore, can clog the market by their redundance, nor afford a motive to pay anyone a reduced value in order to get rid of them.

Fullarton (pp. 64–65) went on to give a remarkably incisive explanation of why an overissue of banknotes was not possible:

12 The relationship between Say's Law and the Law of Reflux was never recognized in the literature until I associated the two in Glasner (1985a). The closest approach to a recognition of their basic identity is by Frank Fetter (1965, p. 232), although he speaks of the real-bills doctrine rather than the Law of Reflux. "In the setting of inconvertibility the policy thrust of the real bills doctrine was that if banks loaned only on good short-term assets there was no danger of inflation. In the setting of the gold standard there were subliminal traces of the idea that if banks continued to loan on good assets the total means of payment would increase with the volume of business, and that hence, even though the gold supply did not increase as rapidly as production, there was no danger of price decline from an inadequate monetary supply."

However prone individuals may be to abuse at times the facility of borrowing, no merchant can ever desire to keep by him a larger sum in bank-notes than is indispensably necessary for his payments; and if any one were disposed to indulge in so unprofitable a fancy, it would be a matter of not the slightest importance to any one other than himself, for in as far as the public are concerned, notes which are not in use are the same as if they are not in existence. Those notes cannot be obtained from a banker, but by paying interest for the use of them, nor can they be obtained at all but for very short periods, at the expiration of which they must be replaced. Their circulation must always be strictly limited by the wants of those who have value or security to offer for them. And so limited, there can be no redundance; no holder of them can ever be placed in the same predicament with the importers of a double supply of bullion, or the recipients of a forced issue of government-paper, who have no means of turning their acquisitions to use but by submitting to part with them at a reduced value.

What Fullarton did not mention here is that banknotes can be acquired by exchanging goods for them as well as by borrowing from a bank. Nor did he explain why the costs of borrowing would deter spending, especially if, as some were quick to point out, banks competed to issue notes by reducing the interest rates they were charging on loans.[13]

But Fullarton was not as vulnerable to these criticisms as it may seem. For he recognized that competition would lead banks to pay interest on the money they issued. Thus any holder of money had to bear the forgone interest income he could earn by continuing to hold rather than spend the money. Though transactions costs probably made paying interest on banknotes prohibitively expensive, paying interest on deposits was not. Since banknotes could easily be converted into deposits, holders of banknotes would have to bear the cost of holding or using banknotes rather than deposits. The apparent profit margin banks could earn by non-interest-bearing notes would not lead banks to overissue notes because any excess notes would be converted into interest-bearing deposits. Instead of causing excessive spending, an overissue of banknotes would simply be converted into interest-bearing deposits.

Moreover, banks, like other intermediaries, can acquire additional assets only by inducing the public to hold more of their liabilities. So if they are competing for market share, they must do so, not simply by reducing the interest on loans, but by raising the interest they pay on deposits. All deposits that were issued, therefore, would be held willingly, so there would be no tendency for an increase in the quantity of deposits to promote spending and raise prices. Indeed, when money yields competitive interest and is costless to hold, the classical dichotomy obtains, so changes in the quantity of deposits held by the public would not affect spending

13 This was a point originally made by Thornton (1802/1969) and in the Report of the Bullion Committee (Cannan 1925/1969) of which he was the principal author.

decisions: If money balances were larger than desired, people would adjust by using the balances to reduce their indebtedness, not by altering their spending patterns. One last quotation from Fullarton (pp. 92–93)may be in order here:

The joint-stock banks have been far more successful in their efforts to promote and extend the use of banking accounts among all ranks throughout the kingdom, than in their attempts to engross or enlarge the circulation. This they have partly accomplished, by the facilities for that purpose which their numerous offices, dispersed over the country, afford to every man, but chiefly by the practice which they have borrowed from the Scotch bankers, of allowing interest to their depositors, and which, by the force of their example and competition, has become also, I believe, a very general practice among the private bankers everywhere but in London. The inducement which such a system holds out to individuals to become depositors in banks, and to those who are already depositors to increase their deposits, are sufficiently obvious; and it is equally apparent that such circumstances must have a decided influence in reducing the circulation of bank-notes. The tradesman, instead of keeping by him an unproductive hoard of such notes for his daily disbursements, will prefer paying them into a bank which allows him interest for the amount, without any prejudice to his perfect command over the principal. He will make his payments thenceforth by cheque; and those cheques will, in the vast majority of cases, be adjusted by transfer or exchange, without any resort to money.

The Scotch banks, among whom this practice of allowing interest to depositors has been coeval with their existence, are in themselves a standing refutation of the notion that bank-notes can be over-issued at the pleasure of the issuers.

Fullarton may have overstated his case somewhat in asserting that it was almost physically impossible for banks to overissue notes. The point he failed to explain adequately is that the quantity of money a bank creates is governed by the same economic incentives that govern the quantity of output any firm produces. By paying competitive interest on deposits, each bank reaches a point of equilibrium at which it no longer has any incentive, under given cost and demand conditions, to expand. The lesson the Law of Reflux teaches is that an economic process governs how much money a bank creates and that economic incentives can induce a bank to curtail as well as to expand its creation of money.

THE WEAK LINK IN CLASSICAL THEORY

As I have described it, the monetary system envisioned by classical monetary theorists has many attractive features. It relies on a competitive banking system to supply banknotes and deposits that are convertible into gold while market forces ensure that the banking system supplies as much money as (but no more than) the public wants to hold at the price level fixed by convertibility.

The responsiveness of the banking system to the public's demand for money is the most remarkable, though least understood, characteristic of the classical system. Since competitive banks supply as much money as the public demands, inflation cannot be caused by an excess supply of, nor depression by an excess demand for, money. Sadly, the idyllic, seemingly tranquil, world envisioned by classical theory is susceptible to turbulent storms that gather quickly when the value of gold changes substantially.

That the value of gold might change was a problem for the classical theory not only because it could cause inflation or deflation but also because classical theory could not readily explain the mechanism that caused the change. As we saw earlier, classical theory sought to use the cost of production to explain the value of commodities. But changes in production costs could affect the value of a durable good such as gold only over a long period of time. Over shorter periods, other factors affecting supply and demand would be more likely to alter the value of gold.

Although it was understood that large increases in the demand for gold could be deflationary, there was little systematic analysis of the relationship between the price level and the demand for gold. In general, classical theorists were content to assume that the value of gold would be highly stable, taking it almost as an index of commodity prices. And so, in England at any rate, convertibility into gold came to be regarded, without a great deal of serious analysis, as an essential characteristic of a stable monetary system (Fetter 1965).

But the expectation that the value of gold would remain stable over time was more wishful than scientific. Classical monetary theory was therefore on shaky ground because a metallic standard was not a secure basis for the price stability that was the classical economists' fundamental, though not well articulated, rationale for a metallic standard.

Moreover, certain kinds of monetary disturbances really could affect the value of gold or silver. In my earlier discussion of how the banking system responds to an increase in the demand for money, I assumed that the system would supply the additional money without increasing its demand to hold gold reserves. Under normal circumstances, this is a reasonable assumption, because if, at any moment, the public wanted to hold more money than it had, banks could create it without having to add to their gold reserves. Their demand for reserves arises to guard against the possibility of being called upon to redeem their money. Such demands are related to the number of transactions being made and to the public's confidence in the solvency of the banking system (White 1984; Selgin 1988). Thus an increase in the demand to hold money, unrelated to an increase in the number of transactions, occasions no demand by the banking system for additional reserves.

If an increase in the demand to hold money can be met by the banking system without an increased demand for gold, that increase need not have deflationary consequences. But there are obviously circumstances in which an increased demand for money would cause a significant increase in the demand for gold.

An increase in the demand for money is most likely to be transformed into an increase in the demand for gold in a financial panic when the public loses confidence in the banks and begins trying to convert bank-notes and deposits into gold. But since the market for gold is international, an exceptional demand for gold in one country could ordinarily induce a rapid influx of gold from abroad without changing the value of gold, and hence prices, very much in that country or elsewhere.

Only if several countries were simultaneously under severe financial pressure or if the one country under pressure were large compared to the world economy would a sudden increase in the demand for gold in a crisis substantially raise the international value of gold. At least after the gold discoveries of the 1840s and 1850s increased the world's stock of gold, Britain by itself was probably not large enough to have had much influence on the value of gold. But the resumption of convertibility after the Napoleonic Wars, as well as severe financial disturbances in the United States or in Britain in the 1830s and 1890s, probably did force up the value of gold internationally and so helped precipitate depressions in countries on the gold standard.

CONCLUSION

Compared to recent experience, the price level generated by the gold standard in the nineteenth century was remarkably stable. Long periods of slowly falling prices alternated with long periods of slowly rising prices, interspersed every decade or so with an episode of rapid deflation triggered by a financial panic. Despite its considerable strengths, classical monetary theory could not give an adequate explanation for the behavior of prices. Its theory of the gold market simply could not explain short- and medium-term fluctuations in prices.

These fluctuations in prices seemed more amenable to explanation by the quantity theory of money. Thus economists increasingly adopted the quantity theory to explain fluctuations in the value of money. Implicit in the quantity theory, however, was an unfavorable view of the role of competition in the monetary system. In the next chapter we shall see how the gradual ascendancy of the quantity theory came about in the nine-teenth century and how it led economists and statesmen to view compe-tition in banking with an increasingly suspicious eye.

4

The quantity theory of money

Unlike physicists and chemists, economists cannot conduct decisive experiments to find out which of two or more competing theories best explains reality. So economists don't have any simple, straightforward rules
to follow when choosing among rival theories. What determines their
choices? A complex and subtle process in which advocates of rival theories try to offer their colleagues persuasive reasons to accept their theories. A persuasive reason for accepting a theory could be that the theory
explains some well-known facts better than other theories do or that it
casts light on some previously unknown facts that were unilluminated by
the rival theories. A different type of argument in favor of a given theory
is that it fits in better than its rivals with other more general, and widely
accepted, theories. The rival theories are then pejoratively characterized
as ad hoc.

But these types of arguments, though they can be persuasive, are rarely
decisive. Because interpretations of factual situations are so subjective,
or because there may be persuasive arguments for having a special theory
for a particular class of phenomena, or because one can show that the
supposedly ad hoc theory really can be deduced from the more general

one, it is much easier for theories that have fallen out of fashion in economics to make a comeback than it would be for, say, a flat-earth theory to do so in physics. That is why the same arguments recur over and over in economics, though, to be sure, they do so at higher and higher levels of theoretical sophistication.[1]

In the first half of the nineteenth century, most economists believed in something like what I call the classical theory of a competitively supplied money (Schumpeter 1954, p. 729). But the classical theory wasn't the only monetary theory at the time. There was also the quantity theory of money, which, in fact, long predates the classical theory. Its basic proposition – that prices rise or fall in proportion to changes in the quantity of money – was already familiar to late medieval thinkers and the Scholastics, if not, indeed, to the ancients. And in the sixteenth and seventeenth centuries, when Europe imported huge amounts of gold and silver from America, this theory was commonly cited to explain why prices rose dramatically. In the eighteenth century the quantity theory gained considerable authority, particularly in England, owing to expositions by John Locke and, somewhat later and far more ably, by David Hume.

So it was only after the quantity theory was well established that Adam Smith showed that without affecting prices, a competitive banking system would automatically supply as much money as the public demanded. Smith never disputed the relevance of the quantity theory for an inconvertible government paper currency or for a purely metallic one. But unlike Hume, he distinguished between the effects on prices of money issued by a competitive banking system and the effects on prices of an inconvertible paper money or of new discoveries of gold and silver.

The quantity theory did not necessarily deny that there was such a distinction. However, the quantity theory came to be understood in a way that did deny the distinction, and quantity theorists came to reject the notion that the amount of bank money would automatically adjust to the demand for it. They insisted that, just like changes in the quantity of government money or in the quantity of precious metals, changes in the quantity of bank money could alter the price level. So the dispute between two theories ultimately became whether to treat the quantity of bank money as an independent (or exogenous) variable that could alter the price level or as a dependent (or endogenous) variable that simply adjusted to the demand (Girton and Roper 1978, pp. 615–18).

Although Smith's position was ascendant for some time after his dispute with Hume about whether banks raised prices, the same dispute gradually reemerged during the first half of the nineteenth century, par-

---

1 This view of the process by which theories are selected in economics owes a great deal to McCloskey (1983, 1985).

ticularly in Britain, where monetary issues were hotly debated almost continuously. In the first two decades, the debate did not much concern the effect competitive banks had on prices, since almost everyone at the time accepted Smith's view on that question.[2] The issue under debate was whether, and under what conditions, to restore convertibility after it had been suspended in 1797.

But in the next three decades, recurring financial crises that threatened to force another suspension of convertibility shifted the focus of the debate from whether to how to maintain convertibility. At that stage, the debate reverted to the question whether competitive banking disturbed or stabilized the monetary system. Adherents of the quantity theory insisted, while adherents of the classical theory denied, that overexpansion by the banking system had caused those crises. Eventually, in 1844, the quantity-theoretic view was embodied in legislation, the Bank Charter Act, that altered how both the Bank of England and the rest of the British banking system operated.

Although passage of the Bank Charter Act was an institutional victory for the quantity theory, it did not necessarily imply an intellectual victory. Certainly the debates among economists did not produce any decisive resolution of the issue. Only the apparent ability of the quantity theory to explain the effects of the Californian and Australian gold discoveries of the 1840s and early 1850s ensured the intellectual dominance of quantity theory. How the displacement of the classical theory of money by the quantity theory came about is the story we shall be exploring in this chapter. But to understand the story we have to begin with a brief review of the Bullionist Controversies, the first of the great nineteenth-century monetary debates.

THE BULLIONIST CONTROVERSIES

Aghast at the excesses and fanaticism of revolutionary France and aroused by the Revolution's threat to the established order throughout Europe, Britain went to war with France in 1793. For over twenty years, the tide of battle shifted back and forth until the final British victory in 1816. At first, the war went well for the British and their Continental allies. But after Napoleon seized power, France quickly achieved military supremacy in Europe. So great was France's success that when a small contingent of French troops landed in Britain early in 1797, rumors of a full-scale invasion swept the island. Owing to a rising world price of gold, the Bank of England had already been undergoing a gold drain.[3] The

---

2 The one notable exception was Richard Wheatley (1807, 1822), who did hold the country banks at least partially responsible for the wartime inflation.
3 See the discussion in Chapter 5.

bank therefore was unable to withstand the run that the rumors instantly ignited. Only when, on February 26, 1797, the government, at the behest of the bank, forbade the bank from converting any of its notes into gold was the crisis alleviated.

The initial restriction on convertibility extended only till June. But realizing that the suspensions of convertibility enhanced the bank's capacity to extend it credit, the government continued the suspension after the initial restriction expired.

Shortly thereafter, a debate started about whether the Bank of England was adequately controlling the supply of its newly inconvertible notes. The debates about the bank's policy during the restriction period are now known to us as the Bullionist Controversies. Mindful of the two disastrous French experiments with inconvertible paper money in the eighteenth century, opponents of the suspension immediately warned that a prolonged suspension of convertibility of sterling would have similarly disastrous effects. Correctly applying the quantity theory, critics of the restriction (Boyd 1801) cited the premium on gold and silver to show that the bank had already issued too many inconvertible notes. Defenders of the bank responded by blaming the depreciation on bad harvests that had necessitated unusually large imports and on foreign payments needed to support the British army on the Continent.

Although a recovery by sterling quickly quieted the controversy, the initial phase of the debate did leave one important legacy: a remarkable treatise on banking and monetary theory, *An Enquiry into the Nature and Effects of the Paper Credit of Great Britain*. Its author was a successful London banker and member of Parliament, Henry Thornton.[4]

---

4 Biographical material here is drawn from Laidler (1987) and from Hayek (1939).

A man devoted to the performance of good works, Thornton, before marrying in 1796, was in the habit of donating six-sevenths of his substantial income to charity. In his lifetime, and long afterward, Thornton was perhaps better known as a leading member of the Evangelicals, a small but extremely influential group made up of followers of John Wesley who remained within the Church of England, than as an expert on banking and currency. The group came to be more commonly known as the Clapham sect because its informal headquarters was located there in the country house of Thornton's father, John. Efforts of the members of the sect to bring the moral principles that governed their private lives to bear on public issues earned them the appellation "party of saints." Of all his achievements in business and politics, Thornton took greatest pride in his opposition to slavery. It was largely owing to the efforts of the Clapham sect that Parliament ended British participation in the slave trade in 1809 and slavery itself within the British Empire in 1833.

Despite writing what was certainly the finest, if not the most successful, book on monetary affairs of his time, Thornton devoted most of his literary efforts to religious writings. Later in the nineteenth century, after his *Paper Credit* had fallen into relative obscurity, he was known primarily as the author of the posthumously published *Family Prayers*. His great-great-grandson, E. M. Forster, records that *Family Prayers* was a Victorian best-seller and continued to earn royalties for his descendants till the end of the nineteenth century.

Although he was acknowledged by his contemporaries as a leading monetary expert, Thornton gradually sank into obscurity in the second half of the nineteenth century and the first three or four decades of the twentieth. Ironically, his reputation may have suffered because he was too far ahead of his time. Several theoretical contributions usually credited to economists writing almost a century later were first made by Thornton. But his contemporaries did not fully appreciate them; not until later economists worked these points out on their own did they rediscover them in a book that had long been neglected.

By the time Thornton was rediscovered, the classical theory had been largely forgotten as well. So Thornton was interpreted as being an extremely sophisticated quantity theorist. But although he extended and improved on Smith's work – pointing out, for example, the responsibility of the Bank of England, given its privileged position, to ensure the soundness of the English banking system by lending, not contracting, in a panic –Thornton never abandoned the basic Smithian model of a competitive banking system. Thus, while admitting that the quantity of inconvertible notes issued by the Bank of England did affect prices and the exchange rate, Thornton (1802/1969, pp. 211, 215) also argued that since they were convertible into Bank of England notes, the quantity of country banknotes was determined by the demand of the public to hold them and therefore did not affect prices.

What revived the controversies after the initial skirmish of 1800–02 was a series of letters to the *Morning Chronicle* by David Ricardo (1809/1951). In the letters, Ricardo attributed the renewed depreciation of sterling to an overissue of inconvertible pound notes by the Bank of England. He made the point more fully the following year in his famous essay *The High Price of Bullion* (1810–11/1951).

In the letters and the essay, Ricardo maintained that the increase in the price of bullion since the suspension was ipso facto proof of overissue. This claim went beyond Thornton's position because Thornton had mentioned overissue by the Bank of England as just one of several possible causes of depreciation. But for Ricardo, overissue was its one and only cause.

Underlying Ricardo's analysis was a simple version of the quantity theory: If the Bank of England increased the amount of inconvertible paper money it issued, prices, including – or rather, especially – the price of gold, would rise proportionately. But contrary to widespread opinion (O'Brien 1975; Blaug 1985), Ricardo's attachment to the quantity theory was not unconditional. He held that only inconvertible notes issued by the Bank of England affected prices; convertible notes could not have done so.

The concerns about overissue and depreciation so brilliantly raised by

Ricardo led Parliament, in February 1810, to appoint a Select Committee on the High Price of Bullion. The committee, whose membership included Henry Thornton, was asked to study the causes of the premium on gold and the extent of the Bank of England's responsibility for the premium. The committee took evidence and testimony from a variety of experts, including the directors of the Bank of England.

The directors insisted repeatedly, as they had years earlier, that depreciation had been caused by an adverse balance of trade. But they now added a more sweeping assertion. They maintained not only that they had not overissued notes but that they did not even have the power to have done so. Relying on the real-bills doctrine Adam Smith had formulated as a practical guide for bankers under convertibility, the directors asserted (Cannan 1925/1969, p. 46) that so long as they lent only on the security of real bills they could not issue even inconvertible notes to excess – an assertion Smith had explicitly denied.[5]

The testimony of the bank's directors was not treated kindly in the report of the Bullion Committee. And Walter Bagehot's remark that their answers were "almost classical by their nonsense" aptly sums up the nearly universal judgment of subsequent commentators.

But however nonsensical their explanations may have been, the position they were trying to defend is not as absurd as it is usually made out to be. They went too far, to be sure, in arguing that abiding by the real-bills doctrine would prevent the overissue of even an inconvertible currency. But simply to say that the Bank of England had the power to affect prices does not prove that an enlarged quantity of banknotes was the exclusive cause of rising prices.

Once the anchor of convertibility was removed, all sorts of things besides changes in the quantity of notes issued by the Bank of England could cause sterling to fluctuate. With the bank no longer committed to maintaining a particular value of the pound, the demand for pounds fluctuated with the market's estimate of the likelihood that convertibility would be restored at the prewar parity. It should not surprise us, therefore, that during a long war in which British prospects were not uniformly favorable, the premium on bullion was highly variable.

Nevertheless, the report of the Bullion Committee, which was largely written by Henry Thornton, blamed the depreciation of sterling entirely

5 That doctrine, which Smith did not invent but was the first to record, held that banks should lend only on the security of commodities that were already in the process of production and would eventually come to market. It was later interpreted to mean that if banks lent only on the security of such bills, they could not affect the price level, even if their notes were not convertible. But that is not what Smith meant by the real-bills doctrine. To him, as Laidler (1981) points out, it was simply a prudent way for bankers operating under the constraint of convertibility to avoid liquidity problems, since such loans would tend to be self-liquidating.

on an overissue of inconvertible notes by the Bank of England. The report did not go quite as far as Ricardo had in blaming the depreciation on overissue;[6] it recognized that a poor harvest or remittances abroad could also cause depreciation. It simply held that since nonmonetary factors were likely to be self-reversing, a prolonged depreciation of sterling could have been caused only by overissue. To restore the value of the pound and discipline the bank, the Bullion Committee recommended that the convertibility of Bank of England notes be resumed within two years.

Parliament rejected the recommendations of the Bullion Committee. The reasons are not entirely clear. It is possible that Parliament accepted the arguments advanced by the bank's directors even though the committee did not. But fears that restoring convertibility might hinder the war effort also seem to have militated against the report. Thus Spencer Perceval, the prime minister and chancellor of the Exchequer, warned that to adopt the report's recommendations "would be tantamount to a declaration that they would no longer continue those foreign exertions which they had hitherto considered indispensable to the security of the country . . . the house in adopting it would disgrace themselves forever, by becoming the voluntary instruments of their country's ruin" (Fetter 1965, pp. 54–55). Rather than restore convertibility at a definite future time, Parliament chose instead to postpone the resumption of convertibility until six months after the cessation of hostilities. So it appears that recognition of the national defense role for money which I discussed in Chapter 2 did figure in the decision not to restore convertibility in the midst of the Napoleonic Wars.

What significance do the Bullionist Controversies have in our survey of the rivalry between the classical and the quantity theories of money? At one level, the Bullionist Controversies affirmed the position of Adam Smith that a convertible paper money could not be issued to excess. Thornton, Ricardo,[7] and the Bullion Committee all agreed on this point. Yet at another level, by concentrating so much on the relationship between the quantity of money and the price level, critics of the Bank of England fostered the view that the direction of causation always ran from

6 In fact, the difference between Ricardo and Thornton over whether a depreciation was possible without an overissue by the Bank of England was more semantic than substantive. Ricardo's definition of an overissue was any quantity of money greater than that which could have been maintained under convertibility. If there were a bad harvest under convertibility, the consequence, Ricardo agreed, would have been for the note issue to contract. If there was no contraction, that was tantamount to an overissue. Thornton, on the other hand, agreed that it was always possible for the bank to force up the exchange rate by contracting the currency. So there was little if any substantive difference between them on this issue.

7 Samuel Hollander (1979) has shown that on the basis of notes Ricardo made on Bentham's criticisms of Smith's treatment of banks, Ricardo's views on banking were essentially the same as Smith's.

money to prices. Because of that view, later monetary disturbances, as we are about to see, would be widely ascribed to an overissue of bank-notes, convertible or not. This, as I shall now show, is what happened in the succession of monetary crises that followed the resumption in 1819.

MONETARY INSTABILITY AFTER THE RESUMPTION

The economic effects of wars have sometimes been most devastating after the fighting has stopped. Postwar attempts to restore debased or deval-ued currencies to their prewar standards have usually been unsettling, and on occasion traumatic. The most tragic such episode will be the sub-ject of Chapter 6. Our concern here is with the less disastrous, but still unpleasant, consequences of the resumption of gold payments in Britain after the Napoleonic Wars.

In 1816, after Napoleon's final defeat, Parliament enacted legislation defining the pound for the first time as a fixed weight of gold and limiting the legal tender status of silver to payments of less than £2. As early as 1812, after Napoleon's defeat in Russia, the pound began appreciating on the foreign exchanges. And by 1816 the pound had risen to within 5 percent of its prewar parity. Nevertheless, the government asked for and got a two-year postponement of the resumption. In 1819 the prewar par-ity was restored, although gold payments were not formally resumed un-til May 1821.

The postwar period was severely deflationary. Not only was sterling appreciating in relation to gold, but gold itself was probably appreciating in relation to commodities because additional gold was needed to rein-troduce a gold coinage. Suffering from the deflation and the consequent depression of trade, agricultural and some manufacturing interests began agitating against resumption at the old parity and even against the gold standard itself.

Sensitive to these difficulties, Ricardo proposed scrapping a gold coin-age and restoring convertibility by making Bank of England notes con-vertible into gold ingots rather than into coin. The idea was partly just to economize on the use of precious metals for monetary purposes. But Ricardo also wanted to cushion the deflationary impact of the resump-tion by minimizing the increase in the demand for gold entailed by the resumption.

Parliament had intended to give Ricardo's plan a trial by postponing convertibility into coin until two years after convertibility into bullion was restored. But the bank frustrated the intent of the plan by accumu-lating an enormous reserve of bullion. Between 1819 and 1821, the bank's gold reserves rapidly grew from £4 million to £12 million. The savings

Ricardo had expected from substituting a paper for a metallic currency were dissipated in accumulating that hoard.

At the same time, public resentment against the bank and its management of a paper currency was fed by an entirely different source. Counterfeiting Bank of England notes had been made a treasonable offense in 1773. As use of the notes spread during the suspension, so did counterfeiting. The number of executions and the special intervention by officials of the bank to save a few well-connected offenders from the gallows created a public outcry against the bank and against the very idea of a paper currency.

Responding to public sentiment, Parliament abandoned Ricardo's plan and required the Bank of England to begin redeeming its notes in gold coin by May 1821. Although not obligated to do so, the bank began withdrawing from circulation notes in denominations below £5. Believing that the bank had already undermined his plan by accumulating a vast gold hoard, Ricardo did not resist transforming that hoard into coin.

Another way of countering deflation would have been to restore convertibility at a parity below that which prevailed before the war. Ricardo would not have strongly opposed going back at a lower parity, and in his correspondence, he wrote (1952b, p. 73) that he would "never advise a government to restore a currency which had been depreciated 30 per cent to par." But by 1819, when the premium on gold was only about 5 percent, Ricardo saw little reason not to go back on gold at the old parity. What disturbed him was the bank's excessive accumulation of gold. The same issues, as we shall see in Chapter 6, would reappear after World War I, when the whole world tried to restore the gold standard that had broken down during the war.

In 1823, the postwar deflation having run its course, economic conditions quickly began to improve. In 1824 and 1825 Britain enjoyed a boom. As tends to happen during prosperity, when expectations grow increasingly optimistic, credit was readily extended and indebtedness rose. Some observers feared that credit had been extended too freely and warned of a reaction. And indeed, that December, when some country banks could not meet a drain on their reserves, there was a spreading panic that drove many country banks into insolvency. The panic was so bad that in some areas, where all local banks had failed, rendering local banknotes worthless and causing coin to be hoarded, no money was available. The drain on the country banks was transmitted to the Bank of England, and before long, its ability to maintain convertibility came into question.

The bank asked the government to suspend the convertibility of its notes into gold as it had done in 1797. This the government, having only just restored convertibility, would not do. Instead, the bank, prompted by the government and aided by foreign loans and an inflow of specie from abroad, embarked on a policy of virtually unrestricted lending on any valid security.

The massive extension of credit by the bank relieved the panic, and although the bank nearly exhausted its gold reserves, it did not suspend payment. The episode had two main consequences for policy. First, the bank had assumed, however reluctantly, a responsibility (urged on it twenty years earlier by Henry Thornton) to maintain the credit of the nation by lending, not contracting, in a crisis. Second, the failures of the country banks provoked charges that their unsound practices had precipitated the crisis. Misgivings about how the banking system was working inspired proposals to limit the right of issuing notes to the Bank of England or to a special government department analogous to the mint.

That lax lending practices by the country banks may have contributed to the crisis of 1825 is certainly possible.[8] But the collapse of the note issue of the country banks was also caused by two restrictions on the banking system that increased its vulnerability to runs by noteholders.

One restriction deterred banks from issuing notes in small denominations. During the suspension, country banks had been issuing notes of as little as £1. (I should point out that £1 at that time was probably the equivalent of between $50 and $100 in current dollars.) The resumption legislation required that banknotes in denominations less than £5 not issued by the Bank of England be retired from circulation. The small notes still had not been withdrawn before the panic of 1825, but country banks were discouraged from issuing any new small-denominational notes by the expectation that such notes would later have to be withdrawn from circulation and redeemed with coin.

Why did the restriction on small-denominational notes matter? Because whenever the public tried to convert larger denominations of currency into smaller ones, all the banking system could do was convert the notes into coin. The banking system had to undergo a drain on its metallic reserves totally unrelated to a loss of confidence in its soundness.

England, in 1825, was prospering. As incomes rose among the working classes, so did their demand to hold money, which was largely a demand for coin. Moreover, there is ordinarily a seasonal increase in the demand for smaller denominations in the fall. The combination of the two factors led to a drain on the gold reserves of the country banks.

Initially, therefore, the drain on the country banks probably stemmed

---

8 By lax lending practices, I mean acquiring a portfolio of assets that is poorly diversified or that has high market risk so that the probability that the bank will always have positive net present value is significantly less than one. When the net worth of the bank drops below zero or when the public realizes that it has done so or is likely to do so, there is an incentive for the depositors and noteholders to seek redemption. A bank that acquires an excessively risky portfolio is not necessarily overissuing its liabilities. And a bank could overissue liabilities without having an excessively risky portfolio.

from an attempt by the public to shift its holdings from large to small denominations, not from doubts about the banks' solvency. Scottish banks, which issued notes in denominations as low as 10 shillings, were able to respond to that shift in preferences without suffering a drain on their reserves. Had the English country banks done so as well, they might have avoided insolvency and averted the panic.

The second damaging restriction on the banking system was the prohibition on joint-stock banking. The one exception to that prohibition was, of course, the Bank of England. The country banks that issued notes outside London could not legally be owned by more than six partners. The country banks, therefore, were frequently small, undercapitalized entities that could not merge to reduce risks or exploit economies of scale in holding reserves.

In Scotland, where there were no restrictions on note denominations or on joint-stock banking, during neither the panic of 1825 nor any subsequent panic, before Peel's Acts of 1844 and 1845 restricted their right to issue notes, was there any shortage of currency.

Although the timely issue of £1 notes by the Bank of England was instrumental in stopping the panic, the issue of small-denominational notes was singled out by many observers as the source of unsound practices and instability. Consequently, after 1826 small-denominational notes issued by the country banks and the Bank of England were withdrawn from circulation.

However, the panic did cause the restriction on joint-stock banking to be lifted. In 1826 Parliament permitted new joint-stock banks to be formed. Yet Parliament still sought to preserve the bank's monopoly privileges by using criminal penalties to prohibit joint-stock companies from engaging in banking within a sixty-five-mile radius of London. A consolidation of country banks ensued, and within two years their number declined from over 500 to 330.

At first the prohibition on joint-stock banking in and around London succeeded in excluding joint-stock banks from operating in the metropolis. But since the courts construed the criminal prohibition on joint-stock banking in the London area narrowly to include only the issue of banknotes, the joint-stock banks eventually circumvented the prohibition by creating only deposits. To expand their business, they encouraged the increased use of deposits and checks. Thus the attempt to preserve the monopoly over notes accelerated their displacement by deposits and checks. As has happened again and again in the history of money and banking, restricting one form of money only caused money to take on a different form while retaining its essential character.

Panics recurred in 1831, 1835–36, and 1839. Although convertibility was never suspended, each time the gold reserves of the Bank of England declined to such low levels that its continued maintenance was doubted. The crises did ensure that the debate about how the Bank of England was conducting its affairs would not die down. However, the debate increasingly concerned not just the responsibility of the Bank of England for panics but the alleged tendency of the country banks to cause panics by overissuing banknotes.

THE CURRENCY PRINCIPLE

Trying to account for the crisis of 1825, some writers at the time, including Thomas Joplin (1823/1970), and James Pennington (1827/1963), suggested that a necessary condition for monetary stability was that a currency consisting of both convertible bank money and precious metals fluctuate in quantity exactly as would a purely metallic currency. This meant that in a non-gold-producing country, the total quantity of money should change only when gold flowed in or out. From this perspective, the cause of a financial panic was the failure of an inflow or outflow of gold to occasion an equal change in the quantity of money created by the banking system.

This condition was deduced from the quantity-theoretic analysis of international adjustment elegantly described by David Hume. "Suppose," wrote Hume (1752b/1955, pp. 62–63),

four-fifths of all money in Great Britain to be annihilated in one night, and the nation reduced to the same condition, with regard to specie, as in the reigns of the HARRYs and EDWARDs, what would be the consequence? Must not the price of all labour and commodities sink, in proportion, and everything be sold as they were in those ages? What nation could then dispute with us in any foreign market, or pretend to navigate or to sell manufactures at the same price, which to us would afford sufficient profit? In how little time, therefore, must this bring back the money we had lost, and raise us to the level of all the neighboring nations? Where, after we have arrived, we immediately lose the advantage of the cheapness of labour and commodities; and further flowing in of money is stopped by our fulness and repletion.

Thus, when a country lost gold, prices there would fall. Its exports would become more competitive in foreign markets and imports less competitive in domestic markets. An inflow of gold into a country would have the opposite effects. Thus gold flows would eliminate the very disturbance that had originally induced them.

This process, known as the price-specie-flow mechanism, presumed that prices in different countries would adjust to the changes in money supplies caused by the gold flows. But in Hume's treatment, money consisted only of gold, so inflows or outflows of gold implied identical changes in the domestic quantity of money. What this reasoning suggested was that the mechanism could be frustrated if gold flows did not elicit the changes in money supplies that would have occurred under a purely metallic currency. By breaking the direct link between gold flows and the quantity of money, banks seemed to disrupt the mechanism that ensured international monetary equilibrium.

Joplin and Pennington concluded that by preventing the domestic money stock from adjusting immediately to gold flows, a competitive banking system made the inevitable final adjustment more destabilizing to domestic trade than if the money stock had responded immediately to the gold flows. The idea that financial crises were caused by the failure of the total money stock to fluctuate in exact correspondence to gold flows was called the Currency Principle. It is easy to see why supporters of that principle, who formed what became known as the Currency School, should have desired to restrict the note-issuing powers of both the Bank of England and the country banks. Viewing a purely metallic currency as an ideal, the Currency School, like its intellectual ancestor David Hume, deeply mistrusted a medium of exchange like banknotes whose quantity could be instantly augmented.

According to the Currency School, the only legitimate reason for the quantity of paper money ever to increase was an inflow of gold. It never occurred to these theorists that by increasing the amount of paper money, a competitive banking system might be satisfying a demand to hold additional money that otherwise would have induced an inflow of gold. Without the money supplied by the banking system, the public could not have added to its holdings of money without reducing imports and increasing exports. Hence, the danger that preoccupied the Currency School, that an overissue of money by an inherently expansionary banking system would cause an outflow of gold, was misplaced. The money supplied by the banking system did not necessarily cause an external drain of gold; it might simply have saved the costs of importing additional gold to satisfy an increased demand to hold money.

A further difficulty for the Currency School was how to treat bank deposits. Deposits are conceptually the same as notes, as Pennington and a few others in the Currency School tradition recognized. But almost no one recommended controlling the quantity of deposits. To rationalize this inconsistency, members of the Currency School tried unsuccessfully to find persuasive distinctions between banknotes and deposits. Yet that failure never undermined their position.

THE BANK CHARTER ACT OF 1844

The shortcomings of its monetary analysis did not prevent the Currency School from winning over to its side the dominant English politician of the time, Sir Robert Peel. The repeated financial crises in the 1820s and

1830s convinced Peel that the power of the Bank of England and the country banks to issue notes had to be curtailed or convertibility could not be maintained. So in 1844 he introduced his Bank Charter Act to reorganize the Bank of England, to reform its operating procedures, and to restrict the power of all other banks in the United Kingdom to issue notes.

The act divided the bank into two independent departments: an issue department and a banking department. The issue department would be permitted a fixed fiduciary issue of £14 million of notes backed by government securities. Additional notes could be issued only if backed by an equal amount of gold. The banking department was given full freedom to conduct a discount and deposit business in it stockholders' interests.

The act immediately restricted the amount of notes that the country banks could issue to the quantity then outstanding.[9] And over the long run, it called for Bank of England notes eventually to replace the notes of all other banks. Though contrary to the spirit of the act, allowing banknotes not issued by the Bank of England to remain in circulation for a substantial length of time was a necessary concession to the country bankers, who otherwise might have opposed the act much more vigorously than they did.

Though tainted by certain compromises, the Bank Charter Act was still the conceptual offspring of the quantity theory. Since quantity theorists believed that increases in the quantity of banknotes were, in some sense, exogenous events not induced by prior changes in demand, the goal they wanted monetary reform to achieve was to ensure that the total quantity of money would behave as if it were entirely metallic.

Nor did supporters of Peel's Act wish the Bank of England to be a central bank overseeing the British monetary system. Their aim, on the contrary, was to create an automatic mechanism for controlling the quantity of banknotes. They hoped that doing so would both guarantee the absolute convertibility of the pound into gold and avoid any occasion for the Bank of England to exercise discretion. However, as we shall see, they were not entirely successful in accomplishing their objectives.

Let me pause here for a moment to observe that the quantity-theoretic analysis of the Currency School was not the only source of support for the Bank Charter Act. There was also a widely shared feeling, ultimately traceable to the national defense role of the state monopoly over money, that the right of note issue was as much the prerogative of the state as the right of coinage. By centralizing the right of issue in a bank, which, though privately owned, was still heavily dependent on the government, the state was surely enhancing its monetary prerogative. The notion that

9 A follow-up act the next year imposed the same restriction on Scottish banks.

control over the money supply is the peculiar prerogative of the sovereign was important in countering the argument that the principle of free trade excluded any restriction on the right to issue banknotes (Fetter 1965, p. 166).

Within three years of its enactment, yet another financial panic forced the government to suspend the ceiling the act had placed on the fiduciary issue of the Bank of England. Similar panics followed in 1857 and 1866, both of which required suspension of the act.

The indifferent success of the Bank Charter Act had been anticipated by its opponents, the Banking School. Their criticism of the Bank Charter Act consisted of three main points:

1. Since the banking system supplied the public with only as much money as it desired to hold, gold flows could not be adjustments to monetary disturbances. Instead, gold flows arose from nonmonetary causes, like bad harvests, that ordinarily were temporary and would be reversed in due course. Ensuring convertibility did not therefore require the quantity of notes to fluctuate with changes in gold reserves. That would just make matters worse. What was needed was a gold reserve large enough to accommodate temporary drains occasioned by nonmonetary factors.

2. The creation of a banking department separate from the issue department would destabilize the financial system. In a panic, when the banking system was seeking to become more liquid by calling in loans and trying to obtain either gold or Bank of England notes, the banking department would be forced to contract along with the rest of the banking system. But to quiet a panic, the banking department should instead be drawing on the issue department for additional funds with which to provide the banking system the liquidity it was demanding.

3. The distinction the act drew between banknotes and bank deposits was untenable. The difference between deposits and notes was one of form, not substance. Even if overissue by the banking system was a potential danger, the act, leaving the creation of deposits totally unconstrained, did nothing to prevent that expansion.

After its suspension, some supporters of the Bank Charter Act defended it by saying that it was never intended to work in a financial crisis, so that its suspension during a crisis was not evidence that it had failed. But it was just such panics that the framers of the Bank Charter Act had intended to avoid. Before the act was passed, Robert Torrens (1837, p. 43), a leading Currency School theorist, had vividly expressed his expectations of what it would achieve:

But does the necessity under which the Bank directors are occasionally placed, of resorting to extraordinary measures for the purpose of mitigating a pressing mischief, afford a justification of the previous deviations from principle by which that mistake was created? Could a surgeon, who had wounded an artery, instead of having opened a vein, vindicate his professional reputation by showing that he had secured the blood vessel before the patient bled to death? Could an incendiary escape condemnation, by proving that he had laboured at the engine by which the conflagration which he had kindled was at length subdued?

I shall have more to say in the next chapter about the panics and how Peel's act helped cause them. The point I want to emphasize here is that the failure of the act to have the effects supporters had predicted did not shake the quantity-theoretic conceptual foundation of the act. Instead, the failure forced those supporters to accept, however grudgingly, that they had not freed the British monetary system from dependence on a "monetary authority" with discretionary power. By making the Bank of England the ultimate provider of currency, the act simply reinforced the bank's position as the lender of last resort. Yet the act formally barred the bank from being a lender of last resort at the precise moment when one was wanted most. So whenever a panic made it necessary, or at any rate, expedient, to have a lender of last resort, the act had to be suspended to allow the Bank of England to act as one. It was these suspensions of the act that helped establish the idea of a central bank with special responsibilities (V. Smith 1936).

THE ECLIPSE OF THE CLASSICAL THEORY

The disappointment of the hopes that had inspired the Bank Charter Act did not lead to a serious reconsideration of the quantity-theoretic assumptions on which it rested. Indeed, it was the classical theory that before very long was largely abandoned. Why the classical theory did not survive in competition with the quantity theory is a puzzle to which there is no simple solution. But there are a few conjectures that, at least, seem plausible.

One of them is that once Peel's act, as it were, institutionalized a quantity-theoretic view of the monetary system, innate British conservatism transformed that view into part of the conventional wisdom that was no longer subject to debate. Such conservatism permeates Walter Bagehot's famous book on monetary policy, *Lombard Street* (1915/1978). After lamenting that the British monetary system had not been permitted to evolve into a decentralized configuration that would have been independent of the Bank of England, Bagehot at once disavowed any intention to reform the system. He simply analyzed it as it was and explained that, given its dependence on the Bank of England, the system would work better if the bank owned up explicitly and unambiguously to its responsibility to act as a lender of last resort in crisis.

In a similar vein, Frank Fetter (1965, pp. 216) suggests that most British statesmen and opinion leaders wished to avoid a renewed debate over the Bank Charter Act because they feared that throwing the question open to discussion again might allow the gold standard itself to become an issue. Recalling only too well the emotional controversies about the gold standard after the Napoleonic Wars, "responsible" people, in the middle of the nineteenth century, regarded the gold standard as sacrosanct and feared that further controversies would only undermine confidence in its continuation. Determined to uphold confidence in the maintenance of the gold standard at all costs, British political leaders, with the support of the best economists of the day, chose not to reopen the controversy over the Bank Charter Act for fear of where any such debate might lead.

Given that institutional reality, economists, especially in Britain, may have been unwilling to embrace a theory that was as obviously at variance with the institutional reality as was the classical theory. I don't wish to imply that British economists betrayed their scientific integrity to curry the favor of politicians. But in choosing between theories, they may have been willing to give the benefit of the doubt to a theory that was consistent with existing institutions, especially when the alternative theory had certain unresolved difficulties of its own.

Two difficulties seem to have worked against the classical theory and in favor of the quantity theory. First, the theory of a competitive supply of money was never worked out clearly enough to withstand the criticisms of quantity theorists who asserted that a competitive banking system was inherently disposed to overexpansion. Today, we know how to write out a formal model that shows the logic of the system and the absence of a tendency to overexpansion. But in the nineteenth century what classical theorists said about competitive banking often appeared to be no more than an unsupported assertion.

The second difficulty was that the quantity theory seemed better able than the classical theory to account for the international response of prices to the enormous gold discoveries in California and Australia in the late 1840s and early 1850s.[10] Those discoveries implied a substantial reduction in the cost of producing gold. So it seemed that the value of gold was bound to fall and that inflation was in the offing. Yet in the decade following the gold discoveries, prices for finished goods, on average, showed little change.

That prices did not soar in the decade after the discoveries was just as problematic for the quantity theory as for the classical theory. According

---

10 Indeed, even today we lack a truly reliable model for explaining the behavior of gold prices. A durable commodity that is being held should tend to appreciate in value through time. Moreover, its current value should respond to anticipated future increases in supply, so the price effect of discoveries should cause an immediate reduction in the price unless the discovery, though not production, is large compared to the existing stock.

to the quantity theory, the increase in the world's stock of gold would expand money supplies and raise prices throughout the world. Yet the two theories described the process that led from gold discoveries to rising prices very differently, and the alternative processes implied that very different patterns of price increases would be observed.

According to the classical theory, prices would rise after the gold discoveries because gold had become cheaper. That cheapening would be reflected in rising commodities prices. But there was nothing to suggest that some prices would rise more than others. Nor, since gold is an internationally traded commodity, did there seem to be any reason for prices to rise more rapidly in some parts of the world than in others. The quantity theory, however, attributed rising prices to the increase in the quantity of money caused by the gold discoveries. The pattern of price increases would be determined by the price-specie-flow mechanism so that the sequence of price increases would follow the movement of gold from the gold mines to the various gold-importing countries around the world.

CAIRNES AND THE AUSTRALIAN GOLD DISCOVERIES

In 1859 the British economist John E. Cairnes published the first of a series of articles tracing the impact of the Australian gold discoveries on world prices. Cairnes's articles (1873/1965) mark perhaps the first time statistical evidence was systematically used to compare competing theories in economics. Although Cairnes did not really provide a crucial experiment that could distinguish between the quantity and the classical theories of money, he was so persuasive that it was almost as if he had. Even if one differs, as I do, with certain elements of Cairnes's reasoning and with some of his conclusions, and even if one deplores, as I do, the success of his articles in persuading economists that the quantity theory better explained the effects of the gold discoveries on prices than did the classical theory, one cannot help admiring the skill and the disinterested and scientific spirit with which he analyzed theoretically and sought to test empirically an important practical problem (Bordo 1975).

Cairnes began by explaining that prices had generally not risen substantially after the gold discoveries owing to the offsetting impact of technological progress, which for three decades had steadily reduced the real costs and prices of manufactured goods. Thus the tendency of the gold discoveries to raise prices and the tendency of rapid technological progress to reduce them had simply canceled each other out. But Cairnes also pointed out that the impact of the gold discoveries could be readily observed in raw materials prices because technological progress increased the supply of raw materials much less than it did the supply of manufactured goods.

Cairnes then tried to show that the increases in raw materials prices after the Australian gold discoveries had, indeed, corresponded to the geographical pattern implied by the price-specie-flow mechanism. Prices first increased in Australia, where gold discoveries had immediately increased the quantity of money. Australian gold exports then caused money supplies and prices to increase elsewhere. Since the banking systems in Britain and America, and to a lesser extent in the continental European countries, allowed money stocks to increase without a corresponding increase in holdings of gold, much of the gold first exported to America and Europe was ultimately reexported to the Orient, where it was added to the existing hoards. Because it was the rise in prices that triggered the further export of gold, Cairnes concluded, prices must have risen a bit more in the United States and Britain than on the Continent and more on the Continent than in the Orient, where much of the gold was finally held.

Only one adherent of the classical monetary theory, William Newmarch, systematically investigated the effects of the gold discoveries. He did so in the sixth and final volume of the monumental *History of Prices,* the classic work started by Thomas Tooke which, in its later stages, Newmarch collaborated on and eventually finished (Tooke and Newmarch 1857). Newmarch, however, was a more skillful statistician than theorist and simply denied that gold discoveries had affected prices in general — a conclusion definitely not implied by the classical theory. After Cairnes demolished Newmarch's argument and W. S. Jevons (1884), using more sophisticated statistical techniques, supported Cairnes's main findings, the classical theory ceased to be taken seriously as a possible explanation of the effects of the gold discoveries.

The irony here is not only that Newmarch's argument was inconsistent with the classical theory as well the quantity theory, but also that Cairnes's empirical analysis did not really support the quantity theory against the classical theory. What Cairnes wanted to show was that the local increases in the quantity of money caused by gold discoveries had governed the local increases in prices. His statistical evidence revealed a distinct correlation between local increases in money supplies and local increases in prices that seemed to support his a priori argument.

However, Cairnes's theoretical argument and his empirical evidence were susceptible of a much different interpretation from the one he gave them. How else could one have interpreted them? First one needs to recall a point that Cairnes himself conceded. Increases in the prices of the internationally traded commodities had to be uniform throughout the world. So when he said that prices increased by more in Australia than in Britain, America, and Europe, and more in Europe than in the Orient, he was referring to increases in the prices of local goods that were neither traded internationally nor subject to the competition of goods that were. Economists distinguish between goods that are internationally traded or subject to the competition of internationally traded goods and those that are not by calling the former "tradables" and the latter "nontradables." Thus the differences in local rates of price change that Cairnes observed were differences in local rates of change in the prices of nontradables.

Cairnes contended that those differences had been caused by differing rates of change in local money stocks. But the differences did not necessarily have to be produced by monetary factors. They could, instead, have reflected the impact of the gold discoveries on the pattern of world trade.

To understand this point, let us look more closely at what happened in Australia after the discovery of gold. The most important effect was a quadrupling of wages for unskilled labor. The quadrupling could not be confined to the gold fields because other employers could not pay workers less than they could earn mining for gold. At those wages, Australian import-competing industries and Australian export industries other than gold became unprofitable, because their output prices, determined in international markets, could not rise correspondingly. Thus most Australians were drawn into either mining gold or producing nontradable goods and services for local consumption. Since they were not constrained by international competition, Australian producers of nontradable goods and services could raise their output prices enough to pay the quadrupled wages.

Thus the apparent inflation in Australia reflected a huge increase in the ratio of nontradable goods prices to tradable goods prices owing to an enormous increase in the value of labor in gold mining that had nothing to do with a monetary disturbance. An increase in the money stock did not cause the quadrupling of wages. The money stock did increase, but only in response to rising real wages and rising nontradables prices that were inevitable concomitants of the gold discoveries. Precisely the same effect on Australian prices would have been observed if, instead of gold, comparable deposits of an unquestionably nonmonetary exportable resource, such as diamonds, had been found. Indeed, Cairnes himself (1873/1965, p. 25) provided evidence that after the gold discoveries there was a shortage, not an overabundance, of money.[11]

In contrast, the oriental countries, which ultimately imported much of the new gold, had to pay for those imports with additional exports or had to forgo other imported goods. Either way, the production of tradables had to expand and the production of nontradables to contract. For

11 See the penultimate section of Glasner (1989) for a more detailed discussion of the question whether there was an excess demand or excess supply of money in Australia after gold was discovered.

that shift in production to occur, the prices of nontradables had to fall in relation to those of tradables. The more gold came into a country, the more prices of nontradables would rise in relation to those of tradables. That relationship alone suffices to explain the pattern of price increases that Cairnes ascribed to the effects of differential rates of money growth. Britain, America, and the Continent imported some gold, but not so much that their tradable-goods sectors had to expand greatly. Thus, in Britain and America and on the Continent, the prices of nontradables did not have to fall in relation to those of tradables as they did in the Orient, but neither could they rise as much as they did in Australia.

What about the fact, so strongly emphasized by Cairnes, that money stocks increased most rapidly in countries where the prices of nontradables increased most rapidly? That fact seems telling, but it cannot prove that it was increases in money stocks that caused prices to increase. It is equally possible that money stocks increased most where the demand for money, owing to rising real incomes and increasing prices for nontradable goods, had increased the most. Indeed, at several points Cairnes recognized the relative-price effect I have described here, but seeking to confirm the price-specie-flow mechanism, he failed to distinguish between this effect and the effects of changes in the quantity of money.

CONCLUSION

Of course, at this level of abstraction, there is little difference between saying that the gold discoveries increased money stocks around the world, which increase, in turn, caused prices to rise, and saying that gold discoveries reduced the value of gold, which reduction, by raising the prices of other things, induced increases in money supplies. In pure theory, to be sure, there is a difference, but the difference would be subtle enough for us to ignore were it not that the alternative formulations suggest such different approaches to conducting monetary policy.

Focusing attention on the quantity of money as a causal factor, the quantity-theoretic approach leads to the view that controlling the quantity of money ought to be the operational objective of monetary policy. That was the view of the Currency School and it was embodied in the Bank Charter Act. The classical approach regards the quantity of money as an intrinsically insignificant variable that responds automatically to market forces. The objective of monetary policy is, then, not to control the quantity of money, which the market can do well enough on its own, but to guarantee its value. To accomplish this, the classical theorists thought it sufficient to make money convertible into gold or silver. On this particular point, the classical theorists were on shaky ground. And we shall see later to what disastrous consequences reliance on gold as a standard eventually led.

My purpose in this chapter has been to explain how, starting in the middle of the nineteenth century, the quantity-theoretic view of monetary policy won out over the classical view. A pivotal episode in that victory was the enactment of the Bank Charter Act in 1844. Owing to that act, notes issued by competing private banks were slowly withdrawn from circulation. The Bank of England was left with a monopoly over all new issues of banknotes that, notwithstanding the aims of the framers of the act, helped to establish it as a true central bank.

But the victory of the quantity-theoretic view, on a practical level, at any rate, was not as complete as it might seem. Restricting one kind of market transaction led, as usual, to alternative transactions in its place. So when the Bank Charter Act restricted ordinary banks in issuing notes, they simply changed their business practices to emphasize what anyway was becoming a preferable form of holding money – checkable deposits.

In their unceasing attempt to identify the particular assets that, in some sense, are uniquely money and therefore have a causal effect on prices, the mid-nineteenth-century quantity theorists – the Currency School – were willing to confer monetary status only on coin, bullion, and banknotes. The notion that a bank deposit, which could do everything that a banknote could, was money was somehow incomprehensible to them. And they dimly perceived that to accept the notion that deposits were money would undermine their central objective of rigidly controlling the quantity of money to prevent fluctuations in prices.[12]

But in leaving the quantity of deposits uncontrolled by the Bank Charter Act, the Currency School left the competitive character of the British banking system largely unaltered. Even the restriction on the issue of new banknotes by the country banks and the Scottish banks was only a mild constraint, since the public was already shifting its demand from notes to deposits. Even if the Bank Charter Act had not been enacted, the number of banknotes in circulation would probably not have increased much, if at all. The British banking system therefore continued to function more or less as the classical theory suggested it would. And ironically, in the

12 Thus when Robert Torrens wrote to Lord Overstone, the unofficial leader of the Currency School in 1857, suggesting that deposits ought, after all, to be regarded as money, Overstone replied: "If you publish this you let loose upon us the Floodgates of Confusion. It will be the Deluge of Monetary science. Tooke will be in third heaven. . . . You give an abstract Definition of the Term Money, which shall include Deposits. But in so doing you attribute to the Term Money a meaning to which all doctrines hitherto applied to Money are inapplicable. . . . Precious Metals alone are money. Paper notes are money because they are representations of Metallic Money. Unless so, they are false and spurious pretenders. One depositor can get metal, but all cannot, therefore deposits are not money." Torrens had no reply, saying only: "I have no confidence unless you approve. I throw deposits to the dogs."

second half of the nineteenth century, despite the institutional and intellectual dominance of the quantity theory, as more and more countries joined Britain on the gold standard, the classical model became a reasonable representation of the international monetary system. As long as the value of gold did not fluctuate much, the system performed admirably. As we shall see in the next chapter, it did so until the start of World War I, when, along with the rest of Western civilization, the gold standard came apart.

5

The heyday of the gold standard, 1879–1914

What an extraordinary episode in the economic progress of man that age was which came to an end in August, 1914! . . . The inhabitant of London could order by telephone, sipping his morning tea in bed, the various products of the whole earth, in such quantity as he might see fit, and reasonably expect their early delivery upon his doorstep; he could at the same moment and by the same means adventure his wealth in the natural resources and new enterprises of any quarter of the world, and share, without exertion or even trouble, in their prospective fruits and advantages. . . . He could secure forthwith, if he wished it, cheap and comfortable means of transit to any country or climate without passport or other formality, could despatch his servant to the neighboring office of a bank for such supply of the precious metals as might seem convenient, and could then proceed abroad to foreign quarters, without knowledge of their religion, language, or customs, bearing coined wealth upon his person, and would consider himself greatly aggrieved and much surprised at the least interference. But most important of all, he regarded this state of affairs as normal, certain, and permanent, except in the direction of further improvement, and any deviation from it as aberrant, scandalous, and avoidable.

J. M. Keynes, *The Economic Consequences of Peace*

The thirty-five or forty years preceding the First World War were an unparalleled period of rapid, often spectacular, economic growth throughout the developed, and much of the underdeveloped, world, of free international trade and open borders, and for the most part, of peace among nations. The international order rested (or so, at any rate, it seemed) on two pillars – the British navy and the gold standard. The latter had evolved, almost by accident, from a strictly British institution into the international monetary system on which an open and integrated international economy depended. By providing reasonably stable international prices, the gold standard facilitated the transfers of European capital that financed enormous investments in the rest of the world, particularly America. For the most part, an international capital market centered in London, with important outposts in New York, Paris, and Berlin, func-

tioned smoothly – almost automatically. During the occasional monetary disorders of the period, the monetary authorities, of which the Bank
of England was by far the most important, usually provided timely and
effective intervention.

That period, to be sure, was not without its discontents. Poverty, even
in the most advanced countries, was still widespread. Workers labored
long hours under unpleasant conditions for low wages. And a business
cycle caused fluctuations in income and employment that exacerbated the
suffering of those least able to bear it. The bitter discontent with that
state of affairs and with the economic system, including the gold standard, that produced it is amply reflected in the literature, fictional as well
as polemical, of the time.

Yet, looking back at the period, one cannot help being impressed with
its remarkable economic growth. In the United States, for example, population doubled, real income more than tripled, and real income per capita rose by two-thirds between 1879 and 1913. There was real economic
growth in twenty-five of those thirty-five years (Friedman and Schwartz
1982, pp. 122–23). So large an increase in real income could not have
failed to raise the living and working conditions of most people. In Great
Britain growth was less spectacular, but still impressive. Population increased by a third, real income doubled, and real income per capita rose
by 50 percent. Although growth in Great Britain was slower than in the
United States, it may have been somewhat steadier, as real income rose
in twenty-seven of the thirty-five years between 1879 and 1913 (Friedman and Schwartz 1982, pp. 130–31). And even though unemployment
constantly threatened the livelihoods of working people in those days, it
is worth noting that rarely, if ever, in that period did unemployment in
the United States or Great Britain exceed 10 percent of the work force.

The gold standard helped create the conditions for this impressive performance by providing the world with what amounted to an international currency. National currency units were merely different denominations of that international currency in almost the same way that a $5
bill and a $20 bill are now different denominations of the same national
currency. In countries on the gold standard, central banks or governments that issued currency stood ready to convert their currencies into
stipulated amounts of gold or into corresponding amounts of foreign
currencies. People had complete freedom to transfer holdings in one currency into another currency or into gold and to transfer those holdings
across international borders.

Contrary to what one might have expected, the unfettered freedom to
hold liquid balances in any desired form or currency unit did not lead to
chaos. The par values of most major currencies remained fixed throughout the period. Only in the 1890s, when political agitation for inflation

and the free coinage of silver threatened to drive the United States off gold, was there a danger that the gold parities would not be maintained. At least among the major countries at the core of the system, recurrent balance-of-payments crises, exchange controls, currency devaluations, fluctuating exchange rates, and other features of subsequent international monetary arrangements were virtually unknown in the heydey of the gold standard.

The stability of monetary values extended over time as well as over space. Thus, in 1913, the price level in the United States was only about 20 percent higher than it had been in 1879. If we set the price level in 1879 equal to 100, then until 1913 the price level never fell below 85 (1896) or rose above 120 (1913). The British price level seems to have fluctuated within an even narrower band (Friedman and Schwartz 1982, pp. 122–131).

Such long-term stability in the value of money created an environment in which the enormous savings that financed the rapid development and economic growth of that era could be undertaken voluntarily. "To save and to invest," Keynes (1923/1971, p. 6) observed,

became at once the duty and the delight of a large class. The savings were seldom drawn on, and, accumulating at compound interest, made possible the material triumphs which we now all take for granted. The morals, the politics, the literature, and the religion of the age joined in a grand conspiracy for the promotion of saving. God and Mammon were reconciled. Peace on earth to men of good means. A rich man could, after all, enter into the Kingdom of Heaven – if only he saved. A new harmony sounded from the celestial spheres. "It is curious to observe how, through the wise and beneficent arrangement of Providence, men thus do the greatest service to the public, when they are thinking of nothing but their own gain"; so sang the angels.

It therefore is not to be wondered at that some would-be monetary reformers view the gold standard as an ideal monetary system. Whether restoring some form of the gold standard is possible, much less advisable, is a question for another chapter. Before we can take it up, we need to understand how, more or less accidentally, the gold standard achieved its brief ascendancy at the end of the nineteenth century and how it worked in those halcyon days.

The previous chapter showed that both the operation of the banking system and the workings of the gold standard were enveloped in conceptual confusion in the nineteenth century. Our concern in this chapter is thus primarily with the institutional consequences for the gold standard of the conceptual confusion that arose from the misapplication of the quantity theory. Once we understand how the gold standard operated in its heyday and what its defects were, we can go on in the next chapter to examine how it broke down in World War I and how trying to recreate it in the 1920s led to the Great Depression.

The heyday of the gold standard, 1879–1914

Although gold coins had circulated since ancient times, one cannot speak of a gold standard having ever existed before the early eighteenth century, when Britain inadvertently introduced it. It will be instructive, therefore, to retrace the path that led from the original introduction of the gold standard in Britain early in the eighteenth century to its universal acceptance late in the nineteenth.

HOW THE GOLD STANDARD CAME INTO BEING

Medieval coinages, I noted earlier, were motley mixtures of gold, silver, and copper coins of varying weight and quality. Copper and silver coins were used for the smaller everyday transactions of common folk and local tradesmen, while gold coins were reserved for the larger transactions between merchants – usually those engaging in international trade. But the money of account in which prices were quoted was ordinarily linked to silver. In England, for example, the pound sterling originally was one pound of silver. Thus silver, not gold, was the dominant monetary metal in Europe.

Silver remained the predominant monetary metal until well into the nineteenth century. Was Europe, then, before the emergence of the gold standard, on a silver standard? Not really. Before the emergence of the gold standard, sovereign money producers sought to exploit their monopolies by raising the face value of coins above their material value. The essence of a gold or silver standard is that the face value of the currency corresponds exactly to its material value or to the material value of what the currency could be redeemed for on demand. So even though individual coinages may have been minted from silver, local differences in seignorage charges and restrictions on the export of specie kept the separate coinages from being integrated as they would have been under a true silver standard.

Since silver was the predominant monetary metal in Europe and since gold coins were not even minted in England until the middle of the seventeenth century, how is it that the gold standard came to be established in England? And how did it achieve such a sweeping triumph in the last quarter of the nineteenth century?

The transition started in late medieval times. The growth of trade increased the number of high-value transactions for which gold, the more valuable metal, is a better medium of exchange than silver. The growing demand for the gold coins already in circulation made it profitable for other mints to begin to strike their own gold coins. Gold and silver coins could circulate side by side because the value of the gold coins fluctuated in relation to the silver coins. If the authorities maintained and could enforce a legal exchange rate between gold and silver coins that differed from the relative value of the two metals in the market, the process described by Gresham's Law ("bad money drives out good money") could begin to operate. Coins of whichever metal was overvalued at the mint (the bad money) would then tend to drive out of domestic circulation coins of the metal that was undervalued at the mint (the good money).

Suppose a mint is striking gold and silver coins weighing exactly one ounce. Say that the mint defines one gold livre to be equal to ten silver sous. But in world markets, let us assume, an ounce of uncoined gold is worth fifteen ounces of uncoined silver. The mint is thus undervaluing gold and overvaluing silver. All sellers, therefore, quote prices assuming that they will be paid in overvalued silver coins, not undervalued gold coins. No debtor will use gold coins to discharge an obligation that he could discharge just as well with silver coins. If they wanted to, transactors could always stipulate in advance that payment would be made in gold coins at a reduced price, but making such a stipulation would ordinarily be prohibitively costly except for large transactions (Rolnick and Weber 1986). That is why undervalued gold coins often remained in circulation at a premium in relation to their mint pars.

If the official exchange rate were effectively enforced, gold would be employed exclusively in foreign trade and disappear from domestic circulation. But gold coins would not be driven out of domestic circulation if the coinage of silver at the mint were quantitatively limited. Even with silver coins overvalued at the mint, the quantitative limit on silver coins would allow gold coins to remain in circulation. In that case, the value of silver coins would equal the value of gold for which they could be exchanged at the mint. Such an arrangement is called a limping standard. Thus quantitative restrictions on minting coins or high seignorage charges at the mint could give metallic currencies many of the characteristics of an inconvertible fiat paper currency.

In the seventeenth century England had such a semi-fiat metallic currency. The face value of silver coins was about 25 percent higher than its silver content would have warranted. But because their quantity was limited, underweight silver coins exchanged at par with the full-bodied gold guinea. When the newly chartered Bank of England issued £1.2 million in new banknotes in 1694, it was as if new silver coins had been minted. Since the exchange rate of gold guineas against silver coins was not legally fixed, guineas appreciated by more than 25 percent against silver coins, and Bank of England notes remained in circulation (Vilar 1969/1984, pp. 218–20).

The decision the government then had to make was whether to ratify the depreciation of the silver coinage by officially reducing the silver content of the pound to the actual level or to restore the silver content of the pound to its legal value. The secretary of the Treasury, William Lowndes, favored the former policy, while John Locke favored the latter. The government followed Locke's advice – providing still another instance in which a currency was restored to its old value after a wartime depreciation – and instituted a recoinage that raised the silver content of the pound.

At the same time, however, the government also fixed the legal value of the gold guinea at 21.5 silver shillings. At this rate gold was overvalued, so that gold began flowing into England from abroad. Even after Sir Isaac Newton, master of the Mint, effected a new currency reform in 1717, which reduced the value of the gold guinea to 21 silver shillings, the implied mint ratio of silver to gold of 15.21 to 1 still slightly overvalued gold. Although it was not intended to do so, Newton's reform confirmed a de facto gold standard in Britain.

The de facto gold standard remained in effect almost till the end of the century. But in 1795 the situation began to change. After its disastrous revolutionary experiment with the inconvertible assignats, France introduced a gold coinage at a 15 1/2 to 1 ratio. At this ratio, France was overvaluing gold, so that gold began flowing into France in exchange for silver. Much of it came from England, where the mint ratio of 15.21 to 1 now undervalued gold. In addition, the Bank of England was also lending heavily to the Government to finance the war effort. That lending was another cause of a drain on the bank's gold reserves. For whatever reason, between August 1794 and August 1796, the amount of coin and bullion held by the Bank of England fell from £6.8 million to £2.1 million (Cannan, 1925/1969, p. xliv).

The outflow of gold left the Bank of England vulnerable to a run on gold triggered by the invasion scare in February 1797 that I mentioned in the previous chapter. The gold holdings of the bank were down to £1.1 million that February. To protect what was left of the bank's gold reserves, the Government, at the bank's request, prohibited the bank from redeeming any of its obligations in gold. But at the prevailing mint ratio of 15.21 to 1, it is likely that, sooner or later, England would have reverted to a silver standard had the free coinage of silver not also been suspended (Hawtrey 1947, pp. 67–69).

Instead, England operated on an inconvertible paper standard until 1816, when Parliament for the first time defined the pound as a particular weight of gold. Parliament declared that a standard ounce of gold, eleven-twelfths fine, was equivalent to £3 17s. 10 1/2d. Silver was relegated once and for all to a secondary role in the coinage.

France, meanwhile, had stabilized the world ratio of silver to gold at its own mint ratio of 15 1/2 to 1. With free coinage of both metals at the prevailing mint pars and both gold and silver coins circulating, France successfully maintained a bimetallic standard. However, silver production increased more rapidly than did gold production between 1820 and 1850, so there was upward pressure on the relative value of gold. By 1850 the 15 1/2 to 1 ratio was tending to undervalue gold. Gold coins were disappearing from the French circulation and France had shifted to a de facto silver standard.

The United States was theoretically on a bimetallic standard also. But from 1792 to 1834, the mint ratio of silver to gold was set at 15 to 1, undervaluing gold. So the United States was on a de facto silver standard until 1834, when the mint ratio was raised to 16 to 1. Silver then became the undervalued metal, and the United States shifted to a de facto gold standard.[1]

Then came discoveries of gold in California in 1848 and in Australia in 1850. Owing to the subsequent increase in gold production, the French coinage, which by 1850 had become mainly silver, gradually changed back to gold. Switzerland, Italy, and Belgium joined France on a bimetallic standard that was shifting increasingly to a de facto gold standard. Allowing each other's currencies to circulate within their own borders, the four countries formed the Latin Monetary Union. They stabilized the world ratio of gold to silver at 15 1/2 to 1. By 1870 only Germany, Holland, and the Scandinavian countries remained on a pure silver standard.

In 1871 Germany, using the indemnity it exacted from France after the Franco–Prussian War, switched to a gold standard. The simultaneous release of silver and accumulation of gold overwhelmed the 15 1/2 to 1 ratio. As silver depreciated in world markets, it became increasingly overvalued at the mint. Countries still on the silver standard faced a rapid depreciation of their currencies while countries on a bimetallic standard anticipated a massive export of gold and a reversion to a rapidly depreciating de facto silver standard. To avoid that outcome, countries on silver or bimetallic standards suspended the free coinage of silver; silver quickly ceased to be a monetary standard anywhere in Europe.

Still further upward pressure on the value of gold came from the United States, which was preparing to restore the convertibility of the dollar after its suspension during the Civil War. At the pre-Civil War ratio of 16 to 1, which had once overvalued gold, gold was now undervalued. So if they wished to return to a gold standard, the U.S. authorities could not allow free coinage of silver at the old mint ratio. That decision was not welcomed by the potent silver interests in the western states. Already injured by the decline in world silver prices, they lobbied for reinstating the free coinage of silver at the old ratio. Although they never achieved

1 This account, as Rolnick and Weber (1986) explain, somewhat oversimplifies what happened in the United States after 1834.

their goal, they did persuade Congress to authorize a substantial, though limited, coinage at the former parity.

While the depreciation of silver rendered it an unsuitable monetary standard, the appreciation of gold made adopting (or, for that matter, maintaining) a gold standard increasingly difficult. During the 1880s and 1890s, the deflationary impact of rising gold prices created a powerful debtor class that advocated inflation to relieve its debt burden. Combining with the silver interests, the inflationists created a political movement on a platform of free coinage of silver that culminated in William Jennings Bryan's unsuccessful campaign for the presidency in 1896.

Instead of competing for gold in a tight world gold market, many countries joined the gold standard by acquiring reserves of foreign exchange. Holding reserves in foreign exchange was less costly than accumulating gold, since foreign exchange at least yielded some interest income. The countries could then peg the value of their currencies in relation to gold by buying and selling foreign exchange in the London money market, instead of by buying and selling gold itself. That was how India took the rupee off the silver standard and tied it to gold and how Austria–Hungary and Russia linked their inconvertible paper currencies to gold. India, Austria–Hungary, Russia, and several other countries which tied their currencies to gold but in which gold did not actually circulate as a currency were said to have adopted not a pure gold standard but a gold-exchange standard.

At the end of the nineteenth century, the steady deflation of the 1870s, 1880s, and early 1890s was reversed by a sharp increase in world gold production. One cause of increased production was the development of the cyanide process that enhanced recovery of gold from existing deposits. And at just about the same time enormous deposits of gold were discovered in both South Africa and Alaska. The sharp increase in the world's production of gold increased the world price level by perhaps 40 percent between 1896 and 1913 (Rockoff 1984).

THE "RULES OF THE GAME" UNDER THE GOLD STANDARD

In the two previous chapters I discussed the two approaches that nineteenth-century economists took when analyzing monetary questions. According to the approach derived from what I called the classical theory, the price level in a country with a convertible currency is determined by the conversion rate of money into gold (or silver) and the value of gold (or silver) in relation to other commodities. The value of gold, classical theorists believed, is determined in an international market. So prices in any country with a currency convertible into gold have to correspond to the internationally determined value of gold. Any divergence of domestic prices from their gold equivalents will create opportunities for profitable arbitrage that will tend to eliminate those differences.

According to the approach derived from the quantity theory of money, the price level in any country depends on the total quantity of money of all kinds – gold, silver, and paper money – in the country. The more gold, silver, and paper money there is in a country, the higher the level of prices in that country has to be. That is why quantity theorists believed that by issuing paper money, banks inevitably tended to raise prices. David Hume (1752b/1955, p. 67), for example, admitted to knowing of no "method of sinking money below its level, but those institutions of banks, funds, and paper-credit." And that attitude has characterized quantity theorists ever since.

But classical theorists maintained that banks would increase the quantity of convertible money only if the public wished to hold more of it. The issue of convertible paper money by banks, therefore, would not raise domestic prices above their international equivalents measured in gold or silver.[2]

Quantity theorists understood that, under convertibility, domestic prices could not deviate very far from their internationally determined gold equivalents. They feared that competing banks would issue so much money that domestic prices would rise far enough above those gold equivalents to cause gold to start flowing out of the country. Unless banks were restrained, the entire gold reserve of the country might be lost and convertibility abandoned.

The whole purpose of a monetary standard, in their view, was to ensure that international flows of gold or silver would prevent the banking system of any country from issuing too much paper money. The increased prices caused by an overissue would make it more difficult both for the country's exporters to sell in world markets and for the country's import-competing producers to sell in domestic ones. The resulting balance-of-trade deficit would cause an outflow of gold that would eventually force banks to contract their issue of paper money. Gold would flow out and the quantity of money would fall until domestic prices were forced down to the same level as in other countries on the gold standard.

Quantity theorists, however, were unwilling to rely exclusively on the

2 Even in the classical view, if the banking system economized sufficiently on gold (or silver) to reduce the international demand for gold substantially, it could affect domestic prices. Whether this happened depended on the size of the country's holdings of gold for monetary purposes compared to the world market for gold. If they were small, the price-level effect would be negligible. And even if they were large, since the value of gold is determined internationally, it is the world price level that would have been affected, not just the price level of the country in question.

operation of the price-specie-flow mechanism (PSFM). Believing the banking system to be inherently expansionary, they argued that even a loss of gold reserves would not induce the banking system to contract its note issues – at least, not right away. Left to itself, a competitive banking system might not begin contracting until the loss of gold had undermined confidence in the safety of banks and in convertibility. And a collapse of confidence could spark panicky bank runs that might degenerate into a vicious downward spiral of contraction and failure, forcing the suspension of convertibility.

That is why quantity theorists proposed monetary reforms aimed at making the total quantity of banknotes in a country fluctuate in step with inflows and outflows of gold. To accomplish this goal, they sought to centralize the right of note issue in the hands of a single authority (or, at least, to constrain the power of competitive banks to issue notes) and to prescribe rules that tied the total quantity of banknotes in a country to its gold reserves. Although the connection was not perceived immediately, it was the attempt to centralize the right of note issue that led before too long to the rise of central banking and to the concept of a lender of last resort (Selgin 1988; Dowd 1989).

There were two types of rules that related to the quantity of banknotes to gold reserves. One was the kind England adopted by enacting Peel's Bank Charter Act. The approach of the Bank Charter Act was to permit a fixed fiduciary issue of banknotes uncovered by gold reserves and to impose a 100 percent gold reserve requirement on any further issues of notes. But as it turned out, the Bank of England did not always increase its note issue as much as an inflow of gold would have allowed it to. By holding some gold reserves in excess of its legal obligation, the bank also avoided having to withdraw notes from circulation whenever it lost gold. So even under the Bank Charter Act, the correspondence between inflows and outflows of gold and the note issue was not perfect.

In other countries the quantity-theoretic view of monetary reform led to a somewhat different approach to constraining the note issue. This approach, followed in several Continental countries, simply required the banks that had been granted a monopoly over the note issue to hold gold reserves equal to some prescribed fraction (less than one) of their outstanding notes. If they did not let excess reserves cushion the impact of gold flows on their note issues, the emerging central banks would have to alter the quantity of outstanding notes by a multiple of the change in their gold reserves. That multiple, of course, would equal the inverse of the required reserve ratio.

Like the first one, this approach had the desired impact on the note issue only if a central bank held no excess gold reserves or kept its holdings of excess gold reserves constant. If a central bank allowed its excess reserves to absorb the impact of a gold inflow or outflow, its note issue would not vary as quantity theorists had expected.

Recognition that central banks could interfere with the international adjustment process promoted the idea that, besides maintaining convertibility and meeting reserve requirements, central banks also had an obligation to allow gold flows to have a corresponding impact on domestic money supplies. Sterilizing gold flows was thought to frustrate PSFM and to prevent the gold standard from operating as it was supposed to. Central banks were supposed to respond to a loss of gold reserves by tightening domestic monetary conditions and to an inflow of gold by loosening them. Thus the notion that central banks under the gold standard were obligated to do more than just maintain the free convertibility of currency into gold at a stipulated rate – that they had to abide by certain "rules of the game" – was derived from a strictly quantity-theoretic view of how the gold standard operated.

Yet it is not at all obvious that, between 1879 and 1914, central banks did follow any rules besides maintaining convertibility. In a well-known study of the gold standard, Arthur Bloomfield (1959) tried to find out whether gold flows among the principal countries on the gold standard between 1880 and 1914 had indeed led monetary authorities to respond as the rules of the game would have required them to do.[3] He found that in more than half the instances in which gold moved into or out of a country in a particular year, the monetary authorities failed to respond in the prescribed manner.[4]

DID THE RULES OF THE GAME MATTER?

Whether monetary authorities were abiding by the rules of the game is an important question. But an even more important one is whether the gold standard was really operating according to the quantity-theoretic model that made such rules seem necessary. That it did appears unlikely for at least two reasons. If the gold standard had worked as the quantity theory and PSFM suggested, inflows of gold should have caused rising

---

3 Although the United States did not have a central bank before 1913, the Treasury was in fact fulfilling many of the functions of a central bank before the creation of the Federal Reserve System.

4 Bloomfield's results have rightly been challenged on the grounds that he imposed too stringent a condition for finding that the rules were being observed. He interpreted the rules as requiring the monetary authorities to reinforce the effects of a movement of gold with a further restriction or expansion of credit in the same direction. It would have been just as plausible to have interpreted the rules of the game as requiring only that the monetary authorities not reverse the effects of a gold outflow with an even greater credit expansion or of a gold inflow with an even greater credit contraction. Even with a less stringent test, however, there were numerous departures from the rules of the game.

price levels, and outflows falling price levels. Not only that, price-level changes in different countries should have been negatively correlated, because an outflow of gold and falling prices in one country should have corresponded to inflows of gold and rising prices somewhere else.

Although it has been long and widely accepted as authoritative, economists have for nearly as long been aware that this view of the gold standard has not fitted the facts very well. For example, many observers have noted that price levels have been remarkably insensitive to gold flows (J. A. Angell 1926/1965; Taussig 1927; Whale 1937). One explanation for that insensitivity has been that changes in money stocks induced by gold flows affect interest rates and incomes before they affect prices. Rising interest rates and falling incomes in countries losing gold attract capital and discourage imports, thereby eliminating the need for gold to leave the country. The opposite happens in countries into which gold flows. Thus, even within the basic framework of the quantity theory and PSFM, price-level adjustments are rendered unnecessary or of secondary importance.

But more recently, a fundamental challenge to the quantity-theoretic interpretation of the gold standard was mounted by Donald McCloskey and J. Richard Zecher (1976). Reviving in part the analysis of Adam Smith and the Banking School, McCloskey and Zecher denied that PSFM was the means for achieving international equilibrium under the gold standard. Nor did they accept that the monetary authorities either did or were supposed to follow any rules other than to maintain convertibility. If, as the law of one price requires, all countries adhering to the gold standard shared a common price level, one would not expect prices to rise faster in countries into which gold flowed than in countries from which gold flowed. Instead, one would expect changes in the price levels of different countries on the gold standard to be highly correlated, because all countries on the gold standard shared a common price level.

In the quantity-theoretic interpretation of the gold standard, gold flows were the means by which national money stocks and price levels were slowly brought into equilibrium. McCloskey and Zecher suggested an altogether different role for gold flows. Gold flows, in their view, simply reflected the decisions of central banks (often, to be sure, under the constraints of legal reserve requirements) about how to divide their assets among gold, foreign exchange, and domestic securities. On their interpretation, changes in the amount of money created by the domestic banking system, and hence in the size of the central bank's asset portfolio and its demand for gold, could just as easily cause gold flows as gold flows could cause changes in the quantity of money created by the banks.

Although they made few references to classical writings on the subject,[5] McCloskey and Zecher lent powerful support to the classical theory of the determination of the price level and international adjustment. So to understand what was going on in the gold standard era, we can't simply take the traditional quantity-theoretic story, with its emphasis on PSFM and the rules of the game, at face value.

Domestic money stocks were largely determined by competitive banking systems. But restrictions on the creation of banknotes by ordinary banks and gold reserve requirements on banknotes issued by central banks prevented the mechanism from working as smoothly as my description of a competitive banking system in Chapter 3 might have led us to expect. So the monetary system that prevailed under the classical gold standard was only imperfectly competitive. Let us now see just how those imperfections affected the performance of the classical gold standard in the years between 1879 and 1914.

HOW THE GOLD STANDARD WORKED

The gold standard, as it operated between 1879 and 1914, differed from the ideal classical system outlined in Chapter 3 in two major ways. First, banking systems were not fully competitive because the issue of banknotes serving as hand-to-hand currency in most countries was monopolized by central banks or the treasuries. The powers that central banks acquired in the latter half of the nineteenth century gave them some limited control over domestic monetary and financial policy. Although that control was sharply limited by the obligation to maintain convertibility, central banks still had some leeway to affect monetary conditions in their own countries, particularly if other central banks were willing to cooperate. And even the constraints of the gold standard could be circumvented if central banks interfered with the mechanism that kept exchange rates within the gold-export and -import points.[6]

But more significantly, the constraints on competitive note issue left the entire monetary system vulnerable to shifts in demand between notes and deposits. Such shifts in demand did not necessarily reflect a loss of confidence in banks. Most of the time, the shifts occurred simply because people wanted to have more cash on hand for making transactions.

---

5   They did, however, acknowledge the important contribution of Whale (1937) as an early version of their approach. For his part, Whale noted the affinities between his version of the gold standard and the view of the gold standard offered by the Banking School.

6   Truman A. Clark (1984) argued that the Bank of England, by using what have been called gold devices, imposed extra costs on the export of gold and thus allowed the dollar-pound exhange rate to fluctuate outside the boundaries imposed by the gold-import and the gold-export points. However, Lawrence Officer (1986) challenged Clark's reasoning and empirical evidence in a subsequent study that argues that there was far less interference with the gold market than Clark suggested.

Had they not been constrained in issuing notes, banks could have satisfied any desire by the public to shift from holding deposits to holding hand-to-hand currency simply by substituting one kind of liability for another. But when banks could not do so because sufficient currency was not forthcoming from the monopolistic supplier of currency, the public lost confidence in the solvency of banks. Thus a temporary liquidity problem was transformed into a financial panic in which people no longer wanted to hold bank liabilities of any kind (Selgin 1988; Dowd 1989).

Even if a central bank could have detected when the public wanted to shift from holding deposits to holding banknotes, it would not have been able to accommodate such a shift unless it had enough excess reserves to be able to issue additional notes. Owing to reserve requirements, that was not always the case. And as long as the issue of notes was monopolized, the monopoly issuer of banknotes was the only recourse available to banks trying to satisfy their customers' demand to convert deposits into notes. That is why monopolistic issuers of banknotes inevitably became lenders of last resort and why suspending reserve requirements was often an essential step in a crisis.

The second way in which the actual gold standard differed from the ideal one was the requirement in most countries that the banknotes be backed by prescribed minimum ratios of gold reserves. Sometimes such required reserve ratios have even been regarded as an essential characteristic of the gold standard (Barro 1979). But reserve requirements were not at all necessary for the gold standard to operate. It appeared that way only to those who viewed the gold standard from the perspective of the quantity theory and PSFM.

Nevertheless, reserve requirements did have important implications for the way the gold standard actually worked, affecting not only the countries imposing them but all countries on the gold standard. First, the monetary authorities had to accumulate stockpiles of gold not only to have a safe margin of excess reserves as a buffer against a sudden withdrawal of gold but just to satisfy the legal requirements. By increasing the world's demand for gold, reserve requirements raised the value of gold in relation to all other commodities. In other words, legal reserve requirements intensified the deflationary effects of the internationalization of the gold standard in the last three decades of the nineteenth century.

Moreover, economic growth or anything else that increased the desire of the public to hold banknotes would increase the required gold reserves correspondingly, adding to the deflationary pressure. If the demand for currency increased gradually, owing, say, to normal economic growth, the deflationary pressure would not be too disruptive. But any sudden demand for additional liquidity or sudden shift in demand by the public from deposits to banknotes might be impossible for the central bank to satisfy unless it had substantial excess reserves on which to draw. If it did not, the result could be a financial crisis that would not be resolved until interest rates rose enough to attract gold from abroad.

This brings me to a further consequence of the reserve requirements, which was that a decline of the excess reserves of a central bank to a low level could cause a financial panic. The problem was not so much that the public feared the insolvency of the central bank or the abandonment of the gold standard. What the public feared was that the central bank, seeking to protect its position, might begin restricting credit because it could make no more advances to the banking system without risking the violation of the reserve requirements.

That is why, after the Bank Charter Act imposed legal reserve requirements on the Bank of England in 1844, England experienced financial crises in 1847, 1857, and 1866. Each time, a crisis was precipitated by a drain of gold from the Bank of England. In no instance did the drain threaten to exhaust the bank's reserves, only to reduce reserves below the legal minimum. Instead, panics arose out of the fear that the bank would not be able to meet a demand for advances because a lack of gold reserves would prevent the issue of any more banknotes. Under those circumstances, the mere anticipation of a credit stringency in the future created one right away.

The crisis of 1847 was resolved when the Government sent the Bank of England a letter that allowed it to satisfy a demand for advances or to discount bills even if it had to issue notes unbacked by equivalent gold reserves. "The panic," Ralph Hawtrey (1932, p. 125) wrote in his account of the crisis and its resolution, "was attributed to the Act of 1844 because the limit placed upon the fiduciary issue was the obstacle to free lending by the Bank, and relief was given by suspending the limit. That once done, the panic subsided and *it was not found necessary actually to exceed the limit*" (my emphasis).

All three crises were cured by the same remedy – a letter from the government allowing the Bank of England to violate the Bank Charter Act by exceeding the limit on its fiduciary issue. In 1847 and 1857 the Government acted on its own initiative in composing such a letter to relieve the crisis. But in 1866 the bank, slowly assuming the responsibilities of a central bank and lender of last resort, approached the Government and asked for permission to exceed the limit on its fiduciary issue to meet demands for credit that arose in the crisis.

It was this doctrine of the Bank of England's duty to lend in a crisis that Walter Bagehot taught in his famous work *Lombard Street* (1873/ 1978). In the years after the crisis of 1866, as Bagehot's teaching grew into orthodoxy, the public stopped worrying that the Bank of England would create a credit crunch to avoid violating the reserve requirements imposed by the Bank Charter Act. As a consequence, England underwent no further serious financial panics until the outbreak of the Great War.

One further consequence of the accumulation of gold reserves by central banks that ought to be mentioned here was that they came to hold an increasing fraction of the world's stock of gold. During the gold standard period, the central banks and monetary authorities of the world were absorbing most of the annual output of the gold mines. Central banks became increasingly influential in the world market for gold. Thus a chief argument for a metallic standard – that it takes the value of money out of the control of the monetary authority – was slowly being undermined.

Before concluding this chapter, I ought to devote a few words to the unique monetary conditions in the United States. The United States had a banking system very different from that of England – one far more susceptible to financial crises. Even though England managed to avoid serious financial panics after the one in 1866, major crises occurred in the United States in 1884, 1893, 1896, and 1907–08. In those of 1884 and 1907, the banking system was forced to suspend convertibility of deposits into gold and into banknotes, so that deposits were selling at a discount in relation to paper currency and to gold.

At the time, the chronic banking difficulties of the United States were blamed on the absence of a central bank like the Bank of England that could satisfy a demand for banknotes. Monetary reformers called for an elastic currency that could accommodate shifts between the demand for banknotes and the demand for deposits. Under the National Bank Act of 1864 that established the framework for the American banking system for the remainder of the century, national banks could issue notes only on the security of Treasury bonds. However, the federal government ran chronic surpluses in the nineteenth century, so the stock of bonds available to back issues of currency declined throughout the period. Banks had no problem meeting the public's increasing demand to hold deposits, but when there was a shift in demand from deposits to banknotes, the banks were constrained by the outstanding stock of Treasury bonds. The simple remedy for this artificially created inelasticity of the currency would have been to permit banks to issue their own notes without restriction. Instead, Congress, which saved interest costs by creating an artificial demand for Treasury bonds, created the Federal Reserve System.

Instability in American banking was also caused by the various prohibitions on interstate banking and often even on branch banking within the same state or county. These prohibitions closed off opportunities for economies of scale and for the diversification of asset portfolios. As a result, many banks were inefficiently small, excessively risky, undercapitalized, and hence vulnerable to adverse shocks or panics. It is evident, therefore, that the financial difficulties the United States endured in the nineteenth century were caused not by the inherent instability of an unregulated banking and financial system but by the rigidities imposed by a range of misguided regulations at both state and national levels.

CONCLUSION

Despite the instabilities that resulted from the monopolization of the note issue, from reserve requirements and other regulations on banking, and from policy errors the monetary authorities committed, the international gold standard performed remarkably well until practically the eve of the Great War. Nevertheless, the buildup of gold stockpiles in the central banks in step with the increase in international tensions in the decades before the war rendered the world more and more susceptible to sharp fluctuations in the value of gold caused by central bank policies. In a sense, therefore, the very success of the gold standard created the conditions that were undermining its continued stability.

When the war finally did come, the gold standard was among its first casualties. Indeed, the gold standard collapsed a week before the guns of August were actually fired. And when, a decade later, the world attempted to put back together what had been smashed to pieces in the fury of August 1914, conditions were vastly more unstable than they had been before the war. The tragic story of the destruction of the gold standard and the catastrophic struggle to replace it with a new one will occupy our attention in the next chapter.

6

The Great War, the Great Depression, and the gold standard

Nor did the needs of Governments come to an end with the restoration of what was called peace. In some countries the spirit of revolution was abroad, while in others the curious belief prevailed that the vast damage wrought by the war would somehow make it easier to maintain a far higher standard of life than had ever existed in the past. . . . Further, the French had to pay for the wanton damage done by the Germans in time of war, and the Germans a few years later had to pay for the wanton damage done by the French in time of peace. The Russians had to fight the other Russians with one hand, and to inaugurate the millennium with the other. The British had to restore order in Ireland, and the Poles to create chaos in Eastern Europe – two processes whose features were less dissimilar than might be supposed. Everybody was in debt to everybody else; and above all everybody had run up an immense account with the great Sir Galahad of the West, whose bill did not seem to be any the smaller because his heart was pure. They were great days: it is to be hoped we shall not see their like again.
D. H. Robertson, *Money*

It is one of the glories of Western civilization that, in the second half of the nineteenth century, it created a world in which people, goods, and money could move virtually without restriction. It is one of the tragedies of Western civilization that, having created such a world, it could then destroy it, perhaps for all time, in August 1914. The gold standard was an integral part of that remarkably free and orderly world.

So, in a way, what happened to the gold standard during and after the war symbolizes what happened to an entire civilization during and after the war. Wartime collapse and disintegration were followed by an ill-conceived attempt to reconstruct a new order – in some respects similar to, and in others, different from, the old one. But after a brief success, another crisis engulfed the world and led it into a new and even more frightful one than the first. That description fits either the world's monetary or its political history between the wars. Our interest here is in the monetary history, but no one, having read this far, will be surprised to find out that I think the two are closely related.

In the financial panic that gripped the world in the last week of July 1914, people struggled to save what they could from the looming catastrophe. No orderly system of international payment that depended on the least bit of mutual trust – and the gold standard surely was such a system – could have survived that panic. Germany, Austria-Hungary, Russia, and France suspended the convertibility of their currencies into gold almost immediately. Indulging their characteristic taste for humbug, the British pretended to maintain convertibility. But so many obstacles were thrown in front of anyone who tried to convert sterling into gold that the legal right to do so was meaningless.

All the belligerents began spending huge amounts of money on the war – far more than they could raise through explicit taxation. When added spending went to domestic recipients, it was financed largely by printing new money. Central banks bought huge amounts of government debt, paying for it by creating new liabilities of their own. Under convertibility, that would have been impossible because holders of central-bank liabilities would have demanded that the liabilities be redeemed in gold.

Governments can force their citizens to accept an inconvertible fiat currency. But they can't compel foreigners to do so – especially not at an official rate that no longer bears any relation to its purchasing power. Spending on imports, therefore, could not be financed by printing new money; it could be financed only by real borrowing or by payment in gold. So the national mobilization of all available gold stocks became a wartime imperative. Gold coins were quickly withdrawn from circulation and token coins or paper substituted in their place.

The flood of inconvertible paper money in all the belligerent countries could have only one consequence: inflation. In 1919 wholesale prices were twice as high in the United States as they were in 1913; in Britain they were two-and-a-half times as high; in France they were more than three times as high; and in Germany they were eight times as high (Palyi 1972, p. 33). But the inflation was not confined to the belligerents. And the reason it wasn't is instructive. What the belligerents did to pay for their imports from nonbelligerent countries was to withdraw all gold coins from domestic circulation. Demonetizing so much gold reduced the world's monetary demand for gold. Without an offsetting rise in the nonmonetary demand for gold, the value of gold in relation to all other commodities could only fall. That, of course, meant inflation.

So even countries like the United States and Sweden that initially did remain on the gold standard also underwent rapid inflation. The United States, of course, went off the gold standard upon entering the war in 1917. But neutral Sweden had already stopped purchasing gold in 1916 at the prewar parity to avoid the inflation that was inevitable while the krona was linked to gold.

I must acknowledge, however, that the mechanism by which inflation in World War I was transmitted to countries that remained on the gold standard is susceptible of more than one interpretation. As I interpret the mechanism, inflation was caused by a falling demand for gold in belligerent countries. By using gold formerly held for monetary purposes to pay for their imports from the rest of the world, the belligerents swamped the international gold market, driving down the value of gold and driving up the prices, measured in gold, of other commodities.

The conventional quantity-theoretic interpretation of the inflation ignores the supply of and the demand for gold. It concentrates, instead, on the accumulation of gold by the nonbelligerent countries. That accumulation provided them with additional reserves against which to expand their domestic money supplies. The inflation, on this interpretation, was caused by domestic monetary expansion, to which the decline in the value of gold in relation to other commodities was only incidental.

Although differing about what is cause and what is effect, the alternative interpretations of the wartime inflation are not wholly incompatible. When I say that the belligerent countries reduced their demand to hold gold and thus forced down its value in relation to other commodities, I implicitly assume that the central banks of nonbelligerent countries into which the gold was flowing did not simply want to hold it all. Unwilling just to hold the newly acquired gold, they used it to acquire earning assets and, in so doing, created new liabilities. This meant that the public had to absorb some of the gold that would otherwise have accumulated within those central banks. At the same time, the expansion of central-bank liabilities meant an increase in the money stocks of those countries.

Thus, when the international market for gold is dominated by central banks, what I call a decline in the demand for, and a fall in the value of, gold can also be described as an inflationary monetary expansion by central banks. One can, as I do, regard the decline in the demand for gold as the cause and rising prices and money supplies as the effects of this process. Alternatively, one can view the increase in money supplies as the cause and the fall in the value of gold as the effect.

The differences between the two interpretations are subtle, and it is not easy to distinguish between them empirically. But analyzing domestic price levels under the gold standard in terms of an international gold market has at least one major advantage. It explicitly recognizes that domestic prices were determined in international markets. For no central bank under the gold standard could change the domestic prices of internationally traded goods unless it also changed the prices of those goods everywhere else.

When, for example, the price of wheat in the United States was 50 cents a bushel, the price in France had to be about Fr 2.59 and the price in England had to be about 24.7 pence a bushel. Arbitrage ensured that the price of wheat in the United States could not diverge from its internationally determined level. And the same must have been true for all other internationally tradable goods. So unless a central bank could somehow affect the level of international prices, it could not have more than a minimal impact on domestic prices.

A tight monetary policy is simply one in which the central bank accumulates gold. And an easy one is one in which the central bank runs down its gold reserves. Neither one affects domestic prices unless the central bank accumulates or loses enough gold to affect international economic conditions, which is to say unless it materially adds to or detracts from the international demand for gold.

When the United States abandoned the gold standard upon entering the war in 1917, the world gold market ceased to exist. Virtually all countries were tightly controlling the export and import of gold, so official gold prices had virtually no relation to the prices of other commodities. Some semblance of a market for gold was not restored until 1919, when the United States again permitted its unrestricted import and export.

While inflation had been rapid in the United States even before convertibility was suspended, inflation speeded up still more after the suspension. For unlike Sweden, which went off the gold standard to avoid the inflation caused by the depreciation of gold, the United States went off gold to be free to resort to inflation to finance its war expenditures. Yet despite the doubling of wholesale prices between 1913 and 1919, convertibility was restored at the prewar price, $20.67 an ounce. That meant that gold had lost half of its value since 1913.

THE WORLD AFTER THE WAR

After the upheavals of the First World War, resurrecting the gold standard as it existed before 1914 was simply not possible. A small indication of how much things had changed was what happened to exchange rates. During the war, officially frozen exchange rates lost all touch with reality. Only after the war did they finally adjust to reflect the changes in their purchasing power. Yet despite — or perhaps because of — those enormous changes in economic relationships, restoring the international gold standard was a widely shared goal of the postwar era.

No less important than the absolute and relative change in the purchasing powers of currencies was the tremendous accumulation of gold by the United States. In 1913 U.S. gold holdings totaled $1.29 billion, or

26 1/2 percent of the reserves held by the world's central banks and governments. By 1918 U.S. gold holdings had more than doubled to $2.66 billion, or 40 percent of the world's reserves; by 1923 U.S. reserves grew to $3.83 billion, over 44 percent of the world's reserves (Palyi 1972, p. 181). For the first time, the monetary authorities of a single country dominated the world gold market.

The dilemma confronting the world as it tried to restore the gold standard was how to reconcile the existing levels of prices with the old gold parities. With its vast gold reserves, the United States could easily restore the prewar gold parity of $20.67 an ounce, although dollar prices were, even after the severe deflation of 1920–21, more than 50 percent higher than before the war.

Perhaps the sharpest in history, the 1920–21 deflation was deliberately engineered by the Federal Reserve Board to halt an inflationary spiral that had accelerated after the end of the war. Although a deflation that steep could not but cause business activity to drop and unemployment to rise, the recession actually seems to have been moderated by the very rapid adjustment of prices and wages. Such rapidly falling wages and prices prevented output from having to bear an even greater burden of the adjustment.[1] And by the summer of 1921, a strong recovery was under way in the United States.

Even though few other countries had rejoined the gold standard by 1920–21, the American deflation created deflationary pressure in other countries. Since the dollar had replaced sterling as the dominant international currency, a country could rejoin the gold standard by stabilizing the value of its currency against the dollar. Countries that were planning to rejoin the gold standard came under pressure to deflate in step with the United States to avoid any further depreciation of their currencies against the dollar.

Prices measured in gold had risen so far above their prewar levels because the demand for gold had fallen when most countries left the gold standard during the war. Restoring the gold standard, therefore, was a potentially deflationary step. If going back on the gold standard meant increasing the monetary demand for gold back to the level of 1913, it could also drive prices down to the level of 1913. Especially after the deflation of 1920–21 had reduced output and increased unemployment, no one wanted to contemplate a deflation two or three times as deep.

Thus, for the world to restore the gold standard on the basis of the

---

1 However, if deflation is too rapid, or, more precisely, if it is expected to be too rapid, it can cause a collapse of investment and a flight into cash as the expected return to holding cash begins to rise above the return on physical capital. See "The collapse of the international financial system," later in this chapter. Presumably this effect was not an important part of the 1920–21 story, although it seems to have played a key role in the 1929–33 episode.

prewar dollar-gold parity, the world's central banks, of which the Federal Reserve System was now the dominant one, had to restrain their monetary demand for gold to prevent gold from appreciating any further. The steady deflation from 1870 to 1896 – a deflation that earned for that era the name "the Great Depression" before the title was transferred to the 1929–39 episode – had been at least partly caused by the widespread adoption of the gold standard by countries all over the world. With the dangers of both inflation and deflation so deeply imbedded in the public consciousness, it was understood that central banks ought to try to limit their demand for gold while reinstituting the gold standard.

That understanding led to the convening of an international conference in Genoa in 1922 to work out the guidelines for national monetary authorities to follow in restoring the gold standard. Resolution Nine of the Genoa Conference (quoted in Nurkse 1944) read as follows:

These steps might by themselves suffice to establish a gold standard, but its successful maintenance would be materially promoted, not only by the proposed collaboration of central banks, but by an international convention to be adopted at a suitable time. The purpose of the convention would be to centralize and co-ordinate the demand for gold, and so to avoid those wide fluctuations in the purchasing power of gold which might otherwise result from the simultaneous and competitive efforts of a number of countries to secure metallic reserves. The convention should embody some means of economizing the use of gold by maintaining reserves in the form of foreign balances, such, for example, as the gold exchange standard or an international clearing system.

Unfortunately, the convention referred to in Resolution Nine was never adopted.

Central banks in the 1920s found themselves in an unprecedented position. After the great gold discoveries of the mid-nineteenth century, no central bank alone could have significantly affected the value of gold. A central bank could take the value of gold to be independent of its own activities and not go very far wrong. The primary duties of a central bank were then to guarantee the convertibility of its currency into gold and, in a crisis, to act as a lender of last resort.

"But the war," as John Maynard Keynes (1923/1971, p. 134) observed,

has effected a great change. Gold itself has become a "managed" currency. The West, as well as the East, has learnt to hoard gold; but the motives of the United States are not those of India. Now that most countries have abandoned the gold standard, the supply of metal would, if the chief user of it restricted its holdings to its real needs, prove largely redundant. The United States has not been able to let gold fall to its "natural" value, because it could not face the resulting depreciation of its standard. It has been driven, therefore, to the costly policy of burying in the vaults of Washington what the miners of the Rand have laboriously brought to the surface. Consequently gold now stands at an "artificial" value, the future course of which almost entirely depends on the policy of the Federal Reserve Board of the United States.

The reserve requirements that I mentioned in the previous chapter only reinforced the tendency for resumption to increase the value of gold. Attempting to reassure the international financial community of their commitment to gold, many countries raised their legal reserve requirements (Palyi 1972, p. 125). Since reserve requirements were expressed as a percentage of central-bank obligations, the amount of gold required to satisfy the obligations depended on the amount of liabilities issued. Central-bank liabilities had increased so enormously since 1913 that satisfying the reserve requirements entailed a significant increase in the monetary demand for gold even without the reintroduction of a gold coinage. As we shall see presently, reserve requirements played a particularly critical role in France after 1928.

Nevertheless, from 1922 through 1928, the United States did manage to prevent any sharp rise in the value of gold. Under the strong-willed leadership of the president of the New York Federal Reserve Bank, Benjamin Strong, the United States avoided accumulating gold in those years as its share of international gold reserves fell from 44 to 36 percent. Strong believed in close cooperation among the central banks (though he usually insisted that it be on his own terms), so he discouraged any competition for gold that might force up its value. Such cooperation helped the British maintain convertibility of the pound after restoring it in 1925; it also aided the French return to gold between 1926 and 1928.

Unfortunately, there were chronic tensions among the central banks, particularly between the Bank of England and the Bank of France. After 1926, Britain's shaky financial position made it especially dependent on the willingnesss of the Bank of France to hold British securities. Strong could mediate effectively between the British and the French, but after his death in 1928, cooperation between them broke down.

BRITAIN AND THE GOLD STANDARD

The gold standard, as we saw in the previous chapter, was a peculiarly British institution. And so great was Britain's attachment to it that during World War I, Britain refused even to acknowledge that it had been suspended. The patriotic feelings and the exchange controls that helped preserve that fiction during the war could not be maintained after the war. When it was finally acknowledged that the gold standard was no longer in effect, its ultimate restoration was taken for granted.

Even before the war was over, the Cunliffe Committee, in its famous *Interim Report* (U.K. Parliament, 1918/1979), while carefully adhering to the fiction that the gold standard had not really been suspended, announced that the British government intended to restore the gold standard as it had operated before the war. At the time, no one doubted that this meant reestablishing the old parity between gold and sterling of £3 17s 10.5d an ounce. But the postwar dominance of the dollar made the key parity the one between the dollar and sterling, of $4.86 a pound.

After exchange controls were lifted, the value of the pound in relation to gold and other currencies was determined daily in the foreign-exchange markets. By February 1920 the pound had fallen from its prewar parity to $3.20, making the departure from gold unmistakable. But after the very sharp deflation of 1920–21, the pound recovered most of the ground it had lost against the dollar and in 1922 rose to within 10 percent of its prewar parity. From 1922 to 1924 the pound fluctuated between $4.30 and $4.60.

A broad range of British opinion accepted the goal of restoring the gold standard at its prewar parity. But Keynes and a few others dissented. Keynes argued that stabilizing the pound at the prewar parity of $4.86 would entail a further deflation, beyond the drastic deflation of 1920–21, of about 10 percent. If the pound were pegged at $4.86, he maintained, Britain's international competitiveness simply could not be restored without a 10 percent deflation.[2] A deflation of that magnitude would inevitably force unemployment yet higher. Even in 1925, Britain had still not fully recovered from the 1920–21 deflation, so Keynes's warnings could not be lightly dismissed. Despite those warnings, however, Winston Churchill, chancellor of the Exchequer, decided in April 1925 to resume convertibility at the prewar parity.

Although Keynes's argument against restoring the prewar parity is rarely challenged any more, the general presumption that high British unemployment after 1925 was Churchill's fault is not entirely convincing. For however sensible an argument Keynes might have made against restoring the prewar parity, it does not explain why, once the restoration had been accomplished, Britain did not undergo the 10 percent deflation needed to restore its international competitiveness within a year or two. Why, instead, did Britain continue to endure for the rest of the decade (until the Great Depression made things even worse) an unemployment rate that stayed higher than it had been in all but two of the preceding sixty-five years? Indeed, by going back on the gold standard, Britain lost control

2 The concept of international competitiveness is rather vague. The basic economic theory of international trade teaches us that every country, however inefficient, will always have a comparative advantage in the production of some products that it will be able to export. Presumably "international competitiveness" in the context of Great Britain in 1925 referred to its traditional export industries and import-competing industries. Without a reduction in real wages, those industries would not be profitable at the prevailing levels of prices in international markets.

of its domestic price level; so deflation and international competitiveness should have been forced on Britain whether it wanted them or not.

Why didn't deflation in the 1920s restore Britain's international competitiveness and eliminate the chronic unemployment of the 1920s? Sometimes it is suggested that trade unions were able to block the wage reductions that might have restored British competitiveness and brought unemployment down to prewar levels. Whether British unions kept labor costs too high for Britain to regain international competitiveness is not a question we need to pursue here. But even an affirmative answer would not fully account for high British unemployment and declining British competitiveness. After all, the percentage of the British labor force belonging to unions declined steadily throughout the 1920s. If labor costs could fall by almost 50 percent in the deflation of 1920–21, why, when the fraction of the labor force that was unionized was lower, couldn't they have fallen just 10 percent?

Some recent research by two American economists, Dan Benjamin and Levis Kochin (1979), has cast new light on why British unemployment was so high between the wars. They deny that an overvalued pound was what caused high British unemployment in the 1920s. They point out that, on average, economic growth in the 1920s and 1930s was as rapid as in any comparable period in British history. Yet as late as 1938, unemployment had still not dipped below 10 percent. Since the pound depreciated after 1931, it would seem that high unemployment was caused by something other than an overvalued exchange rate. Benjamin and Kochin suggest that it was the level and availability of unemployment relief payments.

Benefits had been raised during the wartime inflation to prevent the real level of support from being eroded. Moreover, coverage had been extended and eligibility rules had been progressively liberalized. Despite the deflation of 1920–21, benefit levels were not reduced, and nominal benefits continued to increase despite the mild deflation that took place over the remainder of the decade. So during the 1920s an enormous increase in the real value of unemployment benefits took place.

Benjamin and Kochin were not the first to suggest that unemployment benefits had been the source of high unemployment. That possibility was raised at the time by a few economists, most notably Edwin Cannan (1930) and Jacques Rueff (1925, 1931). But most economists dismissed this intuitive argument as empirically insignificant. What Benjamin and Kochin did was to use modern econometric techniques to estimate the impact unemployment benefits had on unemployment rates. Their findings were startling. They estimated that if the 1913 ratio of benefits to wages had been maintained between 1925 and 1929, British unemploy-

Table 2. *Benjamin-Kochin estimates of unemployment in Britain from 1920 to 1938 without high unemployment benefits*

Year	Actual unemployment (%)	Estimated unemployment assuming 1913 ratio of benefits to wages (%)	
		Upper limit	Lower limit
1920	3.9	3.9	3.9
1921	17.0	17.0	17.0
1922	14.3	12.2	10.8
1923	11.7	9.1	7.5
1924	10.3	6.7	4.5
1925	11.3	7.0	4.4
1926	12.5	8.0	5.4
1927	9.7	5.3	2.9
1928	10.8	6.1	3.4
1929	10.4	5.5	2.8
1930	16.1	10.6	7.1
1931	21.3	15.5	11.5
1932	22.1	17.1	13.4
1933	19.9	14.8	11.4
1934	16.7	11.2	7.8
1935	15.5	9.5	5.9
1936	13.1	6.6	3.0
1937	10.8	4.6	1.3
1938	12.9	6.8	3.3

Source: Daniel K. Benjamin and Levis A. Kochin (1979), "Searching for an Explanation of Unemployment in Interwar Britain," *Journal of Political Economy* 87(3), table 1, p. 467. Copyright © The University of Chicago. Reprinted by permission.

ment would have been an average of at least 4–7 percentage points lower than it actually was.

Table 2 reproduces their annual estimates of what unemployment between 1921 and 1939 would have been if the 1913 ratio of benefits to wages had been maintained. Unemployment in Britain would have risen sharply in the depression, as it did in all countries on the gold standard, even without the dole. But only the dole can explain why unemployment rates were persistently high both before and after the Great Depression, when, by historical standards, the British economy was growing at a rapid rate.

The Benjamin-Kochin-Cannan-Rueff hypothesis gives us a straightforward explanation for the failure of deflation to restore British competitiveness. Deflation increased the real value of unemployment benefits. That induced workers who might otherwise have chosen employment to choose unemployment.[3] It became easier to take time to look for a job or even to take a short paid vacation.[4] And since workers could afford to be choosier about jobs, employers could not retain their workers unless they raised real wage rates.

By increasing real unemployment benefits, deflation imposed higher real wages on British employers and a higher tax burden on those who were still working. Since, under the gold standard, British exporters sold at prices determined in international markets, they could not easily raise prices to compensate for rising wages. Thus rising real wages made much of Britain's traditional export trade, already in decline, unprofitable. High wages substantially raised unemployment in the export industries while high unemployment benefits made unemployed workers less willing to seek employment elsewhere.

Not understanding the causes of the high unemployment, the British monetary authorities sought to reduce it by easing monetary policy as much as possible within the constraints imposed by the restored parity. The inherent contradictions of that policy forced the Bank of England to rely on the forbearance of the Federal Reserve and the Bank of France to avoid gold outflows. The vulnerability of the British monetary policy to the whims of the American and, particularly, the French monetary authorities increased the underlying instability of the international economy. The crucial, and not altogether benign, effects French monetary policy had on the international economy in the late 1920s merit our further attention.

3 To say that unemployment was chosen does not mean that those unemployed always preferred being unemployed to holding a job. What it means is that qualifying for unemployment benefits was easy and that benefits were generous enough to induce workers to accept increased stretches of unemployment and to tolerate being laid off during periods of slack demand in preference to accepting greater job security at lower wages. Nor does it mean that unemployment was not involuntary during the Great Depression itself in a sense that was not true of the late 1920s.

4 Winston Churchill, who drafted the original legislation setting up unemployment insurance, did not reject the idea that the dole was a major contributor to high unemployment rates. Churchill (1930) charged that unemployment was overstated because "every case of unemployment, even for short periods, is recorded in the national register, and the benefit is increasingly applied for, even by those not in actual want, . . . as a contribution toward what may be little more than a needed holiday after years of continuous work. . . . It is significant that after every public holiday – Christmas, Easter, Whitsuntide – there is a very large addition to the unemployment total, which falls off again a few weeks later." Moreover, "many British employers have lent themselves to an abuse of the system of unemployment insurance. . . . They systematically arrange to give their workers just that amount of employment as will enable them to qualify for the benefit."

THE FRENCH STABILIZATION

While Britain was struggling to go back on the gold standard in the early 1920s, France, under a series of unstable and ineffectual governments, allowed inflation to accelerate and the franc to depreciate. Inflation in France during and immediately after the war had been even worse than in Britain, though never reaching the hyperinflationary dimensions of the postwar German inflation. Mesmerized by a vision of German reparations that would solve all its financial woes, the French political process threw off all fiscal and monetary self-discipline. Reflecting the disordered state of French finances, the franc depreciated steadily until 1926, when it dropped to under 2 cents – barely a tenth of its prewar parity against the dollar of 19.3 cents. However, the depreciation of the franc produced an economic and political crisis that led to the formation of a national-unity coalition headed by a respected conservative politician, Raymond Poincaré.[5]

The Poincaré government was committed to a balanced budget and a stable franc. Poincaré's ability to build a national consensus for these goals prompted an immediate reversal of inflationary expectations. The franc recovered strongly in the foreign-exchange markets, quickly reaching 4 cents. So, late in 1926, the Bank of France announced that it would stabilize the value of the franc at 3.92 cents as a prelude to the eventual restoration of convertibility into gold at a corresponding rate.

With the franc pegged at just under 4 cents, French wages, unlike British wages, did not render domestically produced goods internationally uncompetitive. Low real wages helped French exporters adjust without difficulty to the stabilization of the franc in 1927–28. Over those two years France steadily increased its holdings of foreign-exchange reserves. By keeping a large fraction of those reserves in sterling-denominated assets, the Bank of France assisted the British in maintaining sterling at its dollar parity.

On June 25, 1928, France legally went back on the gold standard. Like other countries returning to gold, France did not reintroduce a gold coinage. It made the franc convertible into bullion but not into coin. That was consistent with Resolution Nine of the Genoa Conference. But the legislation that reestablished the gold standard also required the Bank of France to hold gold reserves equal to 35 percent of its demand liabilities and prohibited the bank from purchasing any more foreign exchange. So stiff a requirement was contrary to the spirit if not the letter of Resolution Nine. The momentous consequences of those reserve requirements will become apparent shortly.

5 This account of the French stabilization relies heavily on Hawtrey (1932, chap. 1). An important recent treatment of the episode is presented by Sargent (1986, chap. 4).

The Great War, the depression, and the gold standard

THE ONSET OF TIGHT MONEY IN 1928

While running balance-of-payments surpluses in 1927–28, France was accumulating bills on London and New York. By accumulating bills instead of gold, the Bank of France enabled the British and American authorities to avoid having to protect their own gold reserves by tightening their money markets. Freed from worry about an excessive loss of gold reserves, the Federal Reserve was actually able to ease conditions in 1927 when a recession seemed about to begin. The easy Federal Reserve policy did cause a modest drain on U.S. gold reserves in 1927 and 1928, but was hardly a cause for concern.

That policy was widely thought to have fueled the stock market boom that began in 1927. The Federal Reserve Board thought so too. Concerned about a bull market supposedly driven by speculative borrowing, the Fed tried to check the boom in June 1928 by raising the discount rate to 5 percent and by selling securities. The reversal of policy meant that instead of supplying the additional reserves the Bank of France and other central banks demanded, the Fed itself became a net demander of gold.

Since the reversal of policy was explicitly aimed at checking the stock market boom, the obvious question is whether an easy-money policy could have caused a stock market boom and whether a tight-money policy could have stopped it. Now it is often suggested that an easy-money policy puts extra cash in the pockets of investors who then use it to bid up stock prices. But that reasoning is not easy to follow. Stocks are claims on the present and future earnings of the issuing companies. How much the stock is worth depends, therefore, on potential investors' forecasts of future earnings and the discount factor they apply to those earnings, not on how much cash they have in their pockets. So if investors have excess cash, one can't just assume that it would go into the stock market.

The only way excess cash could raise stock prices is by affecting either future earnings or interest rates. Perhaps the excess cash is spent on goods and services and creates inflation. But there was no inflation in the 1920s, so that could not have been the reason that stock prices rose. Nor could a mere expectation of future inflation raise stock prices; any increase in expected future earnings would be offset by a corresponding rise in nominal interest rates. On the other hand, if the excess cash went into the bond market and thus reduced interest rates, stock prices would rise on that account. But falling interest rates were obviously not the cause of the stock market boom of 1927–29, so the boom must have been generated by rising expectations of future earnings.

Although an excess supply of money cannot generate a stock market

Table 3. *Monthly U.S. net gold movements, 1927–30*

Month	1927	1928	1929	1930
January	72	−6	−14	7
February	22	−11	26	62
March	11	−57	35	70
April	13	−39	72	68
May	−2	−106	41	26
June	−21	−51	23	18
July	−7	4	17	−18
August	8	10	19	−16
September	−17	2	12	10
October	−30	17	14	24
November	−90	−14	−19	36
December	−72	13	−83	22

Source: Charles Cortez Abbott (1937), *The New York Bond Market, 1920–1930* (Cambridge, MA: Harvard University Press), p. 195. Reprinted by permission.

boom, that does not mean that monetary policy was (or is) irrelevant to the stock market.[6] As the Genoa Conference recognized in 1922, the great threat to world prosperity in the 1920s was that restoration of the gold standard would greatly increase the international demand for gold and cause deflation. After Britain rejoined the gold standard in 1925 and France began moving rapidly toward that goal in 1926, the threat of deflation increased correspondingly. The responsibility for avoiding that deflation rested mainly on the United States, which alone had sufficient quantities of gold to support the increased demand. When the underlying deflationary forces seemed about to take over in 1927, the Federal Reserve promptly counteracted them by permitting an outflow of gold.

Table 3 records the monthly net gold movements of the United States from 1927 to 1930. After accumulating gold early in 1927, the United States became a net exporter of gold in every month but one from May 1927 to June 1928. Observing that response by the Fed, investors might realistically have assumed that the probability of deflation (which has adverse implications for real as well as nominal future earnings) had been significantly reduced. As those expectations about the ability and willingness of the Fed to prevent deflation took hold between 1927 and 1929, investors kept raising their forecasts of future earnings. It was those steadily rising expectations that fueled the stock market boom.

6 My account of the relation between monetary policy and the stock market here draws on Earl Thompson (1978, 1981) and on many discussions we have had on the subject over the years, for which I am greatly indebted. The argument is also similar to that of Hawtrey (1932, chap. 4).

The Great War, the depression, and the gold standard

After restoring the gold standard in 1928, the Bank of France was legally obligated to maintain reserve requirements in gold against its demand liabilities, which were rapidly expanding. At first it obtained reserves from domestic sources, but in 1929 it began drawing gold from abroad by liquidating its foreign-exchange reserves. Thus, far from preventing monetary conditions in London and New York from tightening, as it had been doing previously, France began to force tightness on the money markets. The competitive scramble for gold reserves which the Genoa Conference had warned against was finally starting.

Still worried by a continuing stock market boom and now determined to halt the outflow of gold of the previous two years, the Fed began tightening money in the second half of 1928 and continued doing so in 1929. The increased French demand for gold and the unwillingness of the Fed to accommodate that demand in 1929 were reflected in falling commodities prices in the spring of that year. And although the stock market boom continued until October 1929, business activity was already declining that summer. If the stock market boom had indeed been fed by expectations that the Fed would maintain an easy-money policy calculated to avoid deflation, it is possible that the market held up as long as it did in the hope that the Fed would, as it had in 1927, reverse its tight-money policy. When its hopes for a reversal were dashed, the market crashed (Thompson 1978).

The immediate loosening of monetary policy right after the October crash permitted stocks to rebound at the end of 1929 and early 1930. But in early 1930 the Fed returned to a more restrictive stance and began accumulating gold again. The market broke again in March and kept falling almost continuously for three years.

THE COLLAPSE OF THE INTERNATIONAL FINANCIAL SYSTEM

Aside from its vulnerability to an appreciation of gold, the international economy also had to cope with the tremendous burden of allied war debts owed to the United States and of reparations Germany had to make – mostly to the French. To finance those payments, Germany had borrowed heavily from the United States during the 1920s. That borrowing was a partial substitute for German exports that the United States had excluded by the Fordney-McCumber tariff of 1921. The United States had become the world's creditor, but it refused to accept the ultimate payment in goods that others had to make to discharge their debts to it.

This point leads me to consider the impact of the Hawley-Smoot Tariff of 1930. Jude Wanniski (1978) has ingeniously suggested that the stock market crash was precipitated by expectations that the tariff would be enacted. And Allan Meltzer (1981) has also accorded the Hawley-Smoot Tariff an important role in propagating the depression, though the role is still subsidiary to the monetary factors he and other Monetarists normally emphasize.

The Hawley-Smoot Tariff was certainly a tax on efficient world trade. And for that reason alone, it must have caused a contraction of world trade and economic activity (which was Wanniski's point). But it also had important financial effects. In particular, it undermined the ability of foreign debtors to repay their debts to the United States. As it became clear that these loans could not be paid off, confidence in the American and the international banking systems must have been eroded.

One of our foremost economic historians, Charles Kindleberger (1984, pp. 366–67), has challenged the notion that the tariff had much to do with causing the Great Depression. He argues that a tariff tends to increase a country's export surplus. Within a simple Keynesian model, that is an expansionary effect. But such an absolution of the Hawley-Smoot Tariff is hardly persuasive. To argue that the tariff was expansionary is an obvious fallacy of composition. The fallacy of composition incorrectly concludes that what is true for an individual (or a single country) must also be true for a group of individuals (or countries). Even within a simple Keynesian model, the total of contractionary forces in other countries offsets the expansionary effect of the tariff in the country that imposes it. Even more important, though, that simple model totally overlooks the devastating effect the tariff had on the international financial system – the sort of effect that one would have expected the author of *Manias, Panics, and Crashes* and *A Financial History of Western Europe* to be highly sensitive to.

As always, a loss of confidence in the financial system increased the desire for liquidity. Under the circumstances, a demand for liquidity was largely a demand for gold. The increasing demand for gold intensified the deflationary trends that were already spreading to all countries under the gold standard. The rapid deflation increased an already heavy debt burden and forced many otherwise solvent debtors into bankruptcy, further undermining the world financial system.

Since prices measured in gold were more than 50 percent higher in 1930 than they were before the war, an expectation that deflation might drive prices down by 50 or more percent would not have been unreasonable. And once expectations of rapid deflation take hold, economic activity begins to break down. How destructive the mere expectation of rapid deflation is becomes clearer if we look carefully at the Fisher equation. According to that equation, the nominal interest rate (i) equals the real interest rate (r) plus the anticipated rate of inflation or deflation (p).

Most of us have become familiar with this relationship in an inflationary environment in which a premium for expected inflation must be added onto the real interest rate. But the relation holds in a deflation as well. It is easy to see what must happen so long as the rate of deflation is less than the real rate of interest. The nominal rate simply adjusts downward and falls below the real interest rate. But the nominal interest rate cannot fall below zero because the alternative of just holding money ensures that no one will ever lend at a negative nominal rate.

So what happens if the nominal rate has already fallen to zero and people anticipate that deflation will get worse? Since the nominal rate can't fall below zero, the expected rate of deflation cannot exceed the real rate of interest. So the only adjustment possible is for the real rate to rise to match the expected rate of deflation. The economic significance of this is that the expected return to hoarding money begins to exceed the expected return on real investment. People therefore attempt to liquidate their holdings of real assets in order to hold money. Suddenly rendered unprofitable, real investment ceases and the capital stock shrinks until the expected return on investment (the real rate of interest) rises enough to restore the equality with the return to hoarding money. Unless the price level is stabilized, the process feeds on itself, pulling the economy into a downward spiral. And that is just what happened in the Great Depression.

In early 1931 it seemed that the bottom of what was already an un-usually severe recession might have been reached. However, the insolvency of the Austrian Credit Anstalt in May 1931 triggered a massive crisis in financial markets throughout the world, particularly in Germany. Advances to German banks and industrialists were called in and capital began to flee Germany. The crisis forced all German banks and the German foreign-exchange market to close down after the failure of the Darmstadter Bank in July 1931.

After the German debacle, the international financial community focused its attention on Great Britain. As early as February 1931, forward quotations of the pound had fallen below the level at which it became profitable to convert pounds into gold for export. The low forward rate on the pound reflected anxiety that the British, after suffering years of high unemployment before 1930, would not tolerate a downward deflationary spiral just to maintain the gold standard. When France finally ceased absorbing gold in March 1931, the pressure on the pound eased. But the German crisis of July revived fears about sterling, since the British banking system had lent heavily to the German banks.

Fearing that Britain would go off gold, holders of sterling-denominated liabilities sought to convert them into gold. Unwilling to force interest rates, already at 4 1/2 percent in the midst of a violent deflation, any higher, the Bank of England chose instead to suspend convertibility in

September 1931. Although a sustained recovery did not begin in Britain for almost a year, the depreciation of sterling arrested deflation and at least stopped things from getting worse.

On the other hand, the British departure from the gold standard made holding gold that much more attractive and thus intensified deflationary pressures in the countries that remained on the gold standard. The desire to hoard gold and the mistrust of every kind of paper, not only by central banks, which had just suffered heavy losses on their sterling holdings, but also by individuals, was intensified. Yet instead of trying to relieve upward pressure on the value of gold and easing credit conditions, the Federal Reserve immediately raised its discount rate from 1 1/2 to 3 1/2 percent to protect the gold standard. Heroic action by the Fed, had it been willing to supply gold freely to satisfy the world's appetite for it, could perhaps have stemmed the deflationary tide. But the Fed preferred what seemed to be a lower-risk course and looked after its gold reserves.

Although the gold reserves of the United States were enormous, its free reserves – those not required to be held against currency in the hands of the public – were diminishing. The collapse of many banks led to growing public distrust of banks. Many people, therefore, began switching from holding deposits to holding currency. Since the Fed had to hold gold reserves against currency, the growing demand for currency reduced its free gold reserves. Although free reserves were still substantial, rumors spread that dwindling free reserves would force the United States off the gold standard, provoking further withdrawals of gold.

However, when Congress passed the Glass-Steagall Act in February 1932, one of whose provisions allowed currency to be backed by government securities as well as by gold, that threat to the gold standard was eliminated. Freed from the obligation to hold reserves in gold against its currency liabilities, the Fed in 1932 finally embarked on a modest program of open-market purchases that relieved some of the pressure on the gold market.

The Fed's easing of the gold market seemed to bring an end to the deflation in the summer of 1932, and a recovery began that summer and fall. But after the 1932 election, rumors that the incoming Roosevelt administration would devalue the dollar or abandon the gold standard altogether provoked renewed hoarding of gold. For the first time, gold reserves were being withdrawn not only for export but for domestic hoarding. A new wave of bank failures overtook the United States. Many states called bank holidays to halt the runs. And immediately upon taking office on March 6, 1933, Franklin Roosevelt declared a bank holiday, closing all banks in the country for over a week.

In April the new administration halted the free export of gold, taking the United States off the gold standard. U.S. prices were no longer tied to a rapidly falling international price level. Prices in the United States stabilized immediately, and this time a sustained revival of business activity finally began. The strength of the recovery was partially sapped, however, by the National Recovery Administration (NRA) – a New Deal scheme calculated to cartelize much of American industry, restrict output, and raise wages and prices. The NRA slowed the pace of the recovery before the Supreme Court declared it unconstitutional in 1935. The recovery did pick up somewhat after that, but soon thereafter, Congress passed the Wagner Act granting labor unions important new monopolistic privileges. The wage push generated by the subsequent widespread unionization slowed down the recovery just as the NRA had.

At the new official price of gold, $35 an ounce, the United States began attracting large quantities of gold from abroad. The countries remaining on the gold standard, notably France, faced intensified deflationary pressure owing to the increased gold price in the United States and to doubts that they would stay on the gold standard. Low and flexible wage rates had initially cushioned the impact of the depression in France. But in 1935 the depression there was still deepening. So in 1936 France, whose insatiable appetite for gold had helped trigger the depression, finally abandoned the gold standard.

INTERPRETATIONS OF THE GREAT DEPRESSION

Relying mainly on what I have called the classical theory of money, I have offered in this chapter an interpretation of the Great Depression that attributes the catastrophe to an enormous increase in the real value of gold. The real value of gold fell sharply in World War I when the belligerents withdrew gold from circulation and used it to finance their wartime balance-of-trade deficits. At first the return to gold put little upward pressure on the value of gold. And until 1928, an accommodative policy followed by the Federal Reserve Board held the total demand for gold in check. Beginning in 1928, however, the demand for gold increased enormously as France and most other countries sought to convert foreign-exchange reserves into gold. In so doing, by 1933 they had driven the value of gold down to its prewar level.

The sheer magnitude of the increase in the demand for gold was demonstrated by Ragnar Nurkse (1944) in his study of the interwar gold standard. Nurkse calculated the reserves held by twenty-four central banks, not counting the Federal Reserve, from 1924 to 1932 and broke down reserve holdings between gold and foreign exchange. Between 1928 and 1932, the central banks increased their holdings of gold by nearly $2.4 billion, of which $2 billion was accumulated by the Bank of France alone. Meanwhile, total holdings of foreign exchange fell by $2 billion. And this does not even take into account the extent of private hoarding of gold.

As long as a country remained on the gold standard, it could not avoid the deflationary spiral. Either France or the United States could have halted the deflation, the former by not accumulating such huge quantities of gold, the latter by supplying the gold other countries wanted to accumulate. Under the circumstances, the gold standard could not endure, because countries would not tolerate indefinitely the drastically falling prices and incomes it entailed.

How does this explanation compare to other explanations of the Great Depression? Let me consider here three of the better-known ones: the overinvestment theory of the Austrian School;[7] the Monetarist explanation (Friedman and Schwartz 1963), that ascribes the depression to a monetary collapse resulting from bank failures unnecessarily tolerated by the Federal Reserve Board; and the anti-Monetarist, underconsumption explanation of Peter Temin (1976).

The Austrian overinvestment theory holds that the Great Depression was caused by a misdirection of capital that followed from the allegedly inflationary monetary policies of the 1920s. A normal cyclical downturn, in the Austrian view, ought to have been allowed to occur in 1927. But by expanding credit in 1927 to avoid that recession, the Federal Reserve only ensured that a far sharper and deeper depression would ensue two years later.

The charge that monetary policy in the 1920s was inflationary has always seemed paradoxical, since prices actually declined somewhat during the decade. Moreover, even during the allegedly inflationary burst of 1927–28, prices were stable. Some try to argue that the inflation was manifested in rising stock prices rather than in rising output prices. But I have already explained why one cannot assume that an excess supply of money would raise stock prices.

Most Austrian economists have responded to this criticism by pointing out that technological progress in the 1920s led to rapid increases in productivity. In the absence of an expansion of credit, they maintain, the trend of prices should have been more sharply downward. That prices did not fall during a period of such a rapid technological progress shows that there was an inflationary expansion of credit that financed an unsustainable expansion of the capital structure.

I shall not deny that during the 1920s, there may have been some over-

7 The originator of the Austrian business-cycle theory was Ludwig von Mises (1912/1979). It was further developed and elaborated by Friedrich A. Hayek (1929/1966, 1931/1966). Lionel Robbins (1934), then much under the influence of the Austrians, wrote a contemporary account (which he later disavowed) of the depression. Murray Rothbard (1963) presents an extreme, and on many points idiosyncratic, version of the Austrian theory in his history of the depression in the United States.

investment financed by credit creation. Nor do I even wish to deny that such an overexpansion might have had something to do with the downturn in 1929. However, it is difficult to accept the Austrian theory as even remotely accounting for the depth, severity, and duration of the depression. Even if, according to some ideal standard, credit creation during the 1920s was excessive, it is outlandish to suggest that the degree of credit creation was greater than during any number of other boom periods before and since. Yet no other monetary expansion was ever followed by such a severe downturn. The Austrian theory of the Great Depression cannot explain why it was a Great Depression and not simply a garden-variety business-cycle downturn.[8]

In contrast, Friedman and Schwartz do seem to have given an explanation for the unique severity of the Great Depression. They attributed it to three waves of bank failures (the first in late 1930, the second early in 1931, and the last in 1933) that transformed the severe, but not extraordinary, recession of 1929 and 1930 into the worst depression in history. The banking collapse forced a contraction in the money supply which, in their view, pulled the entire economy into the Great Depression.

But in concentrating so intently on bank failures, Friedman and Schwartz lost sight of the international character of the Great Depression. The depression was not, as they contended, simply a monetary shock the United States transmitted to the rest of the world. To support this view, they relied on the simplest version of the price-specie-flow mechanism and looked only at the flow of gold into the United States. They assumed that if the source of the depression had been outside the United States, an outflow of gold from the United States to the rest of the world would have ensued in 1929 and 1930. Since gold was flowing into the United States, Friedman and Schwartz concluded, the United States must have been the source of the depression.

But the entire world, as Gertrude Fremling (1983, 1985) points out in her development of Earl Thompson's alternative monetary explanation for the Great Depression, was accumulating gold reserves at the time. So the mere observation that the United States was, too, provides no ground for inferring whether the depression originated in the United States or elsewhere. So by focusing exclusively on the collapse of the U.S. banking system as the cause of domestic inflation, Friedman and Schwartz ignored the tremendous increase in the international demand for gold. In discussing the panic of 1896, however, they eschewed such a narrow

---

8 Blaming Herbert Hoover for trying to keep big business from cutting wages after the onset of the depression, while fully justified, is not an adequate explanation either, because there have been subsequent more extreme monetary expansions which one would have expected to lead to corresponding downturns and in which strong unions have been able to keep wages from falling also. The uniqueness of the Great Depression is simply not accounted for by the Austrian theory.

interpretation of financial panics and banking disturbances. "Regarding that panic," Friedman and Schwartz (1963, pp. 110–11) wrote,

it is worth emphasizing once again the differences between what we have called the arithmetic and the economics of the situation. The panic had important effects on the banking structure, then and subsequently, and on the climate of political opinion; and it undoubtedly affected the detailed timing, form, and impact of the economic adjustment. At the same time, it was at bottom simply the way in which the adjustment forced by other considerations, worked itself out. The price decline abroad and the distrust of the maintenance of the gold standard by the United States meant that there were only two alternatives: (1) a sizable decline in U.S. prices and a decline or a reduced rate of rise in money income; or (2) the abandonment of the gold standard and the depreciation of the dollar relative to other currencies. Given the maintenance of the gold standard, the adjustments in prices and income were unavoidable. If they had not occurred through the banking panic and the accompanying deepening of the recession under way, they would have taken place in some other way. Indeed, this is clear from contemporary suggestions of a "remedy" for the banking difficulties, namely, earlier loan contraction by the banks through the maintenance of a "higher" quality of loans. That remedy would have produced by design much the same financial adjustments produced inadvertently by the panic.

What Friedman and Schwartz said about the panic of 1896 applies equally to the Great Depression. There was, however, one important difference between the two episodes. The rising value of gold that was the source of the deflationary pressure to which the United States was adjusting between 1929 and 1933 could well have been avoided if the Fed had been willing to supply gold to the rest of the world. Had the Fed dared to risk losing a significant amount of gold instead of jealously guarding its huge hoard, it almost certainly could have saved the world from the deflation that ravaged the international economy. Although the perspective from which Friedman and Schwartz developed their sharp criticism of the Fed was too narrow, that condemnation certainly was not misplaced.

In his controversial book, *Did Monetary Forces Cause the Great Depression?* Peter Temin (1976) attacked the Friedman-Schwartz explanation. His main point was that the decline in the quantity of money in the 1929–33 contraction was actually less than the fall in the price level. So in real terms, the quantity of money actually rose somewhat during what Friedman and Schwartz call the Great Contraction. Temin concluded from this that it could not have been a contraction in the money supply that caused the Great Depression. The reduction in the nominal quantity of money, Temin argued, was simply an automatic response to the deflation associated with the Great Depression. With a lower price level, the public needed to hold fewer dollars. Bank failures were simply one of the mechanisms by which that contraction in the nominal quantity of money took place.

There is much in this argument with which to agree. When money is competitively supplied, as it (more or less) was during the Great Depression, the amount of money produced by a competitive banking system equals the amount the public wants to hold. There is no macroeconomic significance in changes in the amount of money produced by the banking system, though such changes may often be associated with other macroeconomically significant events or changes.

However, the correct assessment of the insignificance of changes in the quantity of money supplied by a competitive banking system did not justify Temin's conclusion that monetary forces did not cause the Great Depression. For the monetary forces were really playing themselves out in the international market for gold, which was dominated by the Federal Reserve System and which Temin ignored. Although the decline in the quantity of money was itself a passive adjustment to the falling price level, the price level fell because of an international scramble for gold reserves.

Failing to see the alternative mechanism by which monetary forces could have caused deflation and depression, Temin contended that an unexplained drop in consumption spending in 1930 is what triggered the depression. But Temin was unable to provide a theoretical explanation to show why that supposedly autonomous reduction in consumption should have caused a reduction in income and prices as large as the one that resulted. Indeed, Temin himself seems to have settled on the consumption explanation because he thought he had eliminated all the others. But he actually considered only one of the possible monetary explanations and ignored the other.

CONCLUSION

Writing about the Great Depression, the eminent economic historian J. R. T. Hughes (1984) contrasted the Friedman-Schwartz and the Austrian accounts of that episode, which he called single-cause explanations, with the more complex international explanations favored by such economists as Folke Hilgerdt, Ragnar Nurkse, W. Arthur Lewis, and Charles Kindleberger. He called the international dimension "almost daunting in scope." "If you believe the trouble was rooted in monetary phenomena," Hughes (p. 139) observed, "you may begin with the characteristics of the pre-1914 gold standard, 'the old financial system,' and then have fun with the *Cunliffe Report* and the problems posed by the wartime disruptions and differential inflation rates."

Although I agree with Hughes that an international monetary explanation of the Great Depression is necessary, it seems to me that, once grasped, the explanation is straightforward and not at all daunting. Its main features were well understood and properly diagnosed at the time by at least one contemporary observer: the great British monetary economist, Keynes's colleague and friend, Ralph G. Hawtrey. And by 1936 a similar explanation was formulated by the venerable Swedish economist Gustav Cassel.

Unfortunately, this international monetary explanation of the Great Depression was largely forgotten in the wake of the Keynesian revolution. And as I have just pointed out, when Milton Friedman and Anna Schwartz suggested their own monetary explanation of the Great Depression, they dismissed the international origins of the catastrophe. Only in the last decade has the earlier monetary approach been revived by Earl Thompson and some of his students.

The tragedy of the failure properly to understand the underlying cause of the Great Depression was obviously the human suffering to which it directly and indirectly gave rise. A related tragedy was the widespread rejection of liberal economic and political values during the 1930s, which stemmed in part from ascribing to the liberal capitalist economic order the misery that was all around. But it also stemmed, unfortunately, from the deflationary policies being urged on governments by many of the leading liberal economists of the time, who, under the influence of the Austrian business-cycle theory, mistook a deflation of unprecedented proportions for a normal business-cycle downturn. In doing so, they not only lost credibility as policy advisers themselves but helped to bring the liberal ideals with which they had become identified into discredit. Into this political and intellectual vacuum, it was easy for a man of John Maynard Keynes's extraordinary and manifold talents to step.

7

The Keynesian revolution and the Monetarist counterrevolution

> Either the quantity of money in circulation is a datum – and the theory of Keynes can be true – or the quantity of money is fixed by the size of the cash balances which the users of money desire to hold, and the Keynesian explanation of permanent underemployment equilibrium falls to pieces.
> J. Rueff, "The Fallacies of Lord Keynes' General Theory"

Before his blistering attack on the Treaty of Versailles and the three leaders – Clemenceau, Lloyd-George, and Wilson – he held responsible for it, John Maynard Keynes's reputation as an expert on the arcane subject of the Indian currency, as the author of a philosophical work on probability theory, as an intimate of the Bloomsbury group, and as an effective and tireless civil servant at the Treasury was confined to a narrow circle of public officials and intellectuals. But so extraordinary was the impact of *The Economic Consequences of the Peace* (1919/1971) on American and European public opinion that from then on, Keynes could count on a large and attentive audience for almost anything he wrote. And after the German hyperinflation of the early 1920s seemed to confirm his warning that the Treaty of Versailles had imposed an unbearable burden on Germany, Keynes's reputation as an economic savant grew larger still.[1]

His sudden fame opened a lucrative career for him as a financial journalist. In his internationally syndicated columns, Keynes tried to rally public support for his proposals for postwar reconstruction. His particular concern was what Britain and the rest of the world might put in place of the prewar gold standard. Although a member of England's intellectual and cultural elite, Keynes enjoyed posing as an outsider whose enlightened advice was forever being spurned by the benighted men in

---

1 Much of the first half of this chapter is based on my article "Where Keynes Went Wrong" (Glasner 1988).

power. That was how he had portrayed his opposition to official policy on war reparations and it was how he would later portray his opposition to Britain's official policy of rejoining the gold standard at the prewar parity of $4.86 a pound.

Keynes may well have been, as he believed himself to be, the most enlightened man of his time. Yet there was something about him that made it impossible for him to acknowledge that an opinion opposed to his own could have merit. Keynes was a man of superior intellect, but his treatment of opposing views often betrayed a pettiness and small-mindedness that ought to have been beneath him.[2]

Keynes dissented from the official policy of restoring the gold standard because he saw no reason for the pound to be stabilized in relation to a single commodity instead of in relation to commodities in general. Going back on the gold standard at the old parity might do the former, but it would almost certainly not do the latter. Although the gold standard had produced a modicum of price stability in the nineteenth century, Keynes attributed that stability to fortuitous circumstances that were unlikely to be replicated ever again. So, Keynes argued, far from stabilizing the value of money over the long run, as its supporters promised, the gold standard would actually undermine that stability.

In his book *A Tract on Monetary Reform* (1923/1971), which even now, more than sixty years after it was written, can be read with profit, Keynes showed that there was an inherent conflict between keeping the domestic price level stable and pegging an exchange rate. The conflict is easy to see under a gold standard. Prices expressed in any currency convertible into gold would be stable only if the value of gold in relation to goods in general were stable. But if the value of gold changed, prices quoted in any gold standard currency would vary inversely with the value of gold. More generally, a country that pegged the exchange rate of its currency to the currency of another country would have no choice but to accept the rate of inflation dictated by the other country. A policy of domestic price stability would therefore dictate a flexible or adjustable exchange rate.

Going back on the gold standard really raised two separate questions. One was whether to return to the gold standard at all. The other was the choice of the parity at which to peg the pound to gold and the dollar. In fact, many of the countries that restored the gold standard in the 1920s did so at less than their prewar parities. For those countries, pegging at the old parity would simply have required too much domestic deflation. But in Britain it was taken for granted that going back on the gold standard meant restoring sterling to its prewar parity against gold and the

---

2 On Keynes's personality and his polemical style see the incisive studies in Johnson and Johnson (1976).

dollar. Indeed, the option of stabilizing the pound at a lower parity was hardly mentioned.

When the pound had settled down at about $4.40 in 1923, Keynes's argument against the gold standard was simple. To restore the old dollar parity would require a reduction of British wages and prices of about 10 percent. But Britain had already undergone a massive deflation in 1920–21. That deflation was tolerated while the United States was also deflating to prevent sterling from depreciating any more than it had just after the end of the war. But the recovery from the slump of 1920–21 had been sluggish, and unemployment remained above 10 percent – a rate scarcely ever seen before the war. So believing that under the circumstances reducing unemployment should be the goal of economic policy, Keynes opposed any policy, including rejoining the gold standard, that might cause further deflation.[3]

Despite Keynes's arguments, political and financial opinion in Britain so strongly favored going back on gold at the prewar parity that when, early in 1925, speculative buying raised sterling to $4.80, the chancellor of the Exchequer, Winston Churchill, felt obliged to restore the pound to its prewar parity against the dollar. Following the great preponderance of expert opinion, yet fearing that Keynes might be right, Churchill announced the formal restoration of convertibility on April 28, 1925. Venting his frustration against the resumption in his brilliantly argued and ingeniously titled essay *The Economic Consequences of Mr. Churchill*, Keynes (1925/1972, p. 212) directed his formidable powers of invective against Churchill's decision and against the expert advice on which he had relied:

If Mr. Churchill had restored gold by fixing the parity lower than the pre-war figure, or if he had waited until our money values were adjusted to the pre-war parity, then these particular arguments would have no force. But in doing what he did in the actual circumstances of last spring, he was just asking for trouble. For he was committing himself to force down money wages without any idea how it was to be done. Why did he do such a silly thing?

Partly, perhaps, because he has no instinctive judgement to prevent him from making mistakes; partly because, lacking this instinctive judgement, he was deafened by the clamorous voices of conventional finance; and, most of all, because he was gravely misled by his experts.

---

3 It may seem puzzling that Keynes did not advocate going back on the gold standard at reduced parity in the neighborhood of the prevailing exchange rate of $4.40 to the pound. But perhaps his approach to this issue was guided by strategic concerns. He was, after all, opposed to the gold standard on principle. Although returning to the gold standard at a reduced parity would, in Keynes's view, have eased the transition, it would not have made the gold standard more desirable from a long-run standpoint. So it probably suited him to portray the consequences of going back on gold as bleakly as possible by emphasizing the problems with the prewar parity and ignoring the expedient of returning to gold at a reduced parity.

And, later (p. 223):

> On grounds of social justice, no case can be made out for reducing the wages of the miners. They are the victims of the economic Juggernaut. They represent in the flesh the "fundamental adjustments" engineered by the Treasury and the Bank of England to satisfy the impatience of the City fathers to bridge the "moderate gap" between $4.40 and $4.86. *They* (and others to follow) are the "moderate sacrifice" still necessary to ensure the stability of the gold standard. The plight of the coal miners is the first, but not — unless we are very lucky — the last, of the Economic Consequences of Mr. Churchill.

Once again, subsequent events seemed to confirm Keynes's warnings. The unsuccessful coal miners' strike and the general strike of 1926 embittered much of the British work force. Unemployment stayed over 10 percent, and the periodic assistance of the Federal Reserve Board and the Bank of France was needed to prop up a chronically weak pound. The high British unemployment was generally attributed to a supposedly overvalued pound and the deflationary monetary policy required to force British wages and prices down to levels in the United States and other countries on the gold standard. That high unemployment was related to the increase in the real value of unemployment benefits, as we now have good reason to suspect, seems not even to have occurred to Keynes or most other economists of the day.

KEYNES'S DISILLUSIONMENT WITH TRADITIONAL ECONOMICS

After losing the battle over the gold standard, Keynes devoted himself to the book he expected to be his definitive contribution to monetary theory, *A Treatise on Money* (1930/1971). No short description can adequately summarize this monumental work in two volumes — a dazzling combination of theoretical insight and practical knowledge. But its major theoretical aim was straightforward: to give a new explanation for fluctuations in the price level and economic activity.

After the inflations, hyperinflations, and deflations that marked the war and its aftermath, the behavior of the price level became perhaps the chief theoretical and policy concern of economists in the 1920s. Economists had always favored a stable price level. But that was mainly to secure justice between debtors and creditors. After the war a different concern dominated their thinking. Economists began to suspect that instability of the price level was a primary cause of the business cycle. If that were so, then stabilizing the price level might be the key to preventing cyclical fluctuations in output.

By the 1920s almost all theorists viewed changes in the price level from the perspective of the quantity theory of money. In the *Treatise*, however,

Keynes suggested an alternative. He tried to show that movements in the price level were caused not by fluctuations in the quantity of money but by differences between total savings and total expenditure on investment. Since decisions to save – to postpone consumption – are made by households, and decisions to invest – to add to productive capacity – by business firms, Keynes saw no necessary reason for the two magnitudes to be equal. But only if they were equal, he argued, would prices be stable. If investment was greater than savings, prices would rise; if less, they would fall.

Despite departing from the quantity theory, Keynes still held to a conventional view of monetary policy in the *Treatise,* since he insisted that the monetary authority could control the price level. Because investment tends to fall and savings tend to rise with increases in the interest rate, the monetary authority could, if it wanted to, equalize investment and savings by setting the appropriate interest rate. This rate of interest Keynes, following the Swedish economist Knut Wicksell, called the "natural rate." The problem with the gold standard, Keynes concluded, was that, to defend the exchange rate, the monetary authority had to keep the interest rate above the natural rate. But then savings would exceed investment. And that, in turn, produced falling prices and high unemployment.

The *Treatise* won widespread acclaim. A commanding presence in Britain ever since he published *The Economic Consequences of the Peace,* Keynes secured his place in the front rank of economic theorists with the *Treatise.* Nevertheless, he drew sharp criticism on some crucial theoretical issues from such sources as his close friend Dennis Robertson, his theoretical antagonist F. A. Hayek, and his future disciple Alvin Hansen. Robertson (1931), for example, argued that Keynes had so defined savings and investment that his theory differed only semantically from the quantity theory. Another criticism was that although Keynes had assumed that changes in the price level triggered fluctuations in output and employment, his formal model held real output constant while the price level changed. So to be consistent, either Keynes had to revise his basic assumption about the relationship between the price level and output, or he had to show in a formal model just how output depended on the price level.

At first Keynes resisted the criticisms, notably in a series of sharp exchanges with Hayek. But before long he conceded that, at some crucial points, his argument in the *Treatise* was inadequate.

By the time the *Treatise* appeared in 1930, economic conditions were changing radically from those Keynes had written about. High unemployment was no longer just a British problem; it was an international disaster. Though not blaming the gold standard directly for the depression, Keynes considered it the chief obstacle to a monetary policy that would promote recovery. But ever the pragmatic political adviser, he refused to continue fighting a battle he had already lost. So his policy recommendations took it for granted that the gold standard would be maintained. That helps to explain why, as early as 1929, Keynes was advocating large-scale public works programs to reduce unemployment. If monetary policy was not available to increase employment, Keynes was quite prepared to seek a fiscal remedy.

By 1931 Keynes was so desperate to find a solution for worsening unemployment that he scandalized many fellow economists by recommending a protective tariff to stimulate domestic production and employment. Keynes's (1931b/1981) response to critics who attacked his change of position on the tariff is instructive for the insight it gives into his manner of responding to criticism: "I seem to see the elder parrots sitting around and saying: 'You can *rely* upon us. Every day for 30 years, regardless of the weather, we have said, "What a lovely morning!" But this is a bad bird. He says one thing one day and something else the next.' "

Keynes did insist that he advocated a tariff as a substitute for devaluing the pound. Yet his willingness to commit what for an economist is the closest thing there is to heresy shows how estranged, even then, he was becoming from traditional economic doctrines.

Only a few months later, in September 1931, the speculative attack on the pound following the collapse of the German and Austrian banking systems caused the Bank of England to let the pound float. Keynes applauded this unexpected move and immediately withdrew his support for a protective tariff. Anticipating an immediate decline in the pound's exchange rate against the dollar and other gold standard currencies, he predicted a recovery in prices and a break in the deflationary spiral in which Britain had been caught. The depreciation of sterling, Keynes (1931a/ 1972, p. 246) asserted confidently, would provide "a great stimulus to employment."

But the recovery Keynes hoped for did not materialize – at any rate, not very quickly. Though their downward spiral was arrested, British output and employment changed little in 1932 despite the departure from gold. And although a strong recovery did begin in 1933, unemployment remained extraordinarily high. The persistence of high unemployment even after Britain left the gold standard undoubtedly forced Keynes to question whether his earlier explanation of unemployment and the orthodox economic theory in which it was rooted were fully adequate.

Early in 1932 Keynes alluded to the criticism of the *Treatise* and the effect that criticism was having on his thinking. "After having had the advantage of much criticism and discussion of my theories," Keynes (1930/ 1971, p. xxvii) wrote,

I have naturally made many *addenda* and *corrigenda* in what follows. It is not, however, my intention to revise the existing text of this *Treatise* in the near future. I propose, rather, to publish a short book of a purely theoretical character, extending and correcting the theoretical basis of my views as set forth below.

So it seems that Keynes's thinking in 1932 was in flux. Forced, on purely theoretical grounds, to reconsider his position in the *Treatise,* he had just begun writing what he then described as a "short book of a purely theoretical character" that eventually evolved into *The General Theory of Employment, Interest, and Money* (1936/1973). His correspondence at the time shows that, at first, he believed he could finish writing his new book within two years. But it took him almost four.

Why the delay? In November 1931, after Britain left the gold standard, Keynes wrote a memorandum for the Treasury on which the subsequent cheap-money policy was largely based. With England off gold and pursuing a cheap-money policy, Keynes's possibly wavering faith in monetary policy was put to a decisive test. If unemployment had been caused by an overly tight monetary policy dictated by the gold standard, it would have been reasonable to expect a sharp recovery to begin once Britain went off gold. But there was no recovery for at least a year. If output and employment had begun to recover in 1932, as he had expected, Keynes, in revising the *Treatise,* would have probably continued to assume that output and employment were related to changes in the price level. Thus the disappointed hopes of 1932 probably drove Keynes to a more fundamental break with orthodoxy than he had contemplated when he set out to revise the *Treatise.*

Moreover, the failure of employment to recover in Britain before 1929 must have been theoretically bothersome, too.

Although Keynes attributed the unemployment to an overvalued pound, deflation should, in theory, have brought wages and prices into line with the exchange rate, thereby reducing unemployment. However painful and unnecessary that process might have appeared to Keynes, he did not suggest – nor, oblivious to the effects of high unemployment benefits, did he yet have any reason to believe – that the process would be endless.

So when Keynes was forced by criticism to consider just how changes in the price level were translated into changes in output and employment, his growing doubts on that score may well have persuaded him to abandon that long-held assumption. Luckily for him, he had at hand an alternative explanation for changes in output and employment that he could easily fit into the savings-investment framework of the *Treatise.* The explanation had been provided by the young Cambridge economist Richard Kahn (1931), who had just developed the concept of the multiplier. Keynes could now abandon the assumption that changes in the price level were what caused output and employment to fluctuate without discarding the whole savings-investment paradigm that he claimed as his unique contribution to economic analysis.

The significance of the multiplier for Keynes is easy to understand. What the multiplier signifies is a relation between an initial injection of investment spending and the amount of additional income and output it generates. One might assume that a given injection of new spending would generate only the same amount of added income. But that would be shortsighted. By tracing the repercussions of the initial spending as it comes into the hands of recipients, the multiplier analysis shows that unless the recipients save all additional income, the initial spending generates further spending and further income. The ultimate increase in income can thus be shown to be a multiple of the injection of new spending. The greater the fraction of additional income the public devotes to consumption spending – the smaller the fraction it devotes to saving – the greater the multiplier.

The income-expenditure approach of the multiplier dovetailed beautifully with Keynes's saving-investment framework. Instead of assuming that a difference between savings and investment would change the price level, and only through price-level changes affect income, Keynes could now assume that the price level remained constant and argue that the difference between savings and investment acted directly on income. Since savings were drawn out of earnings, equality between savings and investment was achieved by multiple adjustments in income until savings changed enough to match investment. If savings exceeded investment, total expenditure out of income would be insufficient to maintain that level of income. Income and expenditure would therefore have to contract by a multiple of the difference. The reduction in income would cause savings to fall as well until the equalities between investment and savings and between income and expenditure were restored. Conversely, if investment exceeded savings, income would increase by a multiple of the difference.

Keynes concluded from this analysis that there was no reason for savings to equal investment at a level of income and output consistent with full employment. He had previously opposed deflation as a method of adjusting to an overvalued pound because deflation was so much more painful, costly, and unjust than simply changing the exchange rate. But he had never actually denied that deflation would eventually restore full employment. He now was prepared to do just that and to explain why.

Keynes felt that he could finally explain the prolonged mass unemployment afflicting the world. The older paradigm, to which he himself had subscribed, could not really cope with that phenomenon. In that paradigm, full employment was the normal state of affairs. Lapses from full employment could be attributed to a deviation of the interest rate, the exchange rate, or the level of wages from its equilibrium value. Keynes now maintained that the problem was not that some price was stuck at the wrong level but that the underlying spending plans of the public would not support full employment. If those spending plans could not absorb what the economy was capable of producing because households tried to save more than business would invest, production, income, and employment would fall until savings declined to the level of investment.

In the *Treatise*, Keynes had maintained that savings and investment could be equalized if the monetary authority kept the market interest rate equal to the natural rate. But once he concluded that changes in income, not in the rate of interest, equalized savings and investment, he had to reject the whole concept of a natural rate of interest. "I had," conceded Keynes (1936/1973, pp. 242–43),

overlooked the fact that in any given society there is . . . a *different* natural rate of interest for each hypothetical level of employment. And, similarly, for every rate of interest there is a level of employment for which that rate is the "natural" rate, in the sense that the system will be in equilibrium with that rate of interest and that level of employment. Thus it was a mistake to speak of *the* natural rate of interest or to suggest that the above definition would yield a unique value for the rate of interest irrespective of the level of employment. I had not then understood that, in certain conditions, the system could be in equilibrium with less than full employment.

Nor was there any guarantee that monetary policy could push interest rates low enough to stimulate enough investment to achieve full employment. Thus, in *The General Theory*, Keynes's proposal for achieving full employment was government spending on public works. Public works were no longer a substitute for an activist monetary policy needlessly immobilized by the gold standard, as he had portrayed them in the *Treatise*. In *The General Theory* public works and an active fiscal policy emerged as the indispensable means for achieving full employment.

LIQUIDITY PREFERENCE AND THE MONEY SUPPLY

The novel element of Keynes's theory was the idea that income, not the rate of interest, is what adjusts to ensure that savings and investment match. The contrary view that it is the rate of interest that adjusts to equalize savings and investment is sometimes known as the loanable-funds theory. In that theory savings constitute the supply of loanable funds and investment constitutes the demand for loanable funds. Both savings and investment are presumed in the loanable-funds theory to be at least somewhat sensitive to the rate of interest. The lower the rate of interest, the greater the amount of investment that business will want to

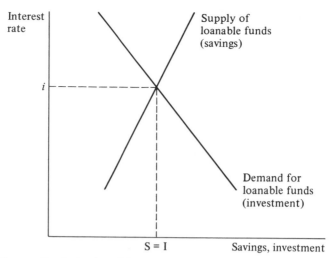

Figure 2. Determination of the interest rate in the loanable-funds theory

undertake and the smaller the amount of savings that households will set aside from their income. So presumably, the supply of loanable funds will just match the demand for loanable funds, or in other words, savings will equal investment at some equilibrium (or, in Wicksell's terminology, natural) rate of interest.

Figure 2 presents a simple diagram illustrating how the interest rate and the amount of savings and investment are mutually determined in the loanable-funds theory. Savings and investment are both measured along the horizontal axis, and the interest rate is measured along the vertical axis. The downward-sloping curve shows the relation between investment by businesses (which constitutes the demand for loanable funds) and the rate of interest: more investment at lower interest rates, less investment at higher ones. The upward-sloping curve shows the relation between savings by households (which constitute the supply of loanable funds) and the rate of interest: less savings at lower interest rates, more savings at higher ones. The point of intersection between the two curves shows the equilibrium interest rate at which households are saving enough to provide financing for the amount of investment that businesses want to undertake.

Keynes saw it differently. He believed that people's saving decisions are based on their incomes, not on the rate of interest. What the rate of interest affects, then, is not savings but how much money people want to hold. Though not original, the latter point was not yet commonplace either. And to explain it, Keynes introduced his concept of liquidity preference, which is really just a fancy term for the demand to hold money.

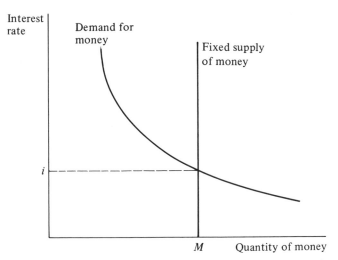

Figure 3. Determination of the interest rate in the liquidity-preference theory

He called it liquidity preference because money, being universally accept-able as payment in transactions, is the most liquid of assets. Moreover, holding money instead of a long-term bond eliminates the risk of a capi-tal loss should the rate of interest increase. The present value of a bond depends on the present value of the future payments it promises to the bearer. The higher the rate of interest, the smaller this present value. So a rise in the interest rate is equivalent to a fall in the value of a bond. Money is the only financial instrument that provides both immediate ac-ceptability in exchange and absolute certainty of nominal value.

The reason even perfectly secure loans bear interest, Keynes argued, is that people have to be compensated for the liquidity they forgo by lend-ing money. It follows that the more money people are holding, the lower the interest rate they will demand as compensation for reducing those holdings when they exchange money for a bond. With a fixed total stock of money in existence, the rate of interest has to adjust to a level that leaves the public content with holding just that amount of money. Since it must adjust to equate the demand for money with the supply of it, Keynes argued, the rate of interest cannot be the variable that adjusts to equate the supply of loanable funds with the demand for them – that is to say, to equate savings and investment.

The Keynesian liquidity-preference approach is represented in Figure 3. The quantity of money is measured along the horizontal axis, and the cost of holding money, the rate of interest, is measured along the vertical axis. The demand to hold money is portrayed by the downward-sloping curve, and the supply of money is portrayed by the vertical line *M* indi-

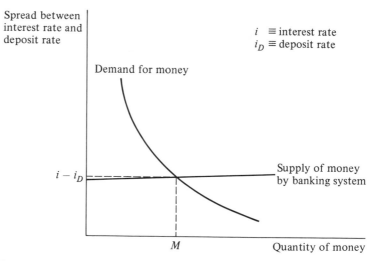

Figure 4. Determination of the cost of holding money and the quantity of money in
a competitive model

cating that the quantity of money in existence is determined by the monetary authority. According to Keynes, the rate of interest adjusts so that
the amount of money people want to hold just matches the quantity in
existence. Since that rate of interest could easily be different from the rate
implicit in Figure 2, something besides interest rates has to adjust to equate
savings and investment. The role of the multiplier analysis was to show
that income would change to equalize savings and investment without
any change in interest rates.

However, the notion that the interest rate is the price of holding money,
which is what Keynes's theory of liquidity preference asserted, requires
that money not bear interest. Keynes took it as axiomatic that money
does not bear interest; to have assumed otherwise would have undermined his argument that interest is a compensation for forgone liquidity.
But nowhere did he explain what keeps money from bearing interest.

We have already seen repeatedly that for money to be non-interest-
bearing, competition in supplying money has to be suppressed. If it is not
suppressed, banks compete by paying interest on deposits, and the price
of money becomes not the interest rate but the spread between the interest rate on loans and the rate paid on deposits.

One more supply-and-demand diagram may be useful to illustrate this
point. Figure 4 differs from Figure 3 in two ways. First, on the vertical
axis, instead of measuring the rate of interest, we measure the spread
between the rate of interest and the rate paid on deposits. Second, the
supply of money is drawn not as a fixed quantity but as an upward-

sloping curve characteristic of a competitive industry. As in Figure 3, the intersection in Figure 4 of the supply-and-demand curves determines the equilibrium quantity of money and the equilibrium cost of holding money. But the cost of holding money is now not the rate of interest but the *spread* between the interest rate and the rate paid on deposits. So what adjusts to achieve equilibrium in the competitive world depicted in Figure 4 is the rate paid on deposits, not the interest rate itself.

In a world of competitive banking in which interest is paid on deposits, the rate of interest on loans does not have to adjust to equate the demand for and the supply of money as it does in Figure 3. It can adjust to equate savings and investment as it does in Figure 2. So Keynes's approach in *The General Theory* was at odds with the notion of a competitive supply of money that adjusts to the demand to hold it.[4]

THE KEYNESIAN REVOLUTION

It took only a few years for the new Keynesian theory to achieve an almost unchallenged ascendancy among economists. In the United States, Keynes's ideas were resisted by many conservatives mistrustful of his desire to enlarge the role of government in the economy and his advocacy of budget deficits. Yet even Republican administrations, which, presumably, were ideologically unsympathetic to Keynes, wound up following Keynesian policies.

The new economic and political consensus was that the duty of a government was not, as once was thought, to comply with the principles of sound finance, but to provide enough aggregate demand to generate full employment. And even though some early critics of Keynes warned that Keynesian policies would lead to inflation (Viner 1937b), Keynesians at first were inclined to regard inflation as either a remote possibility or a minor problem.

Moreover, by insisting that the demand for and the supply of money are what determine the rate of interest, Keynes left the price level theo-

4 This was the point made by Jacques Rueff (1947) in the article from which the epigram to this chapter was drawn. Keynes explicitly assumed in *The General Theory* that the stock of money at any moment was determined by the monetary authority. But in the *Treatise*, where Keynes still believed that the interest rate could adjust to equalize savings and investment, the quantity of money was not treated as if it were entirely determined by the monetary authority. The change in Keynes's assumptions regarding the exogeneity of the money supply has been noted by G. L. S. Shackle (1967, pp. 212–13). "The *General Theory*," writes Shackle, "is more prone to treat the quantity of money as something given, an upshot of central monetary authority decisions to which the non-bank community must respond as best it may. Keynes of the *Treatise* seems, in fact, to have looked on the banking system as more passive, more subservient and more *able* to be subservient to the commercial needs of the country, while Keynes of the *Theory* thought of the system as strongly directed from the centre."

retically undetermined in *The General Theory*. The quantity theory had used the demand for and the supply of money to determine the price level, and the classical theory had pinned it down with convertibility. Lacking either option, Keynes simply took the price level to be a historical datum that was somehow determined outside his theoretical apparatus.

However, in arguing against a policy of cutting wages to reduce unemployment, Keynes did suggest that the price level is governed by the wage level. If unemployment forced wages down, he argued, corresponding price cuts would offset the wage cuts. If they produced no reduction in real wages, falling money wages could not generate an increase in employment. The argument seemed to be symmetrical, so that one could also argue that an excess demand for labor, which would force wages up, would be similarly reflected in rising prices.

Thus the Keynesian model, which was designed to explain the existence of, and to prescribe remedies for, unemployment, was not nearly as well suited to explain, or prescribe remedies for, inflation. The durability of the Keynesian revolution, therefore, required that the fear of unemployment continue to take precedence over the fear of inflation as a social concern (Johnson 1971/1972). For this to be the case either inflation had to remain at low levels or the public had to be willing to support policies promoting full employment regardless of their inflationary consequences. Only when neither condition was met could an alternative to the Keynesian system emerge to compete for the adherence of economists and for influence with policy makers.

THE MONETARIST COUNTERREVOLTUION

The 1940s and 1950s were not easy for dissenters from the new Keynesian orthodoxy. Non-Keynesians who had made their mark before 1936 and could not or would not adapt to the new situation were neither purged nor, with a few exceptions (of whom Keynes's friend and colleague D. H. Robertson was both the most notable and the most unfortunate), harassed for their retrograde opinions. But it could not have been clearer that they were on the losing side of a scientific revolution. They might still hold important academic positions and retain the respect of their colleagues, especially if they were not strident in their criticism of Keynes and Keynesian policies. But it was generally acknowledged that, whatever their individual merits, the viewpoint they represented had been superseded by the Keynesian doctrine. And the inability of non-Keynesians to attract more than a few of the best young economists of those decades to their side was perhaps the truest testimony of the totality of the Keynesian ascendancy.

Only one important academic center, the University of Chicago, housed a group of economists sufficiently self-confident and committed to a non-Keynesian approach to attract younger economists to do research critical of the emerging Keynesian orthodoxy. Keynes never had the impact at Chicago he had at other important research centers in the United States, not to mention in England. Perhaps this was because Chicago economists had called for government stimulation of the economy and an easy monetary policy to combat the Great Depression of the 1930s without feeling a need for a radical change in economic theory to justify doing so. They thus continued to espouse a traditional version of the quantity theory of money that owed a great deal to the work of another great American economist, Irving Fisher.

As quantity theorists, they placed particular importance on the role of the money supply. They held the Federal Reserve Board at least partially responsible for the severity of the depression because it pursued a tight-money policy in 1928–29 and because it did not prevent massive deflation by aggressive monetary expansion thereafter. Achieving effective control over the money supply naturally became an important policy goal of Chicago economists in the 1930s and 1940s. Henry Simons, Milton Friedman's teacher at Chicago, actually proposed a system of 100 percent reserve banking because, among other reasons, it would give the monetary authorities complete control over the quantity of money.

But it was, of course, Milton Friedman, more than anyone else, who revived the quantity theory and made it a serious alternative to Keynesian economics. Friedman was one of the few young economists who, at the peak of the Keynesian revolution, resisted the tide of opinion and adopted the quantity-theoretic approach taught at Chicago. By reformulating the quantity theory in a way that incorporated important Keynesian concepts and that was amenable to estimation and testing by the rapidly advancing techniques of econometric research, he launched a research program that attracted a growing corps of talented young economists.

An important milestone in the success of this research program was the monumental *Monetary History of the United States, 1867–1960* (1963), coauthored by Friedman and Anna J. Schwartz. The *Monetary History* provided a detailed historical account of the role of the Federal Reserve in the financial collapse of 1929–33. Like some earlier quantity theorists, notably Clark Warburton, Friedman and Schwartz suggested that the Fed bore the chief responsibility for the occurrence, length, and severity of the Great Depression. So impressive was the scholarship that supported this argument that those who did not accept it could not ignore it either.

But aside from its purely scholarly and historical concerns, the *Monetary History* also made a more fundamental point. In contrast to the

Keynesian view that the inherent instability of the market economy made it susceptible to events like the Great Depression, the message of the *Monetary History* was that it was the misguided policies or the outright mismanagement of the monetary authorities, particularly the Federal Reserve Board, that had destabilized an otherwise stable private economy.

The manifest technical facility, the command of the fundamental Keynesian concepts, and the important substantive contributions of the Monetarists (as they came to be called) made it impossible for Keynesians to dismiss them as they had earlier non-Keynesians. But the impact of Monetarism would probably have been marginal had inflation not become a major public concern in the late 1960s and 1970s.

Since inflation was not straightforwardly addressed in *The General Theory,* it was natural for Monetarists to choose it as the issue on which to test the relative merits of the Keynesian and Monetarist paradigms. Monetarists, furthermore, had a simple and direct cure for inflation: the Federal Reserve Board should make the stock of money grow at a steady rate of about 3 percent a year. That is about the rate at which the productive capacity of the economy expands. So Monetarists reasoned that a steady rate of monetary growth of 3 percent a year would produce reasonable price stability over time.

Believing that the supply of and demand for money determines interest rates and not the price level, Keynesians could not accept the simple monetary explanation of inflation offered by Monetarists. Instead, taking up Keynes's argument in *The General Theory* about the relationship between wages and prices, they attributed inflation to the pressure of aggregate demand (of which monetary policy is one, but not the only, determinant) on the productive capacity of the economy. When aggregate demand exceeds productive capacity, wages and prices have to rise to soak up the excess purchasing power. When aggregate demand falls short of productive capacity, the resulting unemployment exerts downward pressure on wages and, consequently, on prices.

This theory of inflation underlay the Phillips Curve, which dominated the conduct of economic policy before it started to break down in the 1970s. The Phillips Curve represented a relationship between the rate of unemployment and the rate of inflation that the Australian economist A. W. Phillips (1958) had estimated, using data on inflation and unemployment in Great Britain for almost a century. Phillips found that high rates of inflation corresponded to low rates of unemployment and that low or negative rates of inflation corresponded to high rates of unemployment.

In an influential article, Paul Samuelson and Robert Solow (1960) concluded from this relationship that policy makers could choose, as it were, from a menu of alternative combinations of inflation rates and unemployment rates. The precise combination chosen would depend on how willing a policy maker was to tolerate a bit more inflation in return for a further reduction in unemployment. The Keynesian theory of economic policy codified by Samuelson and Solow came to rest on the presumption of a stable trade-off between inflation and unemployment.

Until the late 1960s, inflation in the United States and in most other developed countries was so low that it seemed doubtful that Monetarists could undermine the Keynesian consensus. And even in 1970 so astute and authoritative an observer of the trend in economic thinking as the late Harry Johnson (1971/1972) argued that the Monetarist challenge to the Keynesian orthodoxy would fail because the public would inevitably assign a higher priority to reducing unemployment than to reducing inflation.

But Johnson made that assertion before the great inflation of the 1970s had yet been unleashed. Foreseeing neither the severity of inflation nor the urgency of the public's reaction to it, Johnson underestimated both the potency of inflation as a political issue and the likelihood that high and persistent inflation would make the public tolerate Monetarist policy prescriptions.

Moreover, Keynesians could not easily explain the unprecedented coincidence of high inflation and high unemployment that became so common in the 1970s. That combination – inelegantly described as stagflation – seemed to vitiate the Phillips Curve relationship that had become the foundation of Keynesian economic policy making. Unable to attribute inflation to excessive aggregate demand when unemployment was rising, Keynesians increasingly took the ad hoc view that inflation is caused by the ability of some resource suppliers, such as organized labor or the oil cartel, to impose price increases on the rest of the economy. So it is not surprising that many Keynesians, some with and some without guilty consciences, began to advocate wage and price controls as a cure for inflation while advocating expansive monetary and fiscal policy to stimulate employment.

Support for wage and price controls served, in a way, to round out the Keynesian approach to economic policy. Whereas Keynes had shifted the responsibility for full employment from the pricing decisions of economic agents in the marketplace to the fiscal and monetary authorities, Keynesian advocates of wage and price controls shifted the responsibility for controlling the value of money from the monetary and fiscal authorities to the pricing decisions of economic agents in the marketplace. But by the end of the 1970s, the role of monetary policy in generating inflation had become too obvious for this Keynesian inversion of public and private economic responsibilities to be convincingly defended any more.

THE MONETARIST EXPLANATION OF STAGFLATION

In contrast, Monetarists not only had a coherent theory of inflation, they had a theory that explained why the Phillips Curve relationship had begun to break down. The theory is that inflation is, in Friedman's words, "always and everywhere a monetary phenomenon." And Friedman (1968/1969) also worked out a Monetarist theory of the Phillips Curve. What is missing from the Keynesian interpretation of the Phillips Curve, he contended, is an understanding of the role played by expectations of inflation by the public. The Phillips Curve, therefore, does not portray an absolute relationship between inflation and unemployment; it portrays a relationship between them that is contingent on the expectations the public holds of future inflation.

Suppose, for example, that the public is expecting prices in the future to be stable. What happens if there is inflation? The effects of inflation are felt in the labor market as well as product markets; so workers will observe rising nominal wages as well as prices. Incorrectly assuming that the increase in the nominal value of wage offers actually corresponds to an increase in real wages, workers accept offers of employment more readily than they would if they correctly evaluated them. That is why the unemployment rate falls.

Conversely, deflation reduces the nominal value of wages offered to workers. But if they expect prices to be stable, workers mistake the reduced nominal wage offers for reduced real wages. Workers are therefore more apt to reject the job offers they get than if prices had been stable. So unemployment rises.

The data Phillips used were mostly drawn from times when Britain was on the gold standard or was committed to returning to it after suspending it during World War I. Thus the relationship between inflation and unemployment that Phillips estimated roughly approximated the relationship corresponding to an expectation of future price stability. That is why Phillips found a negative correlation between inflation and unemployment.

However, after the monetary authorities abandoned their commitment to stable prices, the Phillips Curve became unstable. So, over time, as the monetary authorities began to accept some inflation as the price for reducing unemployment, and as the public learned what was going on, the initial impact of inflation on unemployment was dissipated. That impact required a confusion between nominal and real wage offers that was possible only when inflation was not correctly foreseen. Only an accelerating inflation that fooled workers into constantly overestimating the real value of the wage offers they were receiving could have kept unemployment below the rate corresponding to a condition of actual and expected price stability. Even if it were possible to fool workers in this way, the costs to the economy of an accelerating inflation would probably prevent such a policy from being pursued for long. And if the monetary authority persisted in it anyway, the result would be hyperinflation and economic collapse.

Friedman (p. 102) concluded from this analysis that the economy tends to gravitate toward a "natural rate of unemployment" that is achieved when the expected rate of inflation adjusts to the rate of inflation generated by the monetary authorities. The monetary authorities can reduce unemployment temporarily by increasing the rate of inflation unexpectedly. But that reduction is only transitory and may produce increased unemployment if they decide later to reduce the rate of inflation. The notion that the Phillips Curve offered policy makers a set of alternative combinations from which they could choose was simply not tenable.

CONCLUSION

By the standards of the Keynesian revolution the Monetarist counterrevolution was not a complete success. Despite the inroads of Monetarism, the Keynesian paradigm remains thoroughly imbedded in the discourse of professional economists. However, it is now widely accepted that somehow monetary policy does affect the price level and the rate of inflation. And the belief that government can pursue a countercyclical policy that will continuously maintain full employment is held far less confidently than it used to be.

Indeed, a post-Monetarist development in economics, rational expectations, goes even further than Monetarism in denying the efficacy of countercyclical policies. Many rational-expectations theorists argue that a countercyclical policy is by its nature predictable. So if the government is committed to following a countercyclical policy, the public will be able to anticipate it. Since a policy can affect output and employment only by surprising the public, no consistent countercyclical policy can affect real output and employment. Although the conclusion that countercyclical policy is ineffective has been shown to depend on some special assumptions, the potency of countercyclical policy remains seriously in doubt.

Although the Monetarist counterrevolution did break down the Keynesian consensus on economic policy, it supported another consensus emerging from the Great Depression: that the monetary system should be under strict government control. Unconcerned about controlling the quantity of money as such, Keynesians were nevertheless skeptical about the stability of free markets. They therefore supported the New Deal constraints on the activities of financial intermediaries and commercial banks, particularly the tight ceilings on the interest paid on deposits. This was consistent with Keynesian doctrine, since Keynes seemed to think it was somehow contradictory for money to bear interest.

However, Monetarists are generally less skeptical than Keynesians of the efficiency and stability of free markets and are more sympathetic than Keynesians to proposals for reducing government control over markets. So Monetarists were in a peculiar position when it came to controls over the monetary system. Because they stressed both the overwhelming impact of the money supply on economic activity and the importance of maintaining a steady rate of growth in the quantity of money for a stable economy, Monetarists could not be as noninterventionist when it came to the monetary system as they were inclined to be on other issues.

The consensus that governmental control over the monetary system is necessary reflected basic defects in both the Keynesian and the Monetarist theories. Neither theory could adequately explain how the banking system competitively provides the amount of money demanded by the public. Because it ignored the payment of interest on money, the Keynesian theory incorrectly viewed the rate of interest on loans as equivalent to the cost of holding money. This led to the proposition that liquidity preference could interfere with movement of interest rates to equalize the supply of loanable funds with the demand for them. And Monetarists, not comprehending that a competitive banking system would create only as much money as the public wished to hold, insisted that the quantity of money created by the banking system was a macroeconomically significant variable that had to be controlled by the monetary authorities. Yet from the perspective of classical monetary theory, prescribing the rate of growth of bank deposits makes no more sense than prescribing the rate of growth of any other competitively supplied product or asset.

In Part III we shall explore some of the theoretical, and more important, practical developments that have increasingly forced economists once again to take explicit account of the competitive nature of the process by which money is supplied. The importance of these developments for building a stable monetary regime can hardly be underestimated.

A competitive monetary regime

8

The competitive breakthrough

It is an extraordinary truth that competing currencies have until quite recently never been seriously examined. There is no answer in the available literature to the question why a government monopoly of the provision of money is universally regarded as indispensable. . . . Nor can we find an answer to the question of what would happen if that monopoly were thrown open to the competition of private concerns supplying different currencies.

F. A. Hayek, *Denationalization of Money*

Since the second half of the nineteenth century, the conventional wisdom has been uniformly hostile to the idea of competition in the supply of money. Yet in the nineteenth century that hostility never suppressed the competition. That was because the hostility focused exclusively on competition in issuing banknotes but ignored it in creating deposits.

Why was that distinction made? Mainly because those who most mistrusted competition in the supply of money believed that deposits were not money. That notion was a legacy of the debate over the Bank Charter Act. Members of the Currency School, as we saw earlier, argued against competition in the supply of money and for a legal limit on the quantity of banknotes. They rationalized supporting a limit on banknotes but not on deposits by insisting that only the former, not the latter, were money.

So in the nineteenth century only the supply of banknotes, not the supply of deposits, was constrained. But the constraint was usually ineffective because of the tremendous growth of deposits (absolutely and in comparison with banknotes) during the nineteenth century. All that the limits on note issue did was every so often prevent the banking system from accommodating short-term or seasonal shifts between the demand for deposits and the demand for currency. Much of the monetary instability that marked the nineteenth century was caused by failures to accommodate those shifts. But such failures were the exception.

Eventually, as they thought more about deposits, nearly all economists realized that deposits, no less than banknotes, are money. Unfortunately, the conclusion economists drew was not that the supply of competitively issued banknotes could be left unconstrained. Instead, they concluded that deposits should be controlled as well. But that theoretical conclusion had no immediate practical effect. And so, long after expert opinion had turned against competition in the supply of money and even after the monetary character of deposits had been generally acknowledged, competitive forces were still controlling the creation of deposits.

THE SUPPRESSION OF COMPETITION IN THE GREAT DEPRESSION

Everything changed after the Great Depression. That catastrophe produced a consensus that excessive competition had promoted too much risky lending by banks to uncreditworthy borrowers. So an important goal of the monetary reforms that followed was to suppress competition among banks in the creation of deposits.

The monetary system that emerged from the Great Depression reflected accurately the consensus that money, including deposits, should not be supplied competitively. Three basic reforms shaped the American banking system. The first was the separation between investment banking and commercial banking mandated by the Glass-Steagall Act. The second was the prohibition against paying interest on demand deposits (later followed by ceilings the Federal Reserve System imposed on interest paid on time deposits). And the third was the creation of the Federal Deposit Insurance Corporation (FDIC), which made the federal government the guarantor of most of the deposits created by the banking system.

By suppressing competition, the reforms created a cartel that enriched the banking industry. Banks no longer had to compete by paying interest on deposits, and the government now provided a guarantee for these deposits. Banking became safe, easy, and profitable. But to keep it that way, entry into banking, which would inevitably erode the monopoly profits generated by the cartel, had to be controlled.

Before 1933, entry into banking was easy (Peltzman 1965). Anyone wishing to start a bank could choose between operating the bank under a state charter and running it under a federal charter. That option kept both state and federal chartering agencies from withholding new charters. A prospective entrant who could not get a charter from one source could always go to the other.

The Banking Act of 1933 changed that situation. It required that before granting a charter, the comptroller of the currency establish that the bank would serve the "convenience and the needs" of the community in which it would operate. The Federal Reserve Board had to make a similar finding before admitting a state-chartered bank to membership. But the key to restricting entry was to eliminate the option of a state charter. Here was where deposit insurance made a big difference, for the FDIC also had to make the same finding before it insured a nonmember state-chartered bank. Controlling the availability of deposit insurance, federal authorities could restrict the number of new charters they issued, because banks that were not federally insured could not compete effectively with banks that were.

PRICE STABILITY UNDER THE BRETTON WOODS SYSTEM

For about twenty years after World War II, a heavily regulated and cartelized monetary system worked smoothly. Bank failures were rare, almost nonexistent. And apart from a short burst of inflation during the Korean War, prices were practically stable.

What accounts for this impressive performance just when the U.S. government was acquiring a virtually unchecked domestic and international monopoly over the production of money? Partly it was a sense of restraint and international responsibility felt by the U.S. monetary authorities. But there were also some checks on their exercise of their monopoly. The constraints were embodied in the Bretton Woods System that the United States and Britain drew up in 1944, establishing the international monetary framework for the post-World War II period. Those constraints, reinforced by a residual commitment to balanced budgets and price stability, helped keep prices stable in the two decades after World War II.

That the Bretton Woods System played such a role is not without irony. For one of its chief architects was John Maynard Keynes (in his capacity as an economic statesman), even though less than a decade earlier (in his role as an economic theorist) Keynes had undermined support for the idea of price stability as the primary goal of economic policy.

Why was Bretton Woods so successful? And given its success, why didn't it last longer? Immediately after the war, memories of the hyperinflations of the late 1910s and early 1920s were still fresh and hyperinflations and currency collapses were again taking place in Central and Eastern Europe. In that environment, floating exchange rates were not an option. A country trying to restore confidence in its own currency – a necessary precondition for economic recovery – had little choice but to peg its currency to the dollar at a fixed exchange rate.

Despite the dollar's dominance, other countries would not long have been content to tie their currencies to an unchecked, irredeemable dollar whose purchasing power the American government was not committed to maintain (Johnson 1972b; Batchelder 1986). To induce other countries to accept a system of fixed exchange rates based on the dollar, the United States had an interest in committing itself at Bretton Woods to maintaining a fixed price for gold of $35 an ounce.

I choose my words carefully. I did not say that the United States committed itself to maintaining convertibility between gold and the dollar at $35 an ounce. No true commitment to convertibility was made. Only a select group of foreign central banks was entitled to buy gold from the United States. American citizens could not legally own gold bullion or coin, and many foreign governments also barred their citizens from owning gold. So the international gold market was in no sense a free one. Nevertheless, the promise to keep the price of gold at $35 an ounce at least symbolically committed the United States to price stability. Although American citizens could not enforce that commitment by demanding gold in exchange for dollars at the official price, at least foreign central banks could.

Until about 1965, when signs of inflation first appeared, the U.S. monetary authorities managed the Bretton Woods System with considerable success. Yet even in the late 1950s, some critics charged that the United States was misbehaving (Triffin 1958). Their charges arose from the persistent balance-of-payments deficits, and corresponding outflows of gold, the United States ran in the 1950s and 1960s. Concern about those deficits was never great enough to cause a fundamental shift in monetary policy. What it did lead to, however, was the interest-equalization tax the Kennedy administration imposed in the early 1960s to reduce foreign lending by American individuals and corporations.

It is now clear that the criticisms of the pre-1965 balance-of-payments deficits were misguided. They ignored the responsibility the United States had under Bretton Woods to provide liquidity to the international economy (Despres, Kindleberger, and Salant 1966/1981). Under Bretton Woods, U.S. balance-of-payments deficits were the only way of accommodating the growing demand for liquidity of a growing world economy. There is nothing to suggest that until the early to mid-1960s, additions to the world's holdings of dollar-denominated assets were, in any sense, unwilling. Other countries sought to increase their gold holdings along with, not in exchange for, their dollar-denominated securities. Only France, indulging its chronic national obsession with gold, actually sought to convert a substantial amount of dollar-denominated assets into gold.

Around 1965, however, U.S. good behavior ceased. It stopped when the Johnson administration escalated the war in Vietnam without either cutting back domestic expenditures or raising taxes. The administration, instead, financed the rapid growth in expenditures with monetary expansion. The U.S. monopoly over the dominant international currency greatly facilitated that expansion. Under fixed exchange rates, the United States could shift part of the cost of the war in Vietnam to the rest of the world by exchanging its low-interest liabilities for imported real goods.

As the rest of the world held those liabilities less and less willingly, they became a growing source of friction between the United States and the Europeans and Japanese. By holding those U.S. liabilities at fixed exchange rates, the Europeans and the Japanese had to bear part of the cost of the war in Vietnam. They could have reduced that burden by accepting U.S. inflation and allowing their central banks to increase their liabilities correspondingly. But many of them, particularly the Germans, were set against importing U.S. inflation.

On the other hand, avoiding U.S. inflation required countries to let the exchange rates of their currencies rise against the dollar. But that meant upsetting their exporters and writing off part of the debt the United States owed them. Their only other option was to convert more of their dollar-denominated liabilities into gold and hope to profit when inflation finally forced the United States to raise the official gold price. But when the Europeans showed increasing interest in cashing their dollars in for gold, U.S. officials quietly reminded them that if Europeans could take their gold back to Europe, Americans could just as easily take their troops back to America. When the options were thus laid out before them, the willingness of the Europeans to hold dollars instead of asking for gold was, for a short time at any rate, substantially revived.

Without the anchor of a stable dollar, monetary authorities found it increasingly difficult to maintain the existing currency parities in the face of speculators betting on future changes in those parities. As the numeraire currency (that is, the unit in terms of which exchange rates were typically quoted), the dollar did not at first feel the pressure of such speculation. Speculation focused instead on expected devaluations or up-valuations of other currencies in relation to the dollar. But foreign central banks were rapidly accumulating dollars. And as they did, it became ever more likely that the dollar price of gold would have to rise.

Finally, in 1968, at the height of the Vietnam War, the U.S. monetary authorities and their foreign cohorts lost control of the international gold market they had managed since the end of World War II. So intense was speculation anticipating a devaluation of the dollar that the American and foreign monetary authorities gave up trying to control the price of gold in the international market. From then on, the $35-an-ounce price was used only in the gold transactions of the central banks and to evaluate official gold reserves. Meanwhile, the price of gold in the open market quickly rose to about $38 dollars an ounce.

Although it seemed an ingenious solution, the two-tier gold market did no more than buy a little more time. A permanent solution would have required that the United States commit itself to the old gold price and allow its monetary policy to be determined by that commitment. That would have required the Fed either to create no more liabilities than were consistent with its desired holdings of gold or to supply no less gold to the world market than was consistent with its desired creation of liabilities at the $35-an-ounce price.

After Richard Nixon became president, the United States did tighten monetary policy briefly, without committing itself credibly to the old $35-an-ounce price. But as the economy slid into a recession at the end of 1969 and the beginning of 1970, all monetary restraint was abandoned.

By confirming that the official gold price no longer constrained its monetary policy, the United States made the price untenable. Only if foreign central banks had been willing to accumulate unlimited amounts of U.S. liabilities could the price have survived. But despite pressure from the United States not to demand gold, the central banks began cashing in their dollar-denominated assets at the Treasury. In early August of 1971, with the free-market price at a 20 percent premium over the official parity, foreign central banks started a run on the dollar.

Unwilling to tolerate a large-enough loss of gold reserves to drive down the real value of gold, or to tighten monetary policy, or to devalue the dollar officially, Richard Nixon responded to the run on August 15, 1971, by closing the gold window. Although Nixon refused to acknowledge it at the time, his action signaled the demise of the Bretton Woods System.

The collapse of Bretton Woods created a situation unprecedented in monetary history. Never before had all links between the world's currencies and any real commodity been severed. This seemed to give national governments a degree of unconstrained monopoly power over money they had never before exercised.[1] For they were now able to exploit their monopolies without any legal commitment to convertibility or to price stability.

As might have been expected, such an opportunity did not go unseized. Even before the oil shock of 1973–74, inflation rates in many countries, including the United States, were in the double-digit range. And after the oil shock, inflation accelerated to even higher levels. In most countries high inflation persisted well into the 1980s.

However, as I argued in Chapter 2, the inflationary forces unleashed in the 1970s elicited a long-run competitive response that unexpectedly has begun to erode the state monopoly over money. It is to the first man-

---

[1] There had, of course, been previous instances in which national governments had forced inconvertible fiat currencies on their citizens. But such situations had always been regarded as exceptional, and there was usually some explicit or implicit promise by the government to restore convertibility.

ifestation of that response – the emergence of the Eurodollar market – that we now turn our attention.

THE EURODOLLAR MARKET

Perhaps because it has evolved outside the traditional regulatory framework, the Eurodollar market has always seemed exceptionally arcane and even inscrutable.[2] Fritz Machlup, for example, called his early paper on Eurodollar creation (1970) "a mystery story." Because the Eurodollar market seems so hard to understand, it is not difficult to frighten people with the specter of hundreds of billions of Eurodollars sloshing around outside the reach of any government's control.

Yet although it may seem complex and incomprehensible, the Eurodollar market actually exemplifies many of the basic principles I have already discussed. The growth of this market is a classic example of how spontaneous innovations arise in the marketplace to avoid governmental regulation and taxation, including, of course, the imposition of inefficient monopoly. And what they first simply avoid, they often eventually frustrate and undermine. Once we view the Eurodollar market from that perspective, the mystery surrounding it dissolves.

What is it that we call a Eurodollar? Originally, it was a dollar-denominated deposit created either in a European bank or in the European subsidiary of an American bank, usually located in London. It might appear odd that a bank in London would create a deposit denominated in dollars instead of in pounds. But there really is nothing so unusual about a bank and a customer deciding to denominate a deposit in a currency different from that of the country in which a bank resides. Recall that in the early history of European banking, deposits were often denominated in abstract units that had no concrete counterpart in hand-to-hand circulation.

But why would anyone want to hold a dollar deposit in a London bank? If you want to hold dollars, why not hold them in a good old American bank? And if you want to hold a deposit in a London bank, why not have the deposit denominated in sterling?

There might be several motives. Let's explore what they might be by considering an American residing in London and receiving income in dollars. Rather than exchange all his dollar receipts for pounds, he might prefer to hold some dollars. Even if our American friend receives all his income in pounds, he still might want to hold some dollars besides the pounds he needs for immediate transactions. Similarly, an American firm operating abroad might want to hold dollars as well as the local cur-

---

2 Aside from the specific references, the discussion in this section owes a great deal to Johnston (1982) and Niehans (1984, chap. 9).

rency. For such individuals or firms overseas, it might not be convenient to hold all their dollar deposits in banks located in the United States.

Nor would American individuals or firms domiciled abroad be the only demanders of Eurodollars. Many foreign individuals or firms might also want to hold dollar deposits. And they, too, would often find it more attractive to hold those deposits in foreign banks than in banks located in the United States.

By the same token, not everyone who wants to borrow dollars resides in the United States. Many borrowers live outside the country. It will often be easier for someone outside the United States to borrow dollars from a bank also outside the United States than from a bank inside. Because the dollar is the dominant international currency, many borrowers and lenders outside the United States choose to denominate their mutual claims in dollars. There is no reason the financial intermediation between such borrowers and lenders would always be less costly inside the United States than outside.

So there are, evidently, certain natural advantages to creating offshore dollar deposits that account for the emergence of the Eurodollar market. And as the world economy has become more integrated since World War II, not only the emergence but also the growth of a Eurodollar market was inevitable.

But these natural advantages were not the whole story. For the Eurodollar was also exempt from reserve requirements and other regulatory costs imposed on domestic American banks. Free from regulation, Eurobanks could work with narrower spreads between lending and borrowing rates than domestic American banks. Superior terms in the Eurodollar market attracted American borrowers and depositors who would have otherwise patronized domestic institutions.

But without inflation, even the artificial advantage that regulation of domestic banking conferred on the Eurodollar market would not have led to the extraordinary growth of that market. For as inflation accelerated and drove up interest rates in the 1960s and 1970s, the difference between spreads in the Eurodollar market and in the domestic market kept increasing. Moreover, the ceilings the Federal Reserve System's Regulation Q imposed on the interest that banks and thrifts could pay on time deposits drove many depositors, and consequently many borrowers, into the Eurodollar market.

One apparent difference between the Eurodollar market and the domestic market is that Eurodollars are held almost exclusively as time deposits (though often in maturities as short as one night). But the difference is superficial. Since holders of Eurodollars typically have other sources of funds for making payments and could also arrange for direct wire transfer of funds from their Eurodollar accounts to the accounts of others, they have little reason to want to hold Eurodollars as demand deposits, and only a tiny fraction of Eurodollars are held in that form. But if they did want to hold more Eurodollars as demand deposits than they now do, the quantity of demand deposits in the Eurodollar market could easily be expanded, and Eurobanks would have little difficulty in providing the necessary payments mechanism.

The more important difference between the markets is that as it stands now, the Eurodollar market is primarily a wholesale market in which banks, other financial institutions, and corporations borrow and hold deposits. The high efficiency and low spreads between borrowing and lending rates in the market have turned it into a remarkably effective mechanism for international financial intermediation. Much of the Eurodollar market involves interbank borrowing and lending. That makes it a low-cost way for banks in a country with good investment opportunities compared to domestic savings to acquire funds from banks in another country with less attractive domestic investment opportunities compared to domestic savings. So what started as a kind of fugitive banking system seeking escape from domestic regulations has become the center of the international financial market on which domestic banking systems rely as both a source of and an outlet for funds.

Expansion of the Eurodollar market proceeded along several different dimensions. The market originated primarily in the London subsidiaries of American banks. From there it spread to other banks in other parts of Europe. Eventually the market extended to Asia, Latin America, and the Caribbean. A Eurodollar deposit can, in principle, be created in any country in the world – even the United States. But to be considered "offshore," Eurodollar deposits in the United States must be unavailable to domestic residents. A small, but growing, share of offshore deposits has been denominated in currencies other than the dollar, principally the deutschmark and the yen. These deposits are referred to generically as Eurocurrencies. The forces that spurred the growth of the Eurodollar market also cause the other Eurocurrency markets to expand. That the Eurodollar market is still by far the largest of the various Eurocurrency markets simply reflects the currency-holding preferences of the public.

The obvious question at this juncture is why, if governments are as jealous of their control of money as I have been suggesting, they allowed Eurodollar and Eurocurrency markets to develop virtually free from control or regulation. The answer is simple. The only currency monopoly a government has any reason to protect is the one over its own currency. So a government tries to control the supply of deposits denominated in the currency unit it monopolizes, not the supply of deposits denominated in another currency unit. The function of Eurocurrency markets is precisely to create deposits denominated in a currency unit outside the territory of the government that monopolizes that unit.

Few commercial activities are more mobile than banking. So allowing the unrestricted creation of deposits is a way governments can attract significant benefits flowing from additional banking activity.[3] The benefits from taxing deposits denominated in currencies other governments monopolize would be trivial – possibly even nonexistent – in comparison. Although not regulating the creation of Eurocurrency deposits is rational for each government individually, the absence of regulation undermines the monopoly power over their own currencies they otherwise guard so jealously.

How has the rapidly increasing importance of the Eurodollar and Eurocurrency markets affected the domestic monetary systems of individual countries? When inflation became an intractable problem in the 1970s, many observers pointed to the seemingly uncontrollable growth of Eurodollar and Eurocurrency deposits as the reason monetary authorities the world over had lost control over the quantity of money and, hence, over inflation. Free from reserve requirements, Eurodollars seemed to be susceptible of potentially indefinite expansion. The Eurodollar market appeared to have overcome the obstacles that had been erected to keep banks from overissuing their liabilities and driving up prices.

Those fears, we now know, were unwarranted. The continued growth of the Eurodollar market did not prevent the domestic monetary authorities from reducing the rate of inflation during the 1980s. As long as they were restrictive enough in creating high-powered money (that is, currency plus reserves held by the banking system), the monetary authorities could control inflation even as the Eurodollar market kept growing. The Eurodollar market grew because it offered customers terms superior to those available in domestic markets. The growth of the Eurodollar market was not a source of inflation but a reflection of the asset-holding preferences of individuals, corporations, and banks all over the world. The Eurodollar market therefore perfectly illustrates how stable and noninflationary a competitive free banking system is.

But aside from accusing it of being inflationary, critics have also charged that the Eurodollar market leads to other forms of instability. The Eurodollar market is said to have increased U.S. foreign indebtedness and the fragility of the U.S. financial system by allowing the unconstrained creation of dollar-denominated liabilities that are presumed to be, in some sense, claims on the United States. Moreover, an unregulated Eurodollar market supposedly undermines the safety of the domestic financial sys-

3 The Cayman Islands are an extreme example of the benefits to a local economy from allowing the unregulated creation of deposits denominated in foreign currencies.

tem because the integration of the domestic and the Eurodollar markets makes it impossible to insulate domestic money markets from disturbances in the Eurodollar market.

Neither concern is well founded. The Eurodollar market creates no additional indebtedness by the United States to the rest of the world. It is simply a vehicle for exchanging liabilities and for denominating those liabilities in dollars. Borrowers and lenders who would otherwise have incurred liabilities or acquired assets denominated in other currencies now do so in dollars in the Eurodollar market. And other borrowers and lenders who would have incurred liabilities or acquired assets denominated in dollars in the domestic market can now do so on more favorable terms in the Eurodollar market. But none of that alters who is becoming indebted to whom, which at bottom is what determines the balance of international indebtedness. The net foreign indebtedness of the United States depends on the desire of Americans to save or to borrow compared to the desire of foreigners to save and to borrow. Those desires are unrelated to whether dollar-denominated debts are increasing or decreasing as a share of all debts in the world.

Does the absence of regulation increase the riskiness of the Eurodollar market? And does the added risk make the domestic banking system riskier as well? Again contrary to what many suppose, the answer to both questions is no. The Eurodollar market has grown so large and become so liquid that the banks participating in it can reshuffle their assets and their liabilities to ensure that they are never illiquid. Because long-term liabilities in the Eurodollar market have roll-over provisions, banks can achieve almost perfect synchronization of their assets and liabilities, leaving themselves almost perfectly hedged against fluctuations in interest rates. "The Eurodollar market," Jurg Niehans notes (1984, p. 192), "easily survived situations which seemingly competent observers had forecast to become serious crises."

Granting that individual banks in the Eurodollar market can remain liquid and hedge themselves against fluctuating interest rates, critics might still argue that there are systemic risks against which individual banks cannot protect themselves. An unanticipated decrease in the price level, for example, can cause a business downturn and force many borrowers to default on their loans. A wave of defaults could upset the entire banking system. Only monetary policy can avoid, or at least counteract, such a deflationary shock.

So the question is whether the Eurodollar market has weakened the monetary authority so much that it can no longer protect the economy against such shocks. The answer to that question depends on what instruments the monetary authority requires to respond to such a shock. Most economists would agree that it is primarily by controlling the quantity of high-powered money that the monetary authority affects macro-economic conditions. There is disagreement over whether changes in the quantity of high-powered money directly affect prices or directly affect interest rates, but most would agree that the quantity of high-powered money is the instrument by which the monetary authority exercises whatever control it may have.

But the Eurodollar market has certainly not diminished the control the monetary authority has over the quantity of high-powered money. So as long as there is a well-defined demand for currency and reserves, the monetary authority can, by altering the quantity in the appropriate way, still achieve its objectives. In practice, however, that may not be so simple. For although the Eurodollar market does not impinge on the control the monetary authority has over the quantity of high-powered money, it certainly does make the demand for high-powered money increasingly elastic and unstable. Since both banks and the public can substitute Eurodollars for domestic deposits with increasing ease, shifts between the two types of deposits occur in response to ever-smaller differences in the terms on which the two can be held or supplied. Shifts between Eurodollars and domestic deposits, of course, entail corresponding changes in the amount of high-powered money demanded. And as the demand for high-powered money grows less stable, the monetary authority loses its capacity to control the economy by appropriate changes in the quantity of high-powered money.

Let me explain. A modern monetary authority implements its policy by setting targets for the instruments under its control. The monetary authority may target either the quantity of high-powered money or some short-term interest rate that, in the very short term at least, it can control by controlling the quantity of high-powered money. Suppose it estimates that its policy objectives require the quantity of high-powered money to grow at a 5 percent annual rate or that the short-term interest rate should be 6 percent in the next period. How close the monetary authority comes to achieving its objectives depends both on the accuracy of its estimates and on its ability to reach its targets. That is, the correct objectives might prove to be a 5.5 percent annual rate of growth of high-powered money or a 5.8 percent interest rate, so policy turns out to be unintentionally restrictive. Or even if its targets are correct, the monetary authority may err in executing its policy, achieving only a 4.5 percent annual rate of growth of high-powered money or a 6.2 percent interest rate. Policy again turns out to be unintentionally restrictive.

The increasing risk that monetary policy may have destabilizing effects as the monetary system has grown more competitive is not a concern that I can dispose of briefly. I shall not discuss it here, but it is the primary concern of Chapters 10 and 11, in which I propose an alternative method to conventional monetary targeting for guaranteeing price stability. The remainder of this chapter continues my short history of how a competitive monetary system emerged in the last two decades and also describes the parallel innovations in monetary theory that, after more than a century, have again made competition a respectable idea in monetary theory and policy.

SOME OTHER COMPETITIVE DEVELOPMENTS

The Eurodollar market was not the only competitive response to reserve requirements, ceilings on deposit-interest rates, and high inflation. It would have been remarkable if it had been. Domestic financial institutions and depositors also were seeking to avoid the high costs of inflation and regulation. Doing so was greatly facilitated by the rapid progress of data-processing and telecommunications technologies that was taking place (partly fortuitously, but also partly in response to the incentives those costs had created) at just that time.

The result was an unprecedented burst of financial innovation that generated a broad new array of financial instruments offered by depository institutions. In the late 1960s and early 1970s, rising inflation drove interest rates above Regulation-Q ceilings. As we saw earlier, Regulation-Q ceilings had originally been imposed to suppress competition for deposits among depository institutions and to raise their profits. But when market rates rose above the ceilings, the withdrawals of funds — disintermediation — disrupted the financial system and the industries, particularly home building, dependent on credit. To prevent disintermediation from devastating thrift institutions and crippling the housing and construction industries, thrifts were allowed to offer competitive interest rates on large certificates of deposits (CDs). But once thrifts began paying market rates on CDs, banks had to be allowed to do so, too.

Small depositors, however, unable to afford CDs paying market rates, were stuck with non-interest-bearing demand deposits or Regulation-Q-constrained passbook accounts paying only 5 percent interest. So there were strong incentives to create new instruments paying competitive interest for small savers to take advantage of.

Depository institutions were already providing implicit interest to depositors by offering various free services and promoting credit cards. Using credit cards, prudent individuals could, in effect, borrow at no interest for as long as two months. Interest-free borrowing allowed people to economize on their holdings of non-interest-bearing deposits. Banks and thrifts began competing to make the transfer of funds between accounts easier in order to minimize the cost of holding funds in non-interest-bearing deposits. One way to do this was to allow depositors to transfer funds between their accounts over the telephone. Banks and thrifts also introduced automatic transfer accounts that managed cash for depositors by periodically transferring any funds in the non-interest-bearing checking account to an interest-bearing account. That arrangement effectively merged two accounts, giving the depositor the equivalent of an interest-bearing checking account. Alternatively, banks extended overdraft facilities to depositors equal to the size of their time deposits.

But it was nondepository institutions that introduced the most important innovation: the money-market mutual fund (MMMF). An MMMF offered shares in an asset portfolio made up of highly liquid money-market instruments yielding competitive interest. Those instruments, Treasury bills and CDs, were not available in denominations smaller than $10,000. But savers could invest in mutual funds for as little as $1,000. Thus money-market funds finally enabled depositors who had been trapped in Regulation-Q-constrained accounts to earn market interest rates.

At first, the MMMF was just a way for small savers to avoid Regulation-Q ceilings. But in 1976 Merrill Lynch introduced a Cash Management Account that merged a traditional brokerage account with an MMMF, periodically transferring any idle funds in the non-interest-bearing brokerage account into the MMMF. Customers could make payments either with a credit card provided them or by writing checks. The checks and credit-card drafts would be automatically debited against any cash balance in the account. If there were no cash in the account, shares in the MMMF would be liquidated to cover the payment. If there were not enough shares in the MMMF, Merrill would pledge securities in the customer's portfolio as collateral for a loan to cover the payment.

The success Merrill Lynch enjoyed with its Cash Management Account induced other brokerage houses to offer similar accounts. Pure MMMFs began allowing shareholders to write checks against their shares. The explosive growth of checkable MMMFs virtually forced Congress to enact legislation relaxing the constraints Regulation Q had been imposing on depository institutions.

Thrift institutions and later banks tried to meet the competition from nondepository financial institutions by offering NOW accounts. First introduced in the early 1970s, the NOW account was technically a savings account paying the maximum interest rate permitted by Regulation Q on passbook accounts. A depositor could write a negotiated order of withdrawal – functionally indistinguishable from a check – against this account.

Still another competitive response to high nominal interest rates and to reserve requirements was the withdrawal of an increasing number of banks from the Federal Reserve System. States generally imposed much less stringent reserve requirements on state-chartered banks than the Fed imposed on member banks. As interest rates rose, the costs of holding required reserves became high enough so that for many banks they outweighed the benefits (primarily access to loans from the Fed at its discount window at below-market rates of interest) of belonging to the Fed.

This trend disturbed the monetary authorities for two reasons. First, the withdrawal of reserves from the Fed implied that the Fed, and ultimately the Treasury, would lose seignorage. Second, the Fed worried that if enough banks reduced their holdings of reserves, it would have diminished control over the quantity of money and a diminished capacity to conduct monetary policy. Responding to those concerns, Congress in 1980 imposed uniform reserve requirements on all banks in legislation that partially deregulated banks and thrift institutions.

The first reason for worrying about the withdrawal of banks from the Federal Reserve System was certainly valid from the point of view of the Federal Reserve Board. Reserve requirements constitute a tax on deposits, and the proceeds are collected by the Fed and the Treasury. The reserves that banks hold with the Fed enable it to acquire a corresponding amount of Treasury bonds. The interest on those bonds technically accrues to the Fed, but most of it is returned to the Treasury. By avoiding the tax, banks that withdrew from the Fed forced it to sell a corresponding amount of Treasury bonds to the public. That deprived the Fed of interest income and increased the net interest payments of the Treasury.

But the loss of revenue that might have been expected owing to member-bank withdrawals could not have been more than a few billion dollars a year: a substantial sum, to be sure, but only a tiny fraction of the government's annual revenues.

The second concern is also problematic. In principle, as long as there is a demand for high-powered money, the Fed can conduct monetary policy by controlling the quantity of high-powered money. Since there is a demand for high-powered money apart from the demand to hold required reserves, reserve requirements are not logically necessary for conducting monetary policy. Nor is control over the overall quantity of money necessary for the Fed to operate a monetary policy. All it needs, as noted, is to control the quantity of high-powered money. And it would have that control even if required reserves were zero.

But as we just saw, the stability of the demand for high-powered money is also important. If the demand for required reserves is more stable than the demand for other components of high-powered money, reducing the demand for required reserves makes the overall demand for high-powered money less stable. And as I pointed out earlier, the less stable the demand for high-powered money is, the greater the risk of error in the conduct of monetary policy will be. So the withdrawal of member banks did have implications for monetary policy, even if they were different from what the Fed supposed them to be.

THE DEREGULATORY MOVEMENT

The competitive pressures on domestic depository institutions and the accelerating exodus of domestic banks from the Federal Reserve System made it inevitable that much of the financial regulation inherited from the 1930s would be discarded. As a first step in that direction, Congress in 1980 enacted the Depository Institutions Deregulation and Monetary Control Act (DIDMCA).

The act ordered the gradual removal of Regulation-Q ceilings by April 1986. It established a Depository Institutions Deregulation Committee to decide precisely when to lift the various Regulation-Q ceilings.[4] Although federal courts had ruled that NOW accounts violated the ban on interest-bearing checking accounts, DIDMCA authorized their continuation. The act preempted state usury ceilings on interest rates that were preventing banks and thrifts from lending in a period of unusually high interest rates. It made uniform and, on average, reduced reserve requirements, imposing them on nonmember as well as member banks. Nonmember banks became eligible for Federal Reserve services, including borrowing at the discount window. All services were to be supplied on equal terms to depository institutions according to a published price list.

However, the gradual deregulation of deposit interest rates that followed enactment of DIDMCA did not halt disintermediation. There was a particularly rapid transfer of funds from thrift institutions into MMMFs offering unconstrained interest rates. Between December 1980 and November 1982 assets in MMMFs grew from $76.6 billion to $241 billion. The threat to the survival of thrift institutions moved Congress to pass the Garn-St. Germain Depository Institutions Act of 1982.

The Garn-St. Germain Act required the Depository Institutions Deregulation Committee to allow banks and thrifts to create two new types of deposits that were free from interest-rate ceilings. In December 1982 the committee created the first of these accounts, permitting banks and thrifts to offer money-market deposit accounts (MMDAs) paying interest rates and providing limited transactions services comparable to those of MMMFs. Moreover, MMDAs, unlike MMMFs, were insured by the Federal Deposit Insurance Corporation (FDIC) or the Federal Savings

---

4 The voting membership of the committee consisted of the secretary of the Treasury and the chairmen of the Federal Reserve Board, the Federal Deposit Insurance Corporation, the Federal Home Loan Bank Board, and the National Credit Union Administration. The comptroller of the currency was a nonvoting member (Cooper and Fraser 1984).

and Loan Insurance Corporation (FSLIC). And in January 1983 the committee created the second of these accounts, permitting depository institutions to offer Super-NOW accounts, which, unlike NOW accounts, were free from Regulation-Q ceilings and paid competitive interest rates.[5] The new deposits finally enabled depository institutions to compete effectively with MMMFs. When banks and thrifts were allowed to offer deposit accounts paying competitive interest, the explosive growth of MMMFs came to an abrupt halt.

On April 1, 1986, all remaining interest ceilings and minimum deposit requirements on NOW and Super-NOW accounts were lifted. However, tax considerations and differences in reserve requirements still create incentives for banks to offer accounts paying different interest rates and with different minimum-balance requirements. MMDAs carry no reserve requirements because the MMMFs with which they compete carry none. So to induce the public to hold MMDAs, depository institutions offer higher rates on MMDAs than on other deposits. Yet despite some remaining anomalies, the supply of deposits and monetary services by the financial services industry is now competitive.

That the supply of deposits is competitive means that it is responsive to the incentives reflected in the pattern of interest rates on the whole spectrum of financial instruments. As the character of the monetary system has begun to change, so has the way some economists think about the monetary system and the role competition plays in it. It now remains for me to explain how their thinking has changed and to point out some of the often-unnoticed similarities between the new thinking about money and the classical theory of money I discussed in Chapter 3.

RESTORING COMPETITION TO MONETARY THEORY

From the middle of the nineteenth century to the middle of the twentieth, few economists paid any attention to the competitive forces that determine how much money a banking system creates. The marginal revenue and marginal cost conditions that economists use to analyze the output of any competitive industry were simply absent from monetary analysis. Instead, modern monetary theorists – whether Keynesians or Monetarists – until recently treated the nominal stock of money in existence at any moment as a magnitude determined by the monetary authority.

If the nominal quantity of money is determined not by the choices of individuals, firms, and the banking system, but by the monetary authority, then other economic variables – prices, interest rates, and incomes –

---

5 The difference between the NOW and the Super-NOW accounts was that the former required a minimum balance of $1,000 and the latter required a minimum balance of $2,500.

have to change for the community to be willing to hold that nominal amount of money. If the amount of money in existence is not the amount people want to hold, some process has to achieve a correspondence between the amount of money people want to hold and the amount of money there is to be held. Keynesians typically assume that the interest rate keeps changing until the amount people want to hold just matches the stock in existence. Monetarists assume that the price level is what changes to eliminate the discrepancy. Neither group would entertain the notion that the banking system could, on its own, change the quantity of money to eliminate the discrepancy between actual and desired money balances.

That such an adjustment was possible was almost totally ignored from the middle of the nineteenth century until the late 1950s, when a group of economists raised it again (Gurley and Shaw 1959; Tobin 1963). How ironic that what was a reversion (though not deliberate) to an older and nearly forgotten monetary tradition should have been dubbed the "New View" of monetary theory.[6]

James Tobin's contribution had an especial importance among the New View theorists. Therein lies a further irony, since Tobin and many of his associates were writing from an avowedly Keynesian perspective. By explaining how a competitive banking system adjusts the quantity of money to the demand, they wanted to show that monetary policy can be effective only under special circumstances. As Tobin explained it, the quantity

---

6 It was a Keynesian, James Tobin, who in his classic 1963 paper gave the most direct statement of the mechanism by which the banking system alters the quantity of deposits in response to changes in demand for them. Although never mentioning Fullarton, Tobin's account is very reminiscent of Fullarton's almost a century earlier. Here is Tobin (p. 229):

> Once created printing press money cannot be extinguished. . . . The community cannot get rid of this currency supply; the economy must adjust until it is willingly absorbed. The "hot potato" analogy truly applies. For bank-created money, however, there is an economic mechanism of extinction as well as expansion. If bank deposits are excessive relative to public preferences, they will tend to decline. . . . The burden of adaptation is not placed entirely on the rest of the economy.

Compare Fullarton's argument (1845/1969, p. 64):

> Still more decidedly have the conventional issues of governments all the characteristics of a forced currency. . . . [E]ven after the notes have become depreciated, the law compels the private creditor to accept them in satisfaction of his claim; and the government having no better money to offer, the only alternative left to its creditors and dependents is to take this or none. Bank-notes, on the other hand, are never issued but on demand of the recipient parties. New gold coin and new conventional notes are introduced into the market by being made the medium of payments. Bank-notes, on the contrary are never issued but on *loan,* and an equal amount of notes must be returned whenever the loan becomes due. Bank-notes never, therefore, can clog the market by their redundance, nor afford a motive to anyone to pay them away at a reduced value in order to get rid of them.

of money in a competitive system is determined by the utility- and wealth-maximizing choices of asset holders and the banking system. Given those choices, an injection of reserves into the banking system by the monetary authority would not, as conventional models of the money supply suggested, mechanically increase the stock of money. Since the banking system creates deposits up to the point where the marginal revenue from an additional deposit equals the marginal cost, an injection of reserves can alter the quantity of bank money only if it somehow alters the revenue from or cost of creating additional deposits.[7]

The conventional models break down the money supply into high-powered money and the money multiplier. The money multiplier summarizes the supposedly stable numerical relationship between high-powered money and the total stock of money. Thus an injection of reserves, by increasing high-powered money, is supposed to have a determinate multiple effect on the stock of money. But in Tobin's analysis, the implications of an injection of reserves were ambiguous. The result depended on how the added reserves affected interest rates and, in turn, the costs of and revenues from creating deposits. It was only a legal prohibition against paying interest on deposits, which kept marginal revenue above marginal cost, that created an incentive for banks to expand whenever they acquired additional reserves.

To Tobin and his associates – indeed, to his Monetarist critics as well – this analysis seemed to buttress the early Keynesian contention that monetary policy has little effect on the economy. If the money stock is determined not by monetary policy but by the decisions of the public and the banking system, how can monetary policy be effective? Tobin's analysis seemed to imply that at least in an economy with no ceilings on deposit interest rates, only fiscal policy could be effective.

Yet what Tobin's analysis really did – and this is the irony – was to undermine an important part of the original Keynesian model. For as we saw in the previous chapter, the Keynesian model rested on the assumption of a fixed money supply. In the Keynesian model, when savings exceed investment at the full-employment level of income, aggregate demand stays below the amount needed to generate full employment because the rate of interest does not fall enough. Government spending is needed to create enough aggregate demand to support full employment. But what keeps the rate of interest from falling sufficiently to permit aggregate demand to reach its full employment level? Liquidity preference.

Liquidity preference, remember, was Keynes's term for the desire to

---

7 There is a further irony: Just this point about the crucial role played by Keynes's assumption of a fixed, noncompetitive, non-interest-bearing money in generating his result of an unemployment equilibrium was made by the French economist Jacques Rueff (1947). It was Tobin (1948) who replied defending Keynes against Rueff's attack.

hold money instead of an interest-bearing bond. Since, in the Keynesian model, the rate of interest adjusts to equate the demand for money with the supply of money, it could not, as Keynes's predecessors had thought, be what adjusts to equate savings and investment. If, however, money is competitively supplied and bears interest, it is not the interest rate in itself which adjusts to equate the demand for money with the supply. Rather, it is the spread between the interest rate on loans and the rate paid on deposits that equilibrates the demand for with the supply of money. If aggregate demand is inadequate when money is competitively supplied, it cannot be, as Keynes maintained, owing to an interest rate that the public's liquidity preference keeps too high.

Given Tobin's Keynesian perspective, it was not difficult for critics like Harry Johnson (1972a)[8] and Leland Yeager (1968, 1978) to dismiss Tobin's argument by charging that it presumed that the price level was somehow determined independently of the amount of money the banking system produced. That might be acceptable to Keynesians, who lacked a clear theory of what determined the price level. But for Monetarists, who maintained that the price level is determined by the demand for and the supply of money, that presumption was clearly unacceptable. The considerations Tobin introduced in his sophisticated analysis of the supply of bank money could all be captured, or so Monetarists maintained, by making appropriate adjustments in the various ratios that defined the money multiplier.

However, had Tobin and his critics had a better grasp of the classical theory I outlined in Chapter 3, they would have seen that his analysis did not necessarily leave the price level undetermined. The classical theory distinguished between gold and bank money. At any moment, the supply of gold is fixed. The fixed stock of gold together with the demand for gold determines its value. Given the convertibility of bank money into gold, bank money must have precisely the same value as the corresponding amount of gold. With the price level determined in the market for gold, the banking system, without affecting the price level, supplies as much money as the public wants to hold.

Similarly, a modern competitive theory of money distinguishes between currency[9] and bank money. The stock of currency at any moment is fixed. That fixed stock of currency together with the demand for cur-

---

8 Johnson (1972a, p. 45n) charged that although Tobin and his associates at Yale recognized the distinction between real and nominal balances, they avoided it "either by assuming stable prices and confining their analysis to the financial sector, or by building models based on the fictional construction of a money whose purchasing power is fixed in real terms, thereby avoiding confusion in the analysis at the expense of creating it with respect to the applicability of the results."

9 Currency will hereinafter be taken as synonymous with high-powered money unless otherwise indicated.

rency determines its value. Being convertible into currency, bank money or deposits must have the same value as currency. And given a price level determined by the supply of and the demand for currency, the banking system, without affecting the price level, supplies whatever quantity of deposits the public wants to hold.

Interestingly, some post-Keynesians (Kaldor 1982) have taken the Monetarist contention that Tobin's analysis leaves the price level undetermined and have used it as the basis for polemics against trying to control inflation with monetary policy. Since the quantity of money is determined by the public and the banking system, not the monetary authority, the latter cannot control inflation by limiting the quantity of money. Yet amazingly, what starts out as a theory that monetary policy cannot stop inflation somehow ends up as a theory that tight monetary policy creates a financial disaster and deflation by not providing as much high-powered money as the banking system demands.[10]

However, as I have explained, both Monetarists and Keynesians miss the point when they contend that the price level is not determined if deposits are competitively supplied. The price level is determined not by the demand for and the supply of deposits but by the demand for and the supply of currency into which deposits are convertible. And the stock of currency, surely, is under the control of the monetary authority. Yet by seeking to conflate the demand for and the supply of currency with the demand for and supply of bank money, both Monetarists and mainstream Keynesians ignore that the two sets of demands and supplies are equated by totally different mechanisms. Variations in the price level equilibrate the demand for and the supply of currency, while variations in the spread between the rate of interest banks charge borrowers and the rate they pay depositors equilibrate the demand for and the supply of deposits.

RECENT ADVANCES IN THE THEORY OF A COMPETITIVE MONEY SUPPLY

Although Tobin's work was widely read and cited, no one at first drew the conclusions implicit in his approach. But in the early 1970s, a few younger economists, Fischer Black (1970/1987), Benjamin Klein (1974), and Earl Thompson (1974a), working independently, did develop explicit models of a competitive money supply. Initially their work, especially Black's and Thompson's, was not widely noticed. Only after one of the world's most famous economists, Nobel Laureate F. A. Hayek

---

10 One economist who has consistently developed the view that the monetary authority has no control over the quantity of money or over the price level, except by maintaining convertibility into a real asset, is Fischer Black (1972/1987, 1974/1987).

(1976, 1978), proposed totally eliminating the state monopoly over money and leaving the supply of money entirely to the market did interest in the possibility of competition in the money supply start to spread.

Since Hayek's proposal has received the most attention, and since it raises some essential issues for any discussion of monetary reform in a competitive environment, let us consider it now in some detail. He suggested that if banks were freed from all legal restrictions, they would begin competing to issue currencies denominated in new units of their own definition, rather than in existing governmentally defined units, such as the dollar, pound, and franc. Writing when inflation was at its peak, Hayek insisted that holding a money whose purchasing power the issuing bank had staked its valuable reputation on preserving would be so attractive that banks could easily induce the public to switch from government currencies to their own. Given the opportunity, Hayek argued, private moneys would soon displace the rapidly depreciating state currencies.

Although Hayek was remarkably insightful in perceiving that, contrary to received opinions, competition in supplying money could check inflation, his contention that private monetary units would replace the existing state units overlooked a key distinction. Switching from one money to another is much less costly when both are denominated in the same monetary unit than when they are denominated in different units. The cost is even greater if one of the units is not even being used. Thus, if banks issued moneys denominated in new monetary units, they would somehow have to overcome the cost of inducing people to hold moneys denominated in units that were not yet being used.

Even at high rates of inflation, banks would find it cheaper to issue moneys denominated in existing monetary units and pay money holders competitive interest than to induce people to hold, and transact with, a money denominated in a new unit. Paying competitive interest on deposits denominated in existing monetary units would compensate depositors for inflation nearly as effectively as creating a deposit denominated in a new noninflating unit. So why would banks bother with creating a brand new monetary unit?

The Eurodollar and Eurocurrency markets perfectly illustrate this point. The banks creating Eurocurrencies are in fact free from any government regulation, so there is nothing to prevent them from denominating deposits in some new currency unit. That they, nevertheless, have chosen to denominate those deposits in dollars or in other major monetary units, not in some new unit, shows that the public prefers holding interest-bearing deposits denominated in existing monetary units to any new monetary unit.[11]

---

11 Actually, there is a new monetary unit in use, the ECU. But this is a unit that the countries of the European Monetary System have created and have created a demand

I should not disagree with Hayek that a stable monetary unit that can be confidently used by all transactors exchanging future claims on each other confers a great benefit on society. But those benefits are not confined just to those who are holding money; they accrue to everyone planning to make contracts specifying future monetary obligations. A bank would not profit by introducing a new stable monetary unit because all the benefits could not be captured by the bank and holders of its money, yet it would have to bear the costs of inducing people to switch from the existing unit to the new one. Thus a stable monetary unit is a public good, which the government, if it already provides that existing monetary unit, has an advantage in supplying.

To avoid any confusion on this point, however, I hasten to add that, contrary to Tobin (1980), although the monetary unit is a public good, actual money is a private, not a public, good. The distinction here is the same as that between a yard, which is an abstract concept available simultaneously to everyone, and a yardstick, which is a concrete thing that cannot be used simultaneously by more than one person.

But despite their differences in approach, these recent contributions, and numerous others that have followed (Fama 1980, 1983); Hall 1981; Wallace 1983; Greenfield and Yeager 1983), have done much to refute the standard objection to a competitive, unregulated banking system. That objection holds that an unconstrained banking system has an inherent incentive to overissue its liabilities. Such overissue, it is charged, undermines price stability. Yet as I argued earlier, a competitive banking system reduces the revenue a government can collect from any given rate of inflation and reduces the yield in revenue from any given increase in inflation. As a consequence a competitive banking system should, at least in the long term, reduce the rates of inflation chosen by the monetary authorities (Dwyer and Saving 1986; Glasner 1986). This, at any rate, is consistent with recent experience in which inflation rates have fallen just as banking systems all over the world have become increasingly competitive.

The growing interest in the theory of a competitive supply of money and the recognition that competing suppliers of money need not cause monetary instability have also prompted a reexamination of the few historical examples of relatively unconstrained banking. Several economists have been studying the American experience with free banking between 1836 and 1863 (Rockoff 1975; King 1983; Rolnick and Weber 1983, 1984, 1988; Timberlake 1984). Popular historiography portrays the free-banking period as an exceptionally unstable one in which depositors and noteholders of failing banks suffered large losses. Yet recent research into

for. Banks on their own would not bother trying to create a demand for an entirely new private unit.

the period shows that the reality was far different. Few customers suffered losses as a result of bank failures, and the period was not marked by unusual monetary instability. Lars Jonung (1987) has come up with similar findings in his study of the free banking in Sweden in the nineteenth century.

Perhaps the most impressive case of free banking was in Scotland. Lawrence H. White (1984), in his important study of Scottish free banking, has shown that it functioned extremely efficiently and safely for over a century until the Bank Charter Act of 1844 and the follow-up Act of 1845 restricted the operations of the Scottish banks.

CONCLUSION

The competitive breakthrough I have been describing in this chapter has produced a situation similar in some ways to the one in the middle of the nineteenth century. That too was a time of rapid monetary evolution and financial innovation when the quantity of money was largely determined by competitive forces. Unfortunately, it was just then that economists began to abandon the competitive monetary paradigm that Adam Smith and the Banking School had started to work out. That paradigm treated the creation of money as a product of financial intermediation. In that paradigm it made no sense to distinguish between the "moneyness" of the different sorts of liabilities (such as banknotes and deposits) that banks issued when intermediating between ultimate borrowers and lenders. Because those liabilities had to be held willingly by the public, how much of them banks created had no special significance.

But rejecting the competitive paradigm, monetary theorists in the mid-nineteenth century adopted, instead, the anticompetitive paradigm of David Hume and the Currency School. In that paradigm, there was something special about banks and their creation of a certain type of liability – the banknote. Banknotes were somehow different from other liabilities created by banks because only the former and not the latter were money. That meant that a limit had to be imposed on the quantity of banknotes that did not have to be imposed on the quantity of other financial instruments. But as one might expect from monetary reforms grounded in such a misconception of how the monetary system worked, the measures instituted to limit the creation of banknotes, such as the Bank Charter Act of 1844, only added to monetary instability in the nineteenth century.

Because the reforms left deposits unconstrained, most national monetary systems continued to evolve along competitive lines. But after the destruction of the gold standard in World War I and the catastrophic attempt to restore it, the world abandoned the largely competitive monetary system that had evolved in the nineteenth century. And although the distinction between banknotes and bank deposits eventually had to be abandoned, it was replaced by another one: a distinction between banks, which can create money, and other financial intermediaries, which cannot.

Their special status as creators of money meant that banks had to be subject to both special regulation and special protection against competition from other banks and other financial intermediaries. The post-depression financial system reflected the consensus that banks were a special kind of institution that had to be insulated from competitive pressures. But that noncompetitive financial system could not withstand the competitive pressures unleashed when governments sought to exploit their unconstrained monopolies. A burst of financial innovation has obliterated the boundaries regulation once maintained between transactions accounts that don't bear interest and nontransactions accounts that do. One can no longer distinguish a subset of financial instruments which are money from those which are not. With so many institutions now creating interest-bearing instruments that are excellent substitutes for what we used to regard as money, a competitive monetary system has willy-nilly emerged once again. So economists must again choose, as they did in the nineteenth century, between a competitive monetary paradigm in which the creation of money is simply an aspect of financial intermediation and a noncompetitive paradigm in which the creation of money is something special that can only be undertaken by a select group of institutions receiving special regulation and protection.

However, the competitive system we have now must operate within an institutional framework designed for a noncompetitive system dominated by the government. That institutional framework was adopted during the Great Depression because of two kinds of concerns. One was that banks are susceptible to contagious panics that could lead to a financial collapse. To prevent panics, Congress instituted federal deposit insurance, sought to prevent banks from assuming excessive risks, and restricted the payment of interest on deposits. The barriers to risk taking have gradually eroded, and insured institutions are seeking new ways of exploiting the incentives for risk taking that deposit insurance now creates. The new arrangement, it is now clear, is no more viable than the previous one. So the issue is how to reform deposit insurance without undermining the safety of the whole banking and financial system.

The other concern arising out of the Great Depression was that the economic system in general is inherently unstable. An activist economic policy seemed to be a way of coping with that instability. A key element of that activist policy was a discretionary monetary policy. Yet discretionary monetary policy, while avoiding another Great Depression, could not eradicate the business cycle. And it also generated the inflation that helped transform a controlled monetary system into a competitive one. If, as I have argued, discretionary monetary policy becomes more risky as the monetary system becomes more competitive, we must find an alternative that takes away discretion from the monetary authority to do as it wishes when it wishes. But what is that alternative?

If the newly emerging competitive monetary system is to fare better than its predecessor of the last century, we shall have to find better ways of addressing these concerns than were found then. In the final three chapters of this book I suggest reforms that address these concerns.

9

Can competitive banking be safe and stable?

> [The national guarantee system] proposes to tax good banks to sup-
> port bad; to penalize honesty, ability, experience and training to com-
> pensate for incompetency, dishonesty and ignorance; it removes from
> banking the essential characteristic on which success in the business
> has been based, viz., . . . a reputation for prudence, foresight, sagacity
> and conservatism. It proposes to place the reckless and speculative
> banks on the same level with the best managed and the most conserva-
> tive, which will lead to competition calculated to drag all of them
> down to the least meritorious.
>
> > Chicago Clearing House Association (1932)
>
> Metaphorically, deposit-insurance authorities are paying deposit-
> institution managers to overload the deposit-insurance jalopy, to drive
> it too fast, and even to break dance on its hood as it careens through
> interest rate mountains and over back country roads.
>
> > Edward Kane, *The Gathering Crisis*
> > *in Federal Deposit Insurance*

Competition in banking has always drawn criticism from those who believe it is destabilizing. Such criticism, as we have seen, was common in
the eighteenth and nineteenth centuries. And when the banking collapse
of the Great Depression seemed to validate those criticisms, a series of
reforms turned banking into a heavily regulated industry. But now competition and financial innovation are transforming banking and breaking
down the artificial barriers regulation has interposed between banks and
other financial intermediaries. In this new competitive environment, the
old fears about competitive banking have resurfaced.

Criticism of competition in banking takes two forms. In one, attention
is focused on the liability side of bank balance sheets; in the other, it is
focused on the asset side.

The first form of criticism, which I have discussed at length in earlier
chapters, says that competing banks have an incentive to overissue their
liabilities – banknotes or deposits – as they compete for market share.

Overissue implies that banks create more of these liabilities than the public wants to hold. In trying to dispose of excess banknotes or deposits, the public increases spending, causing bank money to depreciate and driving up prices. Under a gold standard, the overissue could not continue very long before a drain on its gold reserves forced the banking system into a sharp, and possibly destabilizing, contraction. But under a flat standard, the overissue could continue until accelerating inflation forced the central bank to restrict credit to the banks.

I have already shown, however, that this supposed incentive to overissue implicitly assumes that banks always find it profitable to expand their liabilities at the margin. But that could only be true if banks were not paying competitive interest on those liabilities. If they were, no such incentive to overissue would obtain. So the fear of overissue, as many classical theorists well understood, is baseless in a competitive banking system.

My previous discussion, however, did not dispose of the second line of argument against competitive banking. That argument says that competitive banks make too many risky and undiversified loans and investments. The riskier a bank's assets are, the more likely it is that the value of its assets will drop below the value of its liabilities, rendering the bank insolvent. Too many insolvencies can undermine confidence in the banking system and trigger a panic. And far from being a source of stability, paying interest on deposits, according to this argument, simply forces banks to take even more risks to generate the revenue they need to pay interest to depositors. It was that concern which provided the rationale for the New Deal reforms prohibiting interest payments on demand deposits.

The competitive breakthrough I described in the previous chapter shattered the banking cartel created by the New Deal and assiduously nurtured by public officials for over four decades. Despite official solicitude, the profit opportunities that high inflation and technological progress opened up in the 1970s left the cartelized structure of interest rates on bank liabilities unsustainable.

Critics of financial deregulation and competitive banking often make it sound as if deregulation were a deliberate policy initiative. If it had been, there might be some point in their proposals for reregulating banks and thrifts. But financial deregulation did not occur because regulators and Congress took a principled stand for competition and against regulation. It occurred because competitive pressures fueled by inflation and technological progress made old regulations and controls unbearable to many of their original beneficiaries.

Advocates of a pure free market are frequently criticized – and with some justification – for ignoring the political forces that promote political interference with market transactions. But advocates of regulation frequently are just as guilty of ignoring the market forces that impinge on regulation.

You cannot, for instance, regulate part of a competitive industry, leave the other part unregulated, and expect the regulated part to survive. You must either regulate or deregulate the entire industry. Moreover, regulation raises costs, which are ultimately borne by consumers;[1] firms in unregulated industries therefore have an incentive to offer goods and services that are close substitutes for those supplied by the regulated industry. So you face the same dilemma again: You must either regulate outside competitors or deregulate the regulated industry.

That is what happened to the regulation of banks in the 1970s.[2] The profits generated by the banking cartel inevitably attracted new entrants into the industry. Although direct entry was effectively blocked, financial innovation inside and outside the United States began to provide a range of increasingly close and low-cost substitutes for the liabilities issued, and the services rendered by, banks.

As long as inflation and interest rates were low, the profits accruing to the banking cartel did not create unmanageable incentives for entry into banking or for financial innovation. But in the inflationary environment of the 1970s, those incentives became irresistible. Financial innovation would have overwhelmed the New Deal banking cartel and the regulations that supported it no matter how dedicated Congress and the regulators were to a philosophy of regulation.

If the transformation of banking into a highly competitive industry was unavoidable, does that mean that financial instability is also unavoidable? However unstable competitive banking may have been in the past — and the instability has been greatly exaggerated — financial competition and innovation are now potentially highly stabilizing forces. But before showing how competition and innovation can be stabilizing, I must first explain why the main destabilizing force in banking is what we used to think was its main bulwark against instability — federal deposit insurance.

DEPOSIT INSURANCE AND THE BANKING CARTEL

I pointed out in Chapter 8 the essential role that federal deposit insurance played in the New Deal banking cartel. The competitive advantage it

1 The proposition that costs are passed forward to consumers assumes that there are no specialized resources in the industry that earn rents – returns higher than the resources could earn in other occupations. If rents are being earned, then regulatory costs will be borne by the specialized resources instead of being passed forward to consumers.
2 In this chapter I shall, for simplicity, use the term "banks" to stand for both commercial banks and savings and loan institutions.

gave to banks made obtaining deposit insurance indispensable to new entrants. The discretion deposit-insurance agencies had over whether to insure new entrants provided them with a barrier with which to block entry into banking.

But if deposit insurance served the banking cartel, it is also true that the banking cartel served the deposit-insurance system. Insuring deposits in banks reduces the losses borne by depositors in case of insolvency. So depositors no longer panic and withdraw deposits at any sign of weakness in the bank's portfolio. But as a result bankers feel far freer to take risks without the threat of a run by depositors hanging over them than they would otherwise.

A similar effect is present in every insurance contract. The insurance literature has long recognized that being insured reduces the incentive to take precautions against the adverse occurrence covered by insurance. The effect is called "moral hazard." If insurance induces people to be too morally hazardous, providing insurance may become unprofitable.

But there are ways of neutralizing, or at least minimizing, morally hazardous behavior. An insurer can try to monitor the behavior of the insured party and adjust premiums accordingly. Another tactic is to require the insured party to avoid risky activities and to take observable precautions as a condition for retaining coverage. Thus fire insurers will charge a higher premium for insuring an oil refinery than for insuring an office building. And they will insist that both the refinery and the office building take precautions against fires: installing fire alarms, fire extinguishers, and sprinkler systems and excluding, insofar as possible, combustible materials from the premises.

However, unlike most private insurers, FDIC and FSLIC did not try to discourage their clients from taking risks by adjusting premiums to reflect risk. That is because Congress required that FDIC and FSLIC charge all clients a uniform premium. That left regulation as the only way to limit morally hazardous behavior by insured institutions. Thus regulation and deposit insurance did not just support a cartel guaranteeing banks and thrifts high profits; they also had to control banks' asset portfolios and prevent them from offering more than a narrow subset of financial services.

Since regulation was used to accomplish more than one goal, not all restrictions were aimed at reducing risk. For example, there were regulations confining savings and loan institutions exclusively to mortgage lending. As a consequence, thrifts wound up with extremely risky and undiversified portfolios. Similarly, state and federal restrictions on interstate and branch banking confined banks geographically, precluding internal diversification and mergers that could have reduced the riskiness of asset portfolios. Moreover, the Community Reinvestment Act requires all banks and thrifts to reinvest in their local communities. That requirement, which subverts the whole notion of financial intermediation, not only prevents small banks from diversifying, it compels them to make uneconomic loans that could not be justified on commercial criteria. So it would certainly not be easy to argue that the combined effect of all regulation of financial institutions has been to reduce risk.

But although regulation prevented banks from diversifying, it was also calculated to ensure the profitability of whatever activities they were allowed to engage in. Thus, when growing competition and financial innovation began eroding the profitability of traditional banking operations, the implicit bargain that confined banks to just those activities became harder and harder to maintain.

Now, with regulatory barriers collapsing, banks are quickly learning how to exploit the subsidy to risk taking that deposit insurance provides them. This is putting the deposit-insurance agencies into an increasingly untenable situation.

BANK FAILURES AND DEPOSIT INSURANCE — BEFORE AND AFTER

To put the current problems in historical perspective, let's look at the historical record of bank failures in the United States. Between 1865 and 1919, there was only one year in which more than two hundred banks failed. And that was out of more than twenty thousand banks in the whole country. Indeed, the bank failure rate of less than 1 percent a year was less than the nonbank failure rate. Even in the 1920s, when banks were failing at a rate of over six hundred a year, most of the failures were among small rural banks in the South and Midwest (Friedman and Schwartz 1963, p. 438). Ninety percent of the failed banks had total assets of less than $100,000 — a tiny sum even in those days (Benston et al. 1986).

Even without deposit insurance, the high rate of failures did not shake public confidence in the banking system. So one can't conclude that a high rate of bank failures automatically starts a panic. It might be argued that the Great Depression, which began at the end of the decade, shows that the high rate of bank failures did eventually cause a panic. But since the rate of bank failures was high for a whole decade without bringing on a crisis, the argument obviously leaves a good deal unexplained.

Whatever did finally cause them, the bank panics of the depression came to a virtual stop after federal deposit insurance was adopted. In 1933 alone, over four thousand banks failed; in 1934 fewer than one hundred failed. From then until 1985 the number of bank failures in a single year never exceeded one hundred. And the number of failures was in single digits every year between 1943 and 1974 (Cooper and Fraser 1984, p. 153).

THE RISING TIDE OF BANK FAILURES —
OPEN AND DISGUISED

But even when bank failures were almost nonexistent, things were not quite what they seemed. The official statistics on bank failures since 1934 include only insolvent banks actually closed by the FDIC. Many other banks that were economically insolvent·stayed open, only because insurance and regulatory officials let them carry assets on their balance sheets at book value, even though the market value of those assets had gone down. For example, many banks that lent to developing countries in the 1970s are now extremely unlikely ever to receive full payment of interest and principal. Yet banks may carry those loans on their balance sheets as if they were impeccable. If banks were required to mark assets to market, it would become apparent that many of them (particularly thrift institutions) were really insolvent. Some banks like the Continental-Illinois Trust Company, have even received direct financial assistance to ensure their continued operation.

Yet even when banks do face insolvency, the insurance authorities usually try to find sound institutions to take them over in order to avoid having to shut them down and compensate insured depositors. Why not close down and pay off the insured depositors of banks that are insolvent even according to the lax standards of the regulators? There are two reasons. First, the authorities try to keep information about bank problems from reaching the public. A bank closure and a payout to depositors get more publicity than a merger. Closing a bank therefore does more to shake public confidence in the banking system, and thus to incite bank runs, than a merger would. Second, a merger has less immediate effect on the reserves of the insurance fund than a closure. This consideration has taken on increasing importance as the liabilities of insolvent or shaky banks and thrifts have soared in relation to the reserves of the FDIC and FSLIC funds.

But in the long run, since a sound bank does not take over an unsound one for free, a merger has more effect. Federal insurance agencies typically either promise to make future payments to the acquiring institution or at least guarantee that the acquiring institution will realize the book value of the assets it acquires.

The unwillingness of the deposit-insurance agencies to close unsound banks has had another, more serious, effect: it has intensified the moral-hazard problem. With the safety net stretched out to catch them as well as their depositors, managers and stockholders have had little reason to avoid risky strategies that have increased the chances of an insolvency. Indeed, the shakier an institution, the greater the incentive to bet the bank on an all-or-nothing strategy.

Thanks to deposit insurance, these unsound institutions can still attract deposits. Not only do they draw deposits away from sound institutions, they offer higher interest rates than sound institutions do because they expect their risky strategies either to fail or to generate a big payoff. In the meantime, though, sound institutions must pay added interest on deposits to stay competitive with these (in Edward Kane's descriptive term) "zombie" institutions, undermining their own solvency in the process.

In an impressive and disturbing study of deposit insurance, Edward Kane (1985, pp. 96–106) estimated that the explicit and implicit guarantees of the deposit-insurance agencies have raised the market value of depository institutions by between $100 and $150 billion. The value of those guarantees dwarfs the combined FDIC and FSLIC reserve funds of perhaps $20 billion. The 1987 multibillion-dollar congressional bailout of the FSLIC did not even come close to restoring it to solvency. By the end of 1988, it became clear that the cost to taxpayers of redeeming FSLIC guarantees in failed or failing thrifts may even exceed $100 billion.

The current situation not only threatens the future of American banking, it also endangers the future of a private enterprise economy in the United States. Should a full-blown crisis occur, a government takeover of a large fraction of the country's banks and thrifts would become a real possibility. The implications of such a step would be profoundly disturbing. Even if we do avoid that outcome, the magnitude of depositors' potential claims on taxpayers is such that unless the budget deficit becomes a surplus much sooner than anyone expects, meeting them is likely to require a major tax increase, substantial inflation, or both.

The current high rate of bank failures and the effective insolvency of the federal deposit insurance system are thus only symptoms of a much more dangerous malady. A simple bailout would do nothing to correct the distorted incentives that are the source of the malady. Before discussing what can be done to treat it, we must think a bit more deeply about the purpose deposit insurance is really supposed to serve. Confusion about what we want deposit insurance to accomplish has led to proposals for reform of deposit insurance that may throw the baby out with the bath water. Of course, we may not really want this baby. But if not, we should face the issue squarely.

WHY DO WE HAVE DEPOSIT INSURANCE?

Why do we have deposit insurance? That question has two possible answers. One is that it is part of the system of social insurance built up in Western economies over the last fifty or one hundred years. The aim of social insurance is to protect individuals against a variety of risks to which nearly everyone is subject, such as old age, disability, unemployment, and ill health. According to this answer, since almost everyone holds deposits, we insure them collectively just as we insure against other universal risks.

If this were the only reason for deposit insurance, it would be easy to show that we ought to get rid of it. The moral-hazard problem I just described makes deposit insurance an excessively costly way of protecting people against the risk of bank failure. To avoid that risk, after all, people could hold government currency, or savings bonds, or some other very safe default-free asset instead of bank deposits. Since people can easily protect themselves against a substantial exposure to this risk we ought to let them do the job themselves.

According to the second answer, however, protecting individuals against losses from bank failures is only a means, not an end. Its real purpose is to prevent a series of bank failures from provoking a panicky run on the banking system that might cause its collapse. By contrast, social security is not designed to prevent old age, only to make collective provision for it.

Deposit insurance, from this perspective, should be viewed not as a component of social insurance but as a component of monetary policy. When I was in college I, like other students for two generations, was taught that deposit insurance was among the reforms that had made the U.S. economy depression-proof. Indeed, even someone as critical of most of what the New Deal stood for as Milton Friedman (1954) not only conceded, but insisted on, that point.

Although deposit insurance is too costly to adopt just to protect individual depositors, if it is saving the economy from another financial collapse and depression, the cost may not be excessive (Karaken 1983a, 1983b). How does deposit insurance prevent a banking panic and a financial collapse? The answer presupposes an understanding of what makes banks vulnerable to runs and panics in the first place. Their vulnerability stems from two of their characteristic features. The first is the nature of the obligation a bank incurs when it creates a deposit. It obligates itself to redeem the deposit for something else – nowadays government currency – at a fixed rate. As long as the assets of the bank are worth more than its liabilities it can redeem those obligations. Even if it doesn't hold enough currency to meet a demand for redemption, it can still do so by liquidating some of its assets or by borrowing currency, using its assets as collateral.

Here is where the second characteristic comes in. The value of a bank's assets can never be known with certainty. So unless its net worth is very large, there is some probability that the bank will default on its obligations. If depositors believe that the bank's chances of defaulting soon are not negligible, they will obviously try to redeem their deposits – and the quicker the better. The longer they wait, the more likely it is that the bank will default first. If it does, they, along with the bank's other creditors, will have to wait for their share of the uncertain liquidated value of the bank's assets.

What can cause the public to begin to doubt the solvency of a bank? Anything that informs the public that the value of the bank's assets and its net worth have fallen. This could be information that a bank's loans are not being paid back on schedule or that a general rise in interest rates, against which the bank is not hedged, has reduced the value of its assets and its net worth. Since it is not easy to ascertain the true net worth of a bank, people are likely to draw inferences about the solvency of one bank from information they have about the solvency of other banks. So when one bank fails, many people, without other sources of information about banks' solvency, raise their estimate of the probability that other banks will fail, too.

That is why bank runs can be contagious. Bank runs are not the irrational outbreaks of mass hysteria they are often portrayed as. Indeed, they can be perfectly rational. Since it is costly to obtain accurate information about the financial condition of a bank and costly to have deposits in a bank when it becomes insolvent, joining a bank run once doubts about a bank's solvency arise may be fully rational.

But if a bank were well-enough capitalized, it could withstand defaults by its debtors or by other banks and rising interest rates and still retain the confidence of its depositors. Even if depositors lost confidence in the bank, with enough equity it could borrow against its capital to meet any demand for redemption. One way of thinking about deposit insurance is as an alternative source of equity for banks. That explains why, before FDIC, banks operated with two or three times as much capital in relation to assets as they do now.

Now if all deposit insurance did were to allow banks to substitute debt for equity, it would be a pure subsidy to owners of bank stocks with no benefit to depositors. So the case for deposit insurance must presume that, on their own, banks would choose too low a level of capitalization. Why would they be undercapitalized? The standard answer goes as follows. Banks decide how capitalized to be by weighing the cost of attracting additional capital against the benefit from reducing the probability of insolvency. But in reckoning the benefit, a bank considers only the losses it would avoid by reducing that probability. It does not consider that the safer it is, the lower the probability is that other banks will fail. Moreover, a banking collapse affects more than just owners of bank stocks, who are partially insulated from the consequence of a collapse by limited liability.[3]

The problem arises, however, only because the demand for currency cannot be met by all banks simultaneously unless the amount of currency in the system is increased. The banks have no control over the quantity of currency.[4] That is controlled by the government. If the quantity of currency is not increased, the unsatisfied demand for currency begins to depress asset prices and quickly degenerates into a general deflation. The deflation produces further bankruptcy in the economy in general and drives formerly solvent banks into insolvency.

This may be an extreme scenario, but the experience of the Great Depression seems, at least on one reading of the facts, to support it. So do some theoretical models of financial intermediation and bank runs (Diamond and Dybvig 1983). In principle, the government can keep a crisis for some banks from degenerating into a general collapse by lending sound banks enough currency to meet depositors' demands for currency. Yet given the risk that the government might fail to respond appropriately in a crisis, as it did in the Great Depression, prudence might seem to dictate never letting a crisis get started in the first place.

This, at bottom, is the rationale for deposit insurance. The point is not to protect individual depositors. It is to eliminate any incentive for depositors to convert their deposits into currency when they fear an insolvency. To do that, deposit insurance must make deposits so safe that the public would never try, out of fear of insolvency, to convert them into currency.

---

3 One may question how significant this externality is. For, after all, why should it matter to a sufficiently capitalized bank if other banks are failing or if the public is losing confidence in the banking system? With enough equity, a bank should be able to meet a demand for redemption by liquidating some of its assets or by borrowing against assets it can put up as collateral. The problem, however, is that the public may lose confidence in banks in general rather than in a small number of banks. The public then has an incentive to try to redeem the obligations of all banks at the same time. In that situation, it becomes exceedingly difficult even for solvent banks to meet their obligations.

4 Banks would have control over the quantity of banknotes if there were no prohibition on their issue of banknotes. Indeed, as Selgin (1988) argues, this prohibition has often triggered insolvencies by banks unable to meet a demand for banknotes with the limited amount of government currency available. However, even if there were no prohibition of or controls on the issue of banknotes, a demand for redemption of bank liabilities of all types could still arise.

Can competitive banking be safe and stable?

THE ROLE OF UNINSURED DEPOSITS

In fact, Congress and the deposit-insurance agencies have never accepted such a sweeping responsibility, at least not in principle. They have deliberately left some deposits uninsured. When first introduced, deposit insurance covered deposits only up to $2,500; but Congress over the years increased the limit, raising it from $40,000 to $100,000 in 1980.

The rationale for leaving some deposits uninsured was that large depositors would respond differently to banking panics from small depositors. The latter are supposedly unsophisticated and given to panic in a crisis. Large depositors, on the other hand, are sophisticated and stay cool in a crisis. This view implied that small depositors ought to be fully insured so that they would not start panicky runs on all banks whenever a bank failure occurred. Large depositors, who presumably could distinguish between sound and unsound banks and would not be panicked into a general run on banks, needed no protection. Moreover, the knowledge that some depositors were not insured and, therefore, would monitor the banks' performance was supposed to deter banks from taking excessive risks.

Unfortunately, the distinction between insured and uninsured depositors has not worked out as it was intended to. For one thing, it was based on a faulty premise: that bank runs are caused by panic-stricken depositors who act irrationally. As I explained earlier, redeeming one's deposits when questions arise about a bank's future solvency may be quite rational. The second reason that the distinction has not worked out is that deposit insurers have not been willing to force unsound banks to shut down. They have shrunk from doing so, afraid to damage public confidence in the banking system and unwilling to accept the loss of reserves entailed by a payout to insured depositors. But by arranging for sound banks to take over unsound ones, they, in effect, also bailed out the uninsured depositors. Thus uninsured depositors have enjoyed a substantial, though uncertain, degree of de facto coverage of their deposits. But that coverage dilutes their incentive to monitor bank performance.

The Continental-Illinois case showed how blurred the distinction between insured and uninsured deposits has become. Continental's difficulties were no secret, but many uninsured depositors assumed that the de facto guarantee on uninsured deposits would protect them. However, when rumors started to circulate that the FDIC might let Continental fall without saving the uninsured depositors, those depositors started a run on the bank. Fearing that the run could be contagious, and unable to induce a sound bank to take over Continental's assets and liabilities, the FDIC itself took over ownership and operation of the bank. Comptroller of the Currency C. Todd Conover gave the following explanation for the bailout:[5]

In our collective judgment [directors of the FDIC, the chairman of the Federal Reserve Board, and the secretary of the Treasury], had Continental failed and been treated in a way in which [uninsured] depositors and creditors were not made whole, we could very well have seen a national, if not international, financial crisis the dimensions of which were difficult to imagine. None of us wanted to find out.

Having observed how quickly uninsured depositors would jump ship and seeking to avoid future panics by uninsured depositors in other banks, the comptroller of the currency announced that none of the nation's eleven largest banks would be allowed to fail.

Backed up by the Fed and Congress, the FDIC did prevent the collapse of a major U.S. bank. In the short run the FDIC succeeded. But at what price? And how long can it continue to act as a backstop for banks that now have little reason to think twice before taking on risks?

CAN DEPOSIT INSURANCE BE REFORMED?

Surveying this frightening situation, many observers are proposing to reform deposit insurance. The proposals include adjusting premiums to reflect the riskiness of insured institutions, encouraging private deposit insurers to compete with government insurance agencies, and restoring the distinction between insured and uninsured deposits while lowering the dollar limit on insured deposits.

Are any of these proposals likely to fix what is wrong with federal deposit insurance?

Consider first the proposal to adjust premiums to reflect the riskiness of the insured institution (Short and O'Driscoll 1983; Kane 1985).[6] If the insured party knew that taking additional risks would increase its insurance premiums by as much as those risks increased its expected losses, it would not take risks unless they promised to generate at least enough revenue to cover the increased premium.

Unfortunately, proposals to adjust premiums to reflect the riskiness of insured institutions will not realize the hopes of their proponents. There are two problems. First, there is the lack of full information. How is the insurance agency to acquire accurate information about the riskiness of a bank until it is too late? When a bank seems headed for insolvency, financial assistance to keep it from failing may seem more appropriate than a higher insurance premium to reflect the riskiness of prior decisions. Nor is it obvious which criteria to use to gauge the riskiness of a

5 Testimony before Congress quoted in Huertas (1986, pp. 14–15).
6 This proposal has been effectively criticized by Huertas (1986) and England (1985).

depository institution. Whatever the criteria are, there will always be a lag between the new risks that the institution is beginning to exploit and the risks that the insurer has learned to identify.

The second problem is that the deposit-insurance agencies are government monopolies. It would be naive to imagine that their pricing decisions would be made on strictly economic grounds. No government agency prices the goods or services it provides solely, or even primarily, on economic grounds. If the insurance agencies had discretion over premiums, political considerations would inevitably control their pricing decisions.

Would politicians from Texas resign themselves philosophically to the notion that, having lent heavily to energy producers and having contributed to the national goal of energy independence, Texas banks and thrifts should be penalized for their good works by being charged higher premiums than banks elsewhere in the United States? The question, of course, answers itself. There is excellent political, if not economic, sense behind the long-standing insistence by Congress that premiums for deposit insurance be uniform across all banks and all thrifts.

Would the entry of private deposit insurers improve matters, as some have argued (England 1985)? That question recalls the earlier question of what the basic goal of deposit insurance is. If it were to protect individual depositors against a default by the institution in which they hold deposits, then private deposit insurance would have an important role to play.

But I have argued that the protection of individual depositors is only incidental to the greater goal of preventing a collapse of the banking system. If I am right, then private deposit insurance cannot substitute for federal insurance. A private insurance scheme – say, fire insurance – works by pooling many independent risks. The insurer collects a small premium from each policyholder to cover the small risk of a fire. If the risks are correctly estimated and moral hazard does not encourage too many homeowners to torch their homes or fall sleep smoking cigarettes, the insurer can collect enough revenue to compensate the few whose homes do go up in flames. This is the normal case in which private insurance is possible.

But private insurance cannot work when the adverse events covered by insurers are heavily clustered. It would not be easy to find someone to insure your home against fire if there were a chance that in case of fire, the conflagration would keep spreading until it burned down every house in the country. The potential loss would be too great to be underwritten privately.

Private insurance, therefore, could not cope with the problem of a banking collapse. The losses would overwhelm it. If a loss of confidence in banks were widespread, private insurance could not eliminate, as does federal insurance, the incentive for depositors to redeem their deposits. The public would realize that private deposit insurance could not compensate their losses in case of a major banking panic, so there would still be an incentive to start runs on banks.[7]

Consider finally the proposals for again distinguishing between insured and uninsured deposits and lowering the dollar limit on insured deposits (Kane 1985; Huertas 1986). The aim is to protect small depositors who are supposedly the most likely to panic and trigger contagious bank runs. At the same time, the existence of large uninsured depositors would prevent banks from taking risks with impunity. And reducing the limit on insured deposits would nudge bank management further in the direction of risk aversion.

Unfortunately, my earlier discussion shows that the distinction between insured and uninsured deposits may not resolve the central dilemma of deposit insurance. All uninsured depositors are rationally disposed to demand redemption once they suspect that the institution in which they hold deposits may fail. If the insurance agency lets the institution fail, contagious runs are still possible. And if they are, deposit insurance is not performing its only defensible function: protecting the banking system against collapse. But if the insurers feel compelled to bail out banks to prevent uninsured depositors from bolting at the first sign of trouble, the formal distinction between insured and uninsured depositors is meaningless.

However, the large uninsured depositors who would withdraw deposits from banks they suspected might become insolvent would be unlikely to demand additional currency. They would be more likely to transfer their deposits to safe banks. Without an increased demand for currency, a run on some banks would not trigger a deflationary spiral that would cause a collapse of the banking system.

But although the nonbank public might not demand additional currency, the banks themselves, anticipating an increased likelihood of interbank transfers, might want to hold additional currency (reserves) to protect themselves against illiquidity. So although it would improve the incentives of banks to operate responsibly, restoring the distinction between insured and uninsured depositors would create some risk that contagious bank runs would recur.

Do the shortcomings of these proposed reforms mean that it is not possible to reform our banking institutions to make them both safe and

---

7 Actually, private insurance might work, if the insurer, realizing the potential for a contagious run, took upon itself to impose such strict standards (e.g., capital requirements) on insured banks that one of them could never fail. But competition among private insurers could be self-destructive, as it would operate to relax standards in order to get business.

competitive? Definitely not. For as I shall now argue, competition and financial innovation show us a way out of the current impasse in deposit insurance.

CAN WE DO WITHOUT DEPOSIT INSURANCE?

I shall come right out and say it. We could do very well without deposit insurance. I suspect that we always could have done so. We certainly could have if monetary policy had been able to stabilize the price level. But financial innovation is now making it far more likely than ever before that we could safely eliminate deposit insurance. That assertion, as I am about to show, would hold even in the worst-case scenario in which the government failed to increase the quantity of currency to keep the price level constant.

But without deposit insurance, what, besides a timely and sufficient expansion of the quantity of currency, would prevent bank runs from leading to deflation and financial collapse?

To understand the answer, recall that the two necessary conditions for a bank run are a loss of confidence in the solvency of the bank and the existence of fixed nominal claims that depositors are entitled to redeem on demand. What this means is that the most important financial innovation of the last decade – the money-market mutual fund (MMMF) – has introduced a run-proof monetary instrument. It is run-proof because a share owner, unlike a depositor, does not have a fixed nominal claim. Instead, he owns shares in the fund's portfolio of assets. As part owners of the fund's assets, shareholders have no incentive to start a run on their fund. What would they gain by doing so? Once depositors find out that the assets of a bank have depreciated, they may reasonably try to protect themselves against default by withdrawing their deposits. But MMMF shareholders hold no fixed claims on which the fund might default. If the value of the fund's assets falls, shareholders bear the loss instantaneously. Since shareholders can't save what they have already lost, they have far less incentive to cash in shares than depositors have to redeem deposits. And even if they do try to liquidate, doing so can't threaten the solvency of the fund because they can withdraw only their pro rata share of whatever is left in the fund.[8]

But the very characteristic that eliminates the possibility of a run on an MMMF – the absence of a fixed, nominal claim – creates a different kind of risk that holders of deposits do not bear. A depositor can ascertain at any moment the exact amount of his claim. The owner of a fund

---

8 Moreover, as the value of a fund of fixed-income securities falls, the anticipated yield of the fund must rise. Thus the incentive to hold shares actually increases as the value of the fund declines.

share bears no default risk,[9] but until the shares are liquidated, the owner of the shares cannot determine precisely how much they are worth.

In a competitive environment, both deposits and fund shares would probably be offered. But since MMMFs can minimize fluctuations in the value of their asset portfolios by holding only the most liquid short-term instruments, banks could not easily compete with funds if depositors were not guaranteed against the risk of default.

Banks do not have to provide that guarantee now because it is provided for them by federal deposit insurance. So the deposit-insurance subsidy gives deposits a competitive advantage over fund shares. But the advantage is hardly absolute. When MMMFs were generating yields over 10 percent and banks were prohibited from paying more than 5 1/2 percent interest on NOW accounts, deposit insurance could not offset the attractions of MMMF shares. A difference of 5 percent in expected returns was more than enough to induce the public to forsake insured deposits for fund shares in droves. The assets of MMMFs grew from $10 billion to over $240 billion between 1978 and 1982. Only when depository institutions were allowed to offer insured Super-NOW accounts and money-market deposit accounts paying competitive interest rates was the massive shift from deposits to MMMF shares halted.

The unfairness of giving a subsidy to one group of competitors while withholding it from another is patent. But that is a minor point. What is more disturbing is that deposit insurance subsidizes a potentially unstable form of money based on debt at the expense of an inherently stable form of money based on equity.[10] If anything, taxing socially risky deposits would make more sense than subsidizing them.[11] If there were no deposit insurance and if services like check clearing and electronic funds transfers were not denied to MMMFs,[12] banks would either offer their own equity accounts (which the Glass-Steagall Act now prohibits them from doing) or make their deposits as free from default risk as MMMFs are.

9 That is perhaps an overstatement, since the owner of an MMMF share does bear a tiny risk that the managers of the fund will commit fraud and steal the money belonging to the shareholders. Nevertheless, the risk of default is still much less for a mutual fund than for a bank; nor would such a failure be contagious.

10 Goodhart (1987b) argues that financial innovation is creating the possibility of an inherently more safe medium of exchange based on equity that in a competitive environment would replace traditional bank deposits. My argument differs only in suggesting that banks would respond by creating new kinds of deposits of similar safety.

11 Perhaps that might explain why deposits are subject to a reserve-requirement tax. But that hypothesis seems to be refuted by the exemption from any reserve requirements of money-market deposit accounts provided by banks and thrifts.

12 There is no reason these services could not be provided by the market instead of the Fed. But believing that it must control these services to ensure the safety of the payments system, the Fed discourages private competition in their provision.

How could they provide such a guarantee? The same way any debtor does: by building up enough capital to eliminate the risk of default, or by pledging collateral to secure redemption of the deposit.[13] To be acceptable to depositors, the collateral would have to be a liquid security with an active secondary market, for example, Treasury bills or commercial paper.

Before FDIC, banks used to compete for deposits by building up their capital. Yet because so many of the assets on their balance sheets were too illiquid to be acceptable to depositors as collateral, there was no competitive pressure on banks to guarantee that depositors could always redeem their deposits. But if there were no deposit insurance, the example of, and competition from, MMMFs would probably compel banks to collateralize their deposits. They would do so by accumulating enough highly liquid assets on their balance sheets to match the liabilities that were redeemable on demand. Those assets would be specifically pledged for the redemption of deposits. Other creditors of a bank would have no claim on those assets until obligations to depositors had been met.

Banks would, in effect, be creating their own money-market funds for depositors. Depositors could be viewed as shareholders in the funds. The difference between a simple fund and the deposit fund would be that the bank would be insuring depositors against fluctuation in the value of their shares. To provide that insurance, banks would have to hold a certain equity position within the fund from which to compensate depositors for any loss in the value of the portfolio. The cost of providing that insurance would be reflected in a slightly lower average yield on deposits than on ordinary MMMFs. Whether deposits continued to be held would depend on the cost of guaranteeing the value of a depositor's share in the fund and how large a return people would sacrifice in exchange for greater certainty.

A bank would undertake to maintain a fund backing its deposits and other sight obligations (such as banknotes if they were issued) whose value was always at least as great as the sum of those obligations. If the value of the collateral fund slipped below the total of its outstanding sight obligations, the bank would have to add securities to the fund, either by drawing on its existing capital or by raising additional capital from the market. If it did neither, the bank would be in default of its guarantee

13 This proposal is similar to ones put forward by Thomas Huertas (1986), Robert Litan (1987), and Kenneth Scott (1987). The difference lies in my contention that this system would evolve spontaneously without regulation and deposit insurance. Huertas, Litan, and Scott propose that banks offering deposits be legally restricted to holding only a very narrow subset of securities, such as T-bills, against which they would be allowed to create liabilities. Their proposal is to substitute one form of regulation for another. Mine is to eliminate it entirely.

to depositors and the fund would automatically become the property of the depositors. In that event, depositors would simply become shareholders in an MMMF, but the loss of depositors would be almost nil.

As financial markets continue to develop rapidly, the classes of assets that can be acceptable collateral keep expanding. Financial innovation is allowing an increasingly large share of once illiquid bank assets like mortgages and consumer loans to be bundled together and securitized. As they become securitized, and active markets develop, the securities will become eligible collateral for banks to hold against their deposits. Here is another example of how financial innovation can increase the safety of the banking system.

Historically, banks have performed two distinct functions. One was to provide a medium of exchange and to execute payments by appropriately crediting and debiting accounts; the other was to intermediate between savers and borrowers. Unfortunately, whenever banks ran into trouble in discharging their second function, their ability to discharge the first was also impaired. The result was often a financial crisis or collapse.

The belief that unsuccessful financial intermediation could undermine the integrity of the monetary system lay behind many past attempts to restrict the kinds of activities that banks could perform. Perhaps the most ambitious of these attempts has been the Glass-Steagall Act, which separates investment from commercial banking and prohibits banks from owning corporate stock. But the international integration of capital markets means that Glass-Steagall is, at most, a minor impediment to banks with foreign offices or subsidiaries that wish to engage in investment banking.

Without regulation and deposit insurance, however, a separation between the creation of sight liabilities (including, if it were permitted, the creation of banknotes) and other types of financial intermediation would occur spontaneously. The provision of monetary instruments would be carried out by self-contained units operating within larger financial institutions or completely independently. The monetary instruments would either be liabilities collateralized by, or shares in, a fund of highly liquid securities. All other forms of financial intermediation would be financed not by the creation of sight liabilities but by issuing debt or equity in the market.

So in the competitive banking and financial system of the future there would be no need to continue trying to enforce the rapidly eroding separation between commercial and investment banking or to restrict access to the payments system to chartered institutions that hold non-interest-bearing reserves with the Federal Reserve System. A whole array of inefficient and costly regulations designed to protect depositors or to keep the turf of particular financial institutions from being trespassed on by others could be scrapped.

ARE BANK RUNS WITHOUT DEPOSIT INSURANCE CONTAGIOUS?

I began the previous section by saying we could get along very well without deposit insurance. Have I made my case? In particular, would the competitive system I described be susceptible to the contagious bank runs and panics that deposit insurance was designed to eliminate?

I have already explained why MMMF shares are immune to runs. My conjecture, based on the popularity of MMMF shares providing only limited payments services, is that in a competitive system, most of the money balances created by financial intermediaries would be equity shares. Even deposits in a modern competitive system would be based on a fund principle. Could a run on institutions creating these deposits still occur? And if it did, could the nightmare of a banking collapse brought about by contagious runs ever come to pass?

I cannot see how it could. If depositors were unprotected by federal deposit insurance, and could hold shares in MMMFs providing a full array of payments services, they would hold deposits in banks or other financial intermediaries only if the deposits provided the equivalent of a share in an MMMF with a guarantee of fixed nominal value. In such a system contagious bank runs would be impossible.

However, until we actually eliminate deposit insurance and deregulate banks and other financial intermediaries, we can't be sure that banks would collateralize their deposits in the manner I have suggested. If banks did no more than increase their capitalization after federal deposit insurance was abolished, the banking system might still be vulnerable to panics and runs. So to keep that from happening, it might be advisable to impose double liability on stockholders of banks that did not collateralize their deposits.

But even if banks did not collateralize their deposits, depositors in shaky banks would have the option of switching their funds to MMMFs or to any banks that were collateralizing deposits. The run on some banks, therefore, would not necessarily raise the demand for currency. Only when bank failures cause the demand for currency to increase do they lead to deflation and a financial collapse.

Even if depositors were not increasing their demand for currency, however, it is still possible that banks might increase their demand for currency (I treat the demand for reserves as a demand for currency) because they perceived an increased likelihood of withdrawals or interbank transfers. But as I observed earlier, a necessary condition for a run is that depositors have fixed claims on the bank. It is the desire to realize their fixed claims before an anticipated insolvency that induces depositors to demand redemption. The absence of fixed claims is what immunizes money-market mutual funds from the risk of a run. If, therefore, a run ever got started and seemed to be out of control, because the stock of currency was not being increased rapidly enough to prevent a falling price level, it could easily be stopped by suspending the obligation of banks to redeem deposits at the stipulated rate.

When any single bank fails to honor its obligation to redeem its deposits, it instantly renders itself insolvent. It could not be otherwise, for only the knowledge that the failure of a bank to redeem its demand liabilities, for any reason, instantly renders the bank insolvent turns those obligations into virtually perfect substitutes for currency. So if its commitment to convert its sight obligations into currency is to have enough credibility for those obligations to serve as money, a bank cannot retain the discretion to renege on that commitment.

However, there have been two historical exceptions to that general principle. One is the so-called option clause that some of the Scottish banks adopted in the eighteenth and early nineteenth centuries. Condemned by Adam Smith (1776/1937, pp. 309–10), this clause gave banks the option of deferring redemption of their liabilities, along with accrued interest, into gold (though they would continue to clear checks) for six months. Rebutting Smith, Kevin Dowd (1987, 1989) has recently argued that reintroduction of the option clause would protect a banking system from contagious runs because sound banks faced with a panicky run could defer the demand for redemption for a time until they could demonstrate their solvency to worried depositors.

Before the Federal Reserve System was instituted, a different method of suspending the convertibility of deposits into currency was followed. The decision was made not by individual banks but by the banks in concert through their clearinghouses. The clearinghouses would even issue their own notes that would circulate in times of panic instead of the notes of individual banks (Friedman and Schwartz 1963, pp. 164–67; Timberlake 1984; Gorton 1985a, 1985b). By taking away depositors' incentives to demand redemption, the suspensions quickly ended the panics. During the suspensions, deposits of different banks exchanged at variable rates reflecting the market's estimate of the relative soundness of the banks. After several months of variable exchange rates among bank deposits, full convertibility at par was restored.

So to summarize: banking panics in a competitive system without deposit insurance could be prevented by the collateralization of deposits that would probably result if MMMFs were allowed to compete freely with banks and Glass-Steagall prohibitions were lifted. Collateralization could be further encouraged by imposing double liability on stockholders of banks that failed to collateralize. Even without collateralization, temporarily suspending the obligation to convert deposits into currency would prevent a panic from degenerating into a deflationary collapse of the banking system. Finally, the stability of the banking system could be maintained if enough currency were made available to keep the price level stable. In the final chapter of this book, I shall describe a monetary regime that would ensure a stable price level. If banking stability can indeed be maintained without deposit insurance, we have no reason to tolerate the insidious damage it is now inflicting on our financial system.

HOW TO GET OUT FROM UNDER DEPOSIT INSURANCE

In this chapter I have made two basic points. First, I have shown something that is already understood by experts in the field but is not yet widely appreciated by others: that the current system of deposit insurance is creating intolerable incentives for depository institutions, particularly those already in difficulty, to take on risks. The added risks are eating away at the foundations of our monetary system. The danger is not a wave of bank runs. Those can be avoided if Congress and the Fed supply enough money to bail out failed institutions or their depositors. The danger is that the bailouts necessary to avoid a collapse will impose an immense burden of future taxation and inflation or lead to a federal take-over of most of the country's financial institutions.

The second, more hopeful, point of the chapter is that financial innovation now offers the possibility of a truly safe monetary system without the dreadful burden of deposit insurance. Such a system would be preferable in every way to any monetary system with deposit insurance.

Unfortunately, it is not enough simply to recognize the superiority of a possible alternative to current arrangements. If the alternative is to have any practical value, it must also be possible to suggest how to get from where we are now to where we should like to be.

The condition of domestic banks and particularly domestic thrifts has deteriorated so badly over the past decade that many of them could not survive without the "goodwill" on their balance sheets generated by deposit-insurance guarantees. Removing deposit insurance now would leave the blood of a lot of domestic banks and thrifts – no one knows how many – on the floor.

Is there any way out of this mess? There undoubtedly is, but unless we are very lucky, it is too late to get out cheaply. Perhaps the first step ought to be requiring banks to carry assets on their balance sheets at market, rather than book, value. If banks had to carry assets on their balance sheets at market value, their true financial condition would be revealed. And it would also expose the present discounted value of the expected liability of the deposit-insurance agencies.

If Edward Kane is correct in estimating that the implied market value of that exposure may be as much as $150 billion, the agencies' reserves, even after the recent temporary congressional bailout of FSLIC, are not nearly enough to meet the claims that are going to be made against them. That is why the deposit-insurance agencies have, in effect, been selling exemptions from a variety of banking regulations, particularly those against interstate banking, to solvent depository institutions willing to take over insolvent ones. The practice, reminiscent of the selling of indulgences by the papacy during the Renaissance to finance its various wars and other projects, shows how bankrupt, in both a real and metaphoric sense, the current deposit-insurance system is.

The second step would be to set a terminal date for the federal deposit-insurance agencies and their coverage of deposits. The phase-out should not take more than ten years. In the interim deposits would continue to be insured up to the maximum legal limit, though it might be advisable to reduce the limit gradually to $40,000 per deposit during the phase-out period. The insurance agencies would be required to close any institution as soon as its non-equity liabilities exceeded the current market value of its assets. Insured depositors would receive cash reimbursement out of the insurance fund. The insurance agencies should be deprived of their authority to grant any concessions to induce sound institutions to take over failing ones. Congress would have to make the appropriations necessary to keep the insurance funds solvent. Step one would allow Congress to make long-term plans for these appropriations.

While deposit insurance is being phased out, money-market mutual funds should be provided full access to the check-clearing and electronic transfer services provided by the Fed. Those services, moreover, ought to be provided by private clearinghouses rather than the Fed. MMMFs ought not to be hindered in providing shareholders full check-writing privileges. Glass-Steagall restrictions on the provision of mutual funds by banks should also be eliminated.

At the same time, other regulations on banks and thrifts ought to be lifted gradually. As an inducement for depository institutions to increase their safety, they should be allowed to opt out of all regulations and deposit insurance as soon as they collateralize their deposits.

The main risk in the transition period would be the possibility that large legally uninsured depositors, realizing that their de facto coverage was being terminated, would begin withdrawing their deposits from shaky institutions and, thereby, precipitate their insolvency. However, the damage would be limited since large depositors would probably not demand currency but would instead transfer deposits from one institution to another.

The transition would not be easy. But it is not as if there were a low-cost, low-risk alternative. The course I recommend at least offers the promise of a competitive banking and financial system of far greater safety and stability than we ever had before.

CONCLUSION

In this chapter I have been concerned with showing how, without deposit insurance, a competitive banking and financial system could eliminate the risk of destructive bank runs. Except in pointing out that the monetary authority could counteract the destructive impact of bank runs by satisfying the public's demand for additional currency, I focused attention solely on the behavior of the banking system and deposit insurers.

However, one might well argue that the major cause of bank runs in the past has been unanticipated changes in the price level or in inflation. When the price level turns out to be substantially lower than it was expected to be, bank failures increase in frequency.

Thus price-level instability leads to banking instability as well as other forms of economic instability. The price level has been unstable both under the gold standard and under our present unbacked dollar standard. In the next two chapters, I discuss ways of constraining the discretion of the monetary authority through convertibility without tying the economy to the vagaries of any single commodity. Achieving price-level stability, I argue, would do more than anything else to dampen the vicissitudes of the business cycle and provide the stable environment people require before they take the long-run view necessary for generating economic growth.

IO

Why we need a new monetary regime

Old fetishes of so-called international bankers are being replaced by efforts to plan national currencies with the objective of giving to those currencies a continuing purchasing power which does not greatly vary in terms of the commodities and need of modern civilization. Let me be frank in saying that the United States seeks the kind of dollar which a generation hence will have the same purchasing and debt-paying power as the dollar value we hope to attain in the near future. That objective means more to the good of other nations than a fixed ratio for a month or two in terms of the pound or franc.

Franklin D. Roosevelt

President Roosevelt is magnificently right.

John Maynard Keynes

In preceding chapters, I worked out a theory of how a deregulated, competitive banking system would work. As I have described it, such a system would be both highly efficient and, contrary to the conventional view, highly stable. But if a competitive banking system would be so wonderful, why, one might ask, has free banking been so uncommon?

I began answering that question in Chapter 1 when I explained why the primitive state established a monopoly over money. It did so, I argued, not to provide better money than private issuers might have offered, but to appropriate a source of revenue vital to its sovereignty. Yet as I explained in subsequent chapters, a largely competitive, though not entirely free, banking system did evolve in the late eighteenth and nineteenth centuries. Despite that promising start, economists in the second half of the nineteenth century reverted to the quantity-theoretic explanation of prices articulated by David Hume – an explanation antithetical to competitive banking.

The quantity theory, in contrast to the classical theory of Adam Smith, implied that the amount of money supplied by banks had to be strictly limited. But since legal limits were extended only to the quantity of banknotes — not to the quantity of deposits — they did not constrain banks as much as they were meant to.

As I showed in Chapter 4, as long as deposits were not constrained, limiting the quantity of banknotes did not fundamentally alter the competitive character of the monetary system under the gold standard. All it did was to make it difficult for people to increase their holdings of banknotes when they tried to switch from deposits into banknotes.

Lacking an adequate theory of a competitive monetary system, economists and the public never fully understood why there were periodic monetary disturbances under the gold standard. There were two problems. First, restrictions on the creation of banknotes prevented banks from meeting large increases in the public's demand for notes, forcing the excess demand into the market for gold. Second, fluctuations in the demand for gold destabilized its value. An unstable value of gold implied an unstable price level, which, in turn, meant an unstable economy.

For most of the gold standard era, the problems were not terribly serious. It was only in the late 1920s, after the international community tried to restore a gold standard shattered by World War I, that instability of the price level proved unmanageable. Even without really understanding what had happened, people intuitively felt that the Great Depression was somehow linked to the gold standard. And so, within a few years, the gold standard in any meaningful sense was abandoned. The contagious bank failures that nearly destroyed their financial systems led governments to suppress, through regulation and deposit insurance, the competition that had been characteristic of banking under the gold standard.

Thus, after the depression, the state monopoly over money became an instrument of economic policy instead of a bulwark of sovereignty. Responding to political demands to ensure high employment, governments everywhere took responsibility for maintaining full employment, but with, at best, a qualified and unenforceable commitment to price stability.

The formidable tax-collecting powers of the modern state and the large standing armies and defense establishments now maintained even by third- and fourth-rate countries make the national defense argument for a state monopoly over money seem less persuasive now than it might have been formerly. If the connection between money and sovereignty has largely vanished, the case for state control of the banking system and the money supply now rests on two more conventional economic arguments: first, that competitive banking is inherently unstable and, second, that the business cycle cannot be avoided without an activist monetary policy.

In the last chapter, I showed how financial innovation has enabled us to immunize a competitive banking system against the threat of instability. So I have already disposed of the first argument for state control over the monetary system. But what about the second? Is an activist monetary policy really necessary to dampen the business cycle and avoid another Great Depression?

If we wanted to, we could combine a free banking system based on convertibility into a government fiat currency with an activist monetary policy. Yet as I have already suggested, increasingly competitive banking makes conducting an activist monetary policy more difficult than it used to be under a controlled banking system. Thus the point of this chapter will be that under either free or controlled banking, an activist monetary policy is inherently undesirable.

THE IDEA OF A MONETARY REGIME

To make the subsequent argument easier to follow, let me introduce the concept of a monetary regime.[1] A monetary regime can be thought of as a set of rules governing the objectives and the actions of the monetary authority. A gold standard is one example of a monetary regime – the monetary authority is obligated to maintain instant convertibility between its liabilities and gold. The monetary authority may have considerable room to maneuver in that monetary regime, but it can do nothing that would cause it to violate its commitment. The same remarks would apply to a monetary regime obligating the monetary authority to maintain a fixed exchange rate between its own and another currency. A monetary regime of a very different sort could be based on a Monetarist rule specifying the rate of growth of some monetary aggregate. The basic distinction is between regimes based on a convertibility or redemption principle and those based on a quantity principle.

Perhaps the most important issue at stake in selecting a monetary regime is what kinds of expectations people would form under the rules it prescribes. To be worth considering at all, a monetary regime must lead individuals to form expectations about future prices that are both stable and mutually compatible, and it must constrain the monetary authority to take actions that validate those expectations.

It is doubtful whether the monetary arrangements under which we now operate deserve to be called a monetary regime. Axel Leijonhufvud (1987, p. 129) best described those arrangements when he called them a random-walk monetary standard. The essential feature of current monetary arrangements is the absolute freedom of the monetary authorities from any commitment to a specific objective concerning either prices or quantities. We, in effect, tell the Board of Governors of the Federal Reserve

1 The concept of a monetary regime was introduced by such rational-expectations theorists as Robert Lucas (1976) and Thomas Sargent and Neil Wallace (1976). The argument of this chapter draws heavily on two papers by Axel Leijonhufvud (1975/1981, 1987).

System to do whatever they think best for the economy at any moment. Obviously they will prefer, other things equal, low inflation, high output, and high employment to high inflation, low output, and low employment. But other things never are equal, and there are at least temporary trade-offs among those objectives. So in practice, we have very little idea of what future path the Fed will choose for the price level.

Some economists (Tobin 1982; Blinder 1984) still regard the freedom of the Federal Reserve Board at all times to do whatever it thinks best as a good thing. Why, they ask, shouldn't the monetary authority be allowed to make the best use of all available information about the state of the economy and make decisions accordingly? Prescribing a rule, in their view, would simply prevent the monetary authority from making use of the information it has about the current state of the economy – information that the author of a rule governing monetary policy could never have had.

Unfortunately, that approach to monetary policy puts the rest of us, who are not making monetary policy but are trying to live with its consequences, at a bit of a disadvantage. Leijonhufvud (1987, p. 129) has cleverly explained the nature of that disadvantage:

In a memorable Peanuts cartoon of quite some years ago, Peppermint Patty was shown in school struggling with a True/False examination. Her efforts to divine the malicious intent of capricious authority went something like this: "Let's see, last time he had the first one False. So this time it should be True." "He wouldn't have just one False, after a single True. So: False, False." "OK, now we've got True, False, False, True . . . (and with a contented smile) Looks reasonable so far."

If this sounds vaguely familiar, it may be because you read the business and financial pages. "This quarter should be GO, because they want interest rates down before the election." "Next quarter will be STOP again, though, because otherwise we risk a revival of inflationary psychology." "Quarter after that is probably STOP too, but then it is bound to be GO because something will have to be done about unemployment." "So, now we've got GO, STOP, STOP, GO . . . Looks reasonable so far."

A monetary regime, if it is set up to achieve its minimal objectives, can at least eliminate that kind of uncertainty. Is the uncertainty created by the random-walk monetary standard a nuisance, or a fundamental problem?

HOW DISCRETION WORKS AGAINST US

The argument of those favoring an activist policy can be restated as follows. Discretionary policy is obviously better than a monetary regime bound by rules because a policy maker with discretion can always do what the rules would have called for when that would be the best policy.

But there will also be times when the policy maker will be able to conceive a policy superior to the one dictated by the rules. So it would seem that discretion allows the monetary authority to do at least as well as, and probably better than, any rule we could think of.

If that sounds a bit suspicious to you, don't worry: Like any argument that promises something for nothing (which is what the argument for discretion does), it is too good to be true. There are any number of homely little examples that illustrate why it is to good to be true. Here is one of them.

Suppose two parents are trying to train their child to go to sleep at the proper bedtime. The typical child, of course, does not want to go to sleep at the proper bedtime. So when Mom and Dad put little Billy to bed, Billy starts crying to get Mom or Dad to let him stay up a little bit longer. Now the rule is that Billy has to go to sleep and that Mom and Dad don't go into his room despite his outbursts. If the parents follow the rule, everyone, including Billy, is better off in the long run. But if Mom and Dad treat the decision to go back into Billy's room as discretionary, they will always go into the room and let him stay up longer – just this once – since Billy's crying is painful to them and to him. Thus everyone is better off tonight if Mom and Dad let Billy stay up past his bedtime. And unless their decision making is somehow constrained in advance, that is what they do. Billy is a bright young fellow, so the next night he will try the same ploy. And as long as Mom and Dad don't agree on a rule and stick to it, the result will be the same every night. And the longer Mom and Dad wait to adopt, and abide by, the rule, the harder and more painful it will be to get Billy to behave in accordance with it.

This insight is now described by economists as the time inconsistency of optimal plans (Kydland and Prescott 1977). Although economists formalized the concept only within the last ten years or so, jurists long ago expressed the same idea in the old dictum "hard cases make bad law."[2]

So it is disingenuous to suggest that a discretionary policy must be at least as good as any possible rule. It is not. Suppose everyone, including the monetary authority, agrees that monetary policy should aim at price stability and that inflation should be avoided. But suppose, too, that the monetary authority has full discretion to do whatever it thinks best for the economy at any moment. If monetary stimulus can increase employment in the short run, then the monetary authority may well find it optimal to provide that stimulus in every time period. It will appear that employment can be increased at the cost of a small increase in inflation, especially if the monetary authority insists that its current behavior is an

---

2 Jurists and legal scholars, it is well to point out, must grapple with the problem of the exercise of discretion by judges in applying general laws, statutory or common law, to specific cases.

exception. But when the next period arrives, the monetary authority will have a similar incentive to apply further monetary stimulus. So the sequence of optimal policies will be inconsistent with the price stability everyone prefers to the inflation generated by those seemingly optimal policies. But what is so bad about some extra inflation if it gives even a temporary stimulus to employment (Phelps 1972)?

THE PERILS OF DISCRETIONARY INFLATION

Economists don't have a very good model of inflation and its effects (Klein 1976; Fischer and Modigliani 1978; Fischer 1981; Leijonhufvud 1975/1981). Thus most economists have always felt uncomfortable with the popular hostility to inflation, because their own models of inflation could not seem to account for that hostility. If anything, the models seemed to rationalize the propensity of most political systems for inflation. Believing in a stable trade-off between inflation and unemployment, many economists used to argue that the benefits from reducing inflation were unlikely to justify the implied sacrifice of output and employment. A good way to embarrass an economist – particularly a Keynesian – was, therefore, to quote the following passage from Keynes's *Economic Consequences of the Peace* (1919/1971, pp. 148–49):

Lenin is said to have declared that the best way to destroy the Capitalist System was to debauch the currency. By a continuing process of inflation, Governments can confiscate, secretly and unobserved, an important part of the wealth of their citizens. By this method they not only confiscate, but they confiscate *arbitrarily;* and, while the process impoverishes many, it actually enriches some. The sight of this arbitrary rearrangement of riches strikes not only at the security, but at the confidence in the equity of the existing distribution of wealth. Those to whom the system brings windfalls beyond their deserts and even beyond their expectations or desires, become "profiteers," who are the object of the hatred of the bourgeoisie, whom the inflationism has impoverished, not less than the proletariat. As the inflation proceeds, and the real value of the currency fluctuates wildly from month to month, all permanent relations between debtors and creditors, which form the ultimate foundation of capitalism, become so utterly disordered as to be almost meaningless; and the process of wealth-getting degenerates into a gamble and a lottery.

Lenin was certainly right. There is no subtler, no surer means of overthrowing the existing basis of Society than to debauch the currency. The process engages all the hidden forces of economic law on the side of destruction, and it does it in a manner which not one man in a million is able to diagnose.

To many economists this diatribe seemed to be one of those unfortunate occasions on which Keynes's rhetorical powers overcame his good sense. In particular, there seemed to be no awareness of the distinction between an inflation that was and one that was not anticipated. If it were not anticipated, there would be arbitrary redistributions of wealth. But those redistributions would not make the economy any less efficient or productive. In the aggregate they would cancel each other out. And if inflation were anticipated, there would be no wealth redistributions because creditors would demand, and debtors would willingly pay, interest rates incorporating a premium for expected inflation. Expected inflation causes a waste of resources insofar as people undertake to buy and sell interest-bearing assets solely to avoid the tax that inflation levies on holding currency and other non-interest-bearing forms of money. But that inefficiency, according to most estimates, is quantitatively small.

But a few economists, most notably Fischer (1981), Klein (1976), and Leijonhufvud (1975/1981), have finally begun to make some progress toward an understanding of why inflation is destructive and why Keynes's impassioned rhetoric was based on more than mere prejudice. The key point is that the economist's model of perfectly anticipated inflation abstracts from much of what is essential about an inflationary environment. When economists dismiss the costs of inflation, they implicitly assume that everyone knows in advance what the rate of inflation and the price level are going to be indefinitely into the future. In that kind of environment inflation really is nothing more than an excise tax on holding cash, and the inefficiencies that result are the mild distortions created by any excise tax.

But to make that assumption is implicitly to assume a very special kind of monetary regime – a regime in which the monetary authority preselects a future path of the price level and communicates its selection with perfect credibility to the public. That does not sound much like the monetary system under which we have been operating. Thus, instead of focusing on just the rate of inflation, Leijonhufvud's analysis invites us to focus on the uncertainty about the future path of the price level caused by a monetary system that does not pin the price level down, and on the costs of that uncertainty.

In that kind of system, as Keynes correctly observed, arbitrary wealth redistributions and windfalls occur constantly. It is not as if people have a good idea about what the rate of inflation is going to be and simply make appropriate adjustments for it in nominal prices and interest rates. Instead of having well-defined expectations of the future price level, they can anticipate only a distribution of possible outcomes – a distribution that depends on political decisions as well as on the decisions of the monetary authority.

An uncertain monetary regime – a random-walk monetary standard – promotes two kinds of actions by people to protect themselves against, or to take advantage of, price-level uncertainty. One is participation in the political process to influence the choices the monetary authority makes about the price level. People who expect to receive substantial wealth transfers from others if there is inflation will try to influence the monetary authorities to follow an inflationary policy, while those who expect to lose to others if there is inflation will try to exert a contrary influence. The other action is to exploit price-level uncertainty by speculating on what the price level will be. And, of course, engaging in the second kind of action only increases the incentive to engage in the former.

The first type of activity makes for an increasingly politicized society. Participating in the political process is not free. But once one incurs the costs of doing so, by, for example, hiring a lobbyist to influence the choice of monetary policy, it becomes much less costly to begin lobbying for other political objectives as well.

However, as competition for wealth in the political process diverts resources from competition in the marketplace, the economy loses productivity and efficiency.[3] The financial and economic success of individuals and businesses will increasingly come to depend on their ability to manipulate the political process and to find loopholes in existing laws and regulations rather than on their ability to provide valuable services and make profitable real investments. The value of lobbyists, lawyers, and accountants will increase in relation to the value of engineers and scientists. Effort and resources will be diverted from productive, positive-sum activities that generate a net yield to society to unproductive, zero-sum activities that are merely redistributive and generate no net yield to society.

The random-walk monetary standard also encourages financial speculation. When the future path of the price level is uncertain, the future price paths of innumerable financial assets become uncertain as well. People can use these assets or derivative financial instruments like futures contracts and options as hedges against inflation. But where there are hedgers there are also speculators. Guessing right about the future price level when the range of possibilities is extremely wide can be extraordinarily profitable if one takes a financial position reflecting that guess.

Thus the random-walk monetary standard makes possible a whole field of speculative activity that would not exist under a monetary regime that pinned down the future path of the price level. The potential profits and losses generated by such speculative activity attract resources commensurate with those gains and losses. The small army of economists now employed to divine the future actions of the Federal Reserve Open Market Committee and thereby forecast the future path of the price level is only a part of the massive amount of financial research now undertaken in pursuit of the profit opportunities created by an uncertain price level.

It has become fashionable lately to decry the subordination of industry

---

3 See my discussion of the effects of different kinds of competition in chapter 1 of my book *Politics, Prices, and Petroleum* (Glasner 1985b).

to finance. Our best brains are said to be forsaking careers in science and industry for the lure of high salaries in the world of interest-rate options, leveraged buy-outs, program trading, and risk arbitrage. At least until October 1987, Wall Street was supposed to be booming even as our industrial base was rusting away. Some of these complaints simply reflect ignorance of how financial activity leads to real changes in the way resources and productive assets are used. Much of recent corporate take-over activity has shifted real corporate assets into more efficient and more highly valued uses. Those shifts in how assets are used help to generate the increases in stock prices that follow the take-overs. In such cases finance creates industrial efficiency and adds to the wealth of society.

However, the resources devoted to predicting the future rate of inflation generate little net yield to society. They mostly enable the better predictors to gain at the expense of the worse predictors. Total wealth, therefore, would be increased if the finance specialists, economists, and traders involved in intrinsically unproductive financial speculation were otherwise employed. A monetary regime that eliminated price-level uncertainty would do away with that unproductive employment.

The adverse impact of inflation is sometimes dismissed by those who argue that if it were a serious problem, there would be many more contracts indexed to inflation than are now being made. Indexed contracts allow people to avoid price-level uncertainty that they supposedly don't want. That argument ignores the costs of negotiating indexed contracts, which certainly are not negligible. Since, when the value of money is not stable, there is no single index that will automatically come into use in contracts, each party to a contract will have an incentive to select the index that he expects to be most advantageous. But the real reason that such contracts are not widespread is more fundamental. Uncertainty about the future path of the price level leads to divergent expectations about that path. People with differing expectations have an incentive to trade or capitalize on what they believe to be the errors of others.[4] Those who criticize the rise of "casino capitalism" in the 1980s (Strange 1986) would do well to focus their attention on the price-level uncertainty that has fueled the increase in financial speculation, rather than seeking to suppress the inevitable response of financial markets to that uncertainty.

Suppose you want to borrow $100 and you expect 10 percent inflation. If you sell an indexed bond with a real rate of 5 percent, you will expect to repay the borrower about $115 next year. However, if there are other people who expect less inflation than you, it will be in your interest to sell one of them a nonindexed bond. A lender expecting only 5 percent inflation and demanding a 5 percent real return would demand

---

4 I am indebted to Earl Thompson for this observation.

a repayment of only $110 in one year in exchange for $100 now. When the price level is uncertain and people making long-term commitments are already devoting substantial research to forecasting, they may view fixed nominal contracts as opportunities to outguess those who are less well informed about the future rate of inflation. Thus the absence of widespread voluntary indexing in no way supports an inference that the costs of price-level uncertainty are insubstantial.[5]

THE FUTILITY OF ACTIVIST MONETARY POLICY

Not only does an activist monetary policy undermine established social relationships and drive people to engage in redistributive rather than productive activities, it must ultimately dilute – and perhaps even destroy – its own effectiveness. In other words, the presupposition of an activist monetary policy is that people will not adjust their behavior in response to the policy choices of the monetary authority.

But the unfortunate lesson we learned in the late 1960s and 1970s, when Keynesian economists had convinced themselves and policy makers that the Phillips Curve embodied a stable trade-off between inflation and unemployment, is that people do adjust. In this view, policy makers could choose, as it were, from a menu of combinations of unemployment and inflation. A policy maker dedicated to full employment could always reduce unemployment by accepting a bit more inflation. Conversely, to get inflation down, the policy maker had to tolerate a higher rate of unemployment. How much inflation and unemployment we had would, in the end, be determined by the preferences of the monetary authority (Samuelson and Solow 1960).

But that trade-off between inflation and unemployment could be reliably exploited for only as long as the public was unaware of the policy the monetary authority was pursuing. Once policy makers tried to exploit it systematically, the public inevitably caught on.

Indeed, in a devastating criticism of activist economic policy, Robert Lucas (1976/1981) argued that standard techniques of forecasting the effects of changes in economic policy are useless. Every forecasting model, he observed, relies on the estimation of empirical relationships from past data which are presumed to remain constant over the relevant time horizon. However, those empirical relationships will generally not remain constant in the face of a change in policy. That is to say, the change in policy

5 To forestall any misunderstanding, let me emphasize that my criticism here is not of the speculative activity and the resources devoted to it but of my monetary conditions that make such activity worthwhile. Where the cause of the problem is obvious and correctable, there is no reason to treat symptoms that would not occur if we first removed the underlying causes.

must change some of the fundamental structural relationships of the fore-casting model. Previous estimates of those relationships are useless for forecasting the effects of a change in policy when the relationships themselves change along with the policy.

For example, the original estimates of the Phillips curve were based on observations of inflation and unemployment between 1861 and 1957. For over 70 percent of that period England was either on, or expected to rejoin, the gold standard. Obviously, estimates of empirical relationships based on those years, when there was no attempt to exploit a trade-off between inflation and unemployment, would reflect the expectations appropriate to such a monetary regime. But in a regime (or, better, non-regime) in which the authorities sought to exploit a trade-off between inflation and unemployment, estimates of the same empirical relationships would reflect much different expectations. One need not accept all the arguments of the rational-expectations movement of which Lucas is a leading figure to recognize how devastating his critique is to the operational basis of an activist monetary policy.

TWO MONETARY REGIMES WE SHOULD AVOID

Unfortunately, the negative case against an activist monetary policy and the random-walk monetary standard does not describe for us what a good monetary regime would be. I offer proposals for a good monetary regime in the next chapter. But before doing that, I must comment on the two most widely discussed proposals for establishing a monetary regime. One of these proposals, now identified with Milton Friedman, is actually the intellectual offspring of Peel's Bank Charter Act of 1844. It would legally obligate the monetary authority to maintain the rate of growth of a selected monetary aggregate within a prescribed range. The second proposal is to restore the gold standard.

In earlier chapters I discussed at length why trying to control the quantity of money and making money convertible into gold have not worked well in the past. The same considerations still apply. Let us first have a look at the monetary growth rule.

A Monetarist rule

In its present form, the monetary growth rule goes back to 1960, when Milton Friedman suggested it in his book on monetary reform, *A Program for Monetary Stability*. In the years since, Friedman has continued to advocate that rule with only slight modifications in the prescribed rate of growth and occasional wavering between applying the rule to M-1 or to M-2.[6] And most recently he has advocated simply freezing the monetary base (Friedman and Schwartz 1986).

Perhaps the most influential economist since Keynes, Friedman made the monetary growth rule the preferred option of most economists who have decided that the discretion of the monetary authority ought to be minimized. Since Friedman wanted and expected his rule to eliminate inflation, an obvious question is why he formulated his rule to control the quantity of money rather than to control the price level.

The reason for his choice was his belief that the price level is subject to too many random influences for the monetary authority to be able to control it in the short run. Thus simply instructing the monetary authority to keep the price level stable would allow the authority too much leeway in conducting monetary policy. Here is what Friedman said on the subject in *Capitalism and Freedom* (1962, p. 53):

> The rule that has most frequently been suggested by people of a liberal persuasion is a price level rule; namely, a legislative directive to the monetary authorities that they maintain a stable price level. I think this is the wrong kind of rule. It is the wrong kind of a rule because it is in terms of objectives that the monetary authorities do not have the clear and direct power to achieve by their own actions. It consequently raises the problem of dispersing responsibilities and leaving the authorities too much leeway. There is unquestionably a close connection between monetary actions and the price level. But the connection is not so close, so invariable, or so direct that the objective of achieving a stable price level is an appropriate guide to the day-to-day activities of the authorities.

Friedman's reasoning here is puzzling. He opposes letting the monetary authority have any discretion at all. Simply requiring it to achieve price-level stability would not, in his view, sufficiently constrain its actions. It would be left with too many degrees of freedom in pursuing that objective. But since the monetary authority has no direct coercive powers, it is not entirely clear why that offends, as it evidently does, Friedman's genuinely liberal sensibilities.[7]

So, instead, Friedman recommends obligating the monetary authority

---

6 M-1 and M-2 are different measures of the total money supply, M-1 including only checkable demand deposits and M-2 including savings and other time deposits.

7 It is ironic that, of all people, Milton Friedman should have been the leading advocate of dictating to the public the rate at which it was to be allowed to increase its holdings of money. Given Friedman's deep philosophical attachment to free markets and free trade, it is not easy to understand why, in this one instance, he advocated that the rate be determined not by the voluntary choices of the public and the banking system but by the monetary authority. The notion that banks and other financial intermediaries would produce an excessive quantity of money if left to their own devices, so that some statistical representation of a purely hypothetical construct – the total quantity of money – must be controlled by the monetary authority, presumes that someone knows better than the market what is and is not excessive. That is a presumption that goes against everything Friedman has ever said about the relative merits of the market and central authority as mechanisms for allocating resources.

to control the rate of growth of the stock of money. But the monetary authority does not directly control the stock of money any more than it directly controls the price level. In technical language, the monetary authority has targets and instruments. The price level is a target. Friedman disdains a rule specifying the target the monetary authority must aim at because it allows the monetary authority too much discretion over its choice of instruments. He therefore recommends targeting the stock of money. But something is obviously wrong here. If Friedman's objection to a rule for stabilizing the price level is that it doesn't sufficiently constrain the monetary authority's choice of instruments, why replace it with another rule that only specifies another target (the money stock) without constraining the monetary authority's choice of instruments?[8]

Since the quantity of money is not an instrument, but only a target, Friedman's preference for it as a target over the price level must reflect his theoretical presumption that the quantity of money produced by the banking system is a causal determinant of the price level. The quantity of money, in Friedman's view, is an intermediate target.

But a major point of this book has been to show that the quantity of money produced by a competitive banking system has no impact on the determination of prices. The quantity of money produced by banks, as I have been insisting from the outset, is determined by optimizing choices of the public and the banking system. The monetary authority can, of course, influence the equilibrium quantity of money demanded by the public and supplied by the banks. But it does so by first affecting the price level or interest rates and thereby affecting the public's demand for money or the banks' costs of supplying it. That means that the price level is really an intermediate target in relation to the quantity of money, not vice versa. Why bother trying to control the quantity of money when the price level is more directly under the control of the monetary authority than is the stock of money?

Friedman has in fact recently shifted his position and now favors freezing the monetary base. Evidently, after the Fed's failure to meet the monetary targets it set during its Monetarist phase from 1979 to 1982, he now believes that only if all discretion over the monetary base is eliminated can the Fed be forced to comply with a Monetarist rule. But although a rule specifying a rate of growth for the monetary base is logi-

---

8 Of course in Friedman's ideal world, banks would be required to hold 100 percent reserves against deposits, in which case the quantity of money would be entirely under the control of the monetary authority and would be thus both a target and an instrument. On the other hand, I have never understood why such a system, with its obvious restrictions on economic liberty, should be less offensive to Friedman's liberal principles than granting the monetary authority discretion in choosing *noncoercive* instruments to achieve a prescribed target.

cally more coherent than a rule specifying a growth rate for any other monetary aggregate, the former would still suffer from the same, if not even more serious, substantive defects as the latter. Such a rule was suggested as far back as the Napoleonic Wars, but David Ricardo, who is often considered an intellectual forefather of Friedman's, rejected it because he realized that a strict quantity rule could destabilize the market whenever there was an unusual demand for liquidity. "Depreciation cannot be effectually checked," Ricardo (1952a, pp. 67–68) wrote to George Tierney,

> by any other means than by depriving the Bank [of England] of the power which they at present possess of adding indefinitely to the amount of their notes. This might be done in a direct manner by limiting the amount beyond which their paper should be issued; but it has been plausibly urged against such a measure that occasions may arise in which sound policy may require a temporary augmentation of bank paper, and to deprive the Bank of the power of increasing their notes at such periods might be the cause of considerable distress and difficulty to the mercantile class.

As we saw in Chapter 4, the Bank Charter Act of 1844 deprived the bank of just this power and thereby caused precisely such distress and difficulty. Indeed, merely the fear that the upper limit on the note issue of the Bank of England would prevent it from providing needed liquidity to the market was sometimes enough to set off a panicky scramble for liquidity. The resulting panics could only be alleviated by temporary suspensions of the Bank Charter Act. Just the reassurance that the demand for liquidity could be met was enough, as Hawtrey (1932, p. 125) pointed out, to allay public fears of a credit crunch. And in the end, it wasn't even necessary for the bank to exceed the statutory limits on its note issue.

Here, by the way, is an excellent example of the Lucas critique I discussed earlier. Under a policy regime in which the quantity of notes was statutorily limited, the demand of the public for money was much different from what it was under a policy regime without such a statutory limitation. Even if Monetarist empirical estimates of the demand for money purporting to show its stability are accurate, they are of no relevance in judging the effect of adopting a Monetarist rule. Since they are estimates of the demand for money based on observations made when the quantity of money was not statutorily limited, they tell us nothing about how stable the demand for money would be if there were a Monetarist rule. Articulating the same insight, Charles Goodhart (1984, p. 96) has proposed the hypothesis, which has come to be known as Goodhart's Law, that any stable relationship between a monetary aggregate and national income will break down as soon as it becomes the object of a policy to stabilize that aggregate.

A competitive monetary regime

The lessons of the Monetarist experiment, 1979–1982

The danger lurking in any Monetarist rule has been perhaps best summarized by F. A. Hayek, who wrote (1978, p. 77):

As regards Professor Friedman's proposal of a legal limit on the rate at which a monopolistic issuer of money was to be allowed to increase the quantity in circulation, I can only say that I would not like to see what would happen if under such a provision it ever became known that the amount of cash in circulation was approaching the upper limit and therefore a need for increased liquidity could not be met.

Hayek's warnings were subsequently borne out after the Federal Reserve Board shifted its policy from targeting interest rates to targeting the monetary aggregates. The apparent shift toward a less inflationary monetary policy, reinforced by the election of a conservative, antiinflationary president in 1980, induced an international shift from other currencies into the dollar. That shift caused the dollar to appreciate by almost 30 percent against other major currencies.

At the same time the domestic demand for deposits was increasing as deregulation of the banking system reduced the cost of holding deposits. But instead of accommodating the increase in the foreign and domestic demands for dollars, the Fed tightened monetary policy. In 1981, M-1 actually grew slightly more slowly than in 1980. The deflationary impact of that tightening overwhelmed the fiscal stimulus of the tax cuts and defense buildup, which, many had predicted, would cause inflation to speed up. Instead, the economy fell into the deepest recession since the 1930s, while inflation, by 1982, was brought down to the lowest levels since the early 1960s. The contraction, which began in July 1981, accelerated in the fourth quarter of 1981 and the first quarter of 1982.

The rapid disinflation was bringing interest rates down from the record high levels of mid-1981 and the economy seemed to bottom out in the second quarter, showing a slight rise in real GNP over the first quarter. Sticking to its Monetarist strategy, the Fed reduced its targets for monetary growth in 1982 to between 2.5 and 5.5 percent. But in January and February, the money supply increased at a rapid rate, perhaps in anticipation of an incipient expansion. Whatever its cause, the early burst of the money supply pushed M-1 way over its target range.

For the next several months, as M-1 remained above its target, financial and commodity markets were preoccupied with what the Fed was going to do next. The fear that the Fed would tighten further to bring M-1 back within its target range reversed the slide in interest rates that began in the fall of 1981. A striking feature of the behavior of interest rates at that time was that credit markets seemed to be heavily influenced by the announcements every week of the change in M-1 during the previous week. Unexpectedly large increases in the money supply put upward pressure on interest rates.

The Monetarist explanation was that the announcements caused people to raise their expectations of inflation. But if the increases in interest rates had reflected a rising inflation premium, the announcements should have been associated with weakness in the dollar on foreign exchange markets and rising commodities prices. In fact, the dollar was rising and commodities prices were falling consistently throughout this period – even immediately after an unexpectedly large jump in M-1 was announced.

For example on April 1, 1982, the Dow Jones index of futures prices stood at 128.86, the Dow Jones index of spot prices stood at 123.84, and an SDR (Special Drawing Right) was worth $1.11309. But by June 18, after several weeks of large increases in the money supply, the indexes stood at 117.14 and 119.12 and an SDR had fallen to $1.09243. That the spot index had fallen below the futures index even though a futures price normally exceeds the spot price shows that deflationary, not inflationary, expectations had taken hold in commodities markets.

However, increases in M-1 during July turned out to be far smaller than anticipated, relieving some of the pressure on credit and commodities markets and allowing interest rates to begin to fall again. The decline in interest rates may have been eased slightly by Federal Reserve chairman Paul Volcker's statement to Congress on July 20 that monetary growth at the upper range of the Fed's targets would be acceptable. More important, he added that the Fed was willing to let M-1 remain above its target range for a while if the reason seemed to be a precautionary demand for liquidity.

By August, M-1 had actually fallen back within its target range. As fears of further tightening by the Fed subsided, the stage was set for the decline in interest rates to accelerate. As the decline quickened, the great stock market rally began on August 17, when the Dow Jones Industrial Average rose over 38 points. Commodities prices began to recover, the normal premium of futures prices over spot prices was restored, and the rise of the dollar was temporarily halted.

But anticipations of an incipient recovery again fed monetary growth. From the middle of August through the end of September, M-1 grew at an annual rate of over 15 percent. Fears that rapid money growth would induce the Fed to tighten monetary policy slowed down the decline in interest rates and led to renewed declines in commodities prices and the stock market, while pushing up the dollar to new highs. On October 5, for example, the *Wall Street Journal* reported that bond prices had fallen amid fears that the Fed might tighten credit conditions to slow the recent strong growth of the money supply. But on the very next day it was reported that the Fed expected inflation to stay low and would therefore allow M-1 to exceed its targets. The report sparked a major decline in interest rates and the Dow Jones Industrial Average soared another 37 points.

Once fears that the Fed would keep money tight to meet its targets were dispelled, a general economic recovery soon got under way. The bottom of the recession seems to have occurred in November 1982, and the economy recorded a mild expansion in the first quarter of 1983. The recovery continued with surprising strength throughout 1983 and the first two quarters of 1984. In 1983, M-1 far exceeded the target range of between 4 and 8 percent annual growth the Fed had set for it. In the first half, although M-1 grew at a 14.5 percent annual rate, interest rates, commodity prices, and exchange rates remained stable. But because of its concern that M-1 was growing too rapidly, the Fed, using the second-quarter money supply as a base, set a new target of between 5 and 9 percent for the growth of M-1 in the second half.

The renewed monetary stringency forced interest rates to rise slightly while driving the dollar ever higher and commodities prices ever lower. Yet the recovery, once under way, was too powerful to be slowed down perceptibly by the monetary pressure. In the event, although the growth of M-1 for the year was above the 9 percent upper range for the year, the 3.7 percent growth rate in the second half was below the lower range for the second half.

The recovery continued in the first half of 1984. But the amazing strength of the recovery pulled the growth of M-1 above its targets, reviving fears that the Fed would have to tighten. Instead of being welcomed, each bit of favorable economic news – strong growth in real GNP, reduced unemployment, higher factory orders – was greeted with fear and trepidation in the financial markets, because such reports were viewed as portents of future tightening by the Fed. Those fears generated continuing increases in interest rates, appreciation of the dollar, and falling commodities prices. In the summer of 1984, monetary stringency and fears that the Fed would clamp down even more tightly to bring the growth of M-1 back within its targets were threatening to produce a credit crunch and abort the recovery.

With interest rates and the dollar's exchange rate again starting to rise rapidly, and with commodity prices losing the modest gains they had made in the previous year, the recovery was indeed threatened. In late July of 1984, two years after the Fed had given up its earlier effort to meet its monetary targets, the conditions for a credit crunch, if not a full-scale panic, were again developing. The most widely reported monetary aggregate, M-1, was above the upper limit of the Fed's growth target, and economic growth in the second quarter of 1984 was reported to have been an unexpectedly strong 7.5 percent. Commodities prices were practically in free fall and the dollar was soaring.

Once again, however, a timely intervention by Mr. Volcker calmed the markets and put to rest fears that the Fed would strive to keep monetary growth within announced target ranges. Appearing before Congress, he announced that he expected inflation to remain low and that the Fed would maintain its policy without seeking any further tightening to bring monetary growth within the target range. This assurance stopped, at least for a brief spell, the dollar's rise in foreign exchange markets and permitted a slight rebound in commodities prices. Mr. Volcker's assurance that monetary policy would not be tightened encouraged the public to stop trying to build up precautionary balances. As a consequence, M-1 growth leveled off even as interest rates fell back somewhat.

All the while Monetarists were loudly protesting the conduct of monetary policy. Before the Fed abandoned its attempt to target M-1, Monetarists criticized the Fed for not keeping monetary growth steady enough. For a time, they even attributed the failure of interest rates to fall as rapidly as the rate of inflation in 1981, or to fall at all in the first half of 1982, to uncertainty created by too much variability in the rate of monetary growth. Later, when the Fed abandoned, or at any rate deemphasized, monetary targets, they warned that inflation would soon start to rise again. In late 1982, just as the economy was hitting bottom, Milton Friedman was predicting the return of double-digit inflation before the next election. Yet inflation, by any measure, has remained at remarkably low levels despite rates of monetary growth that exceeded those of the previous decade.

In retrospect, Monetarists attribute low inflation in the face of rapid monetary growth to a change in inflationary expectations that has increased the demand for money and to financial innovation. Yet at the time, Monetarists dismissed such arguments for allowing monetary growth to exceed the targets. For the Fed to have kept monetary growth in the 1980s within the Monetarist targets would have been the worst policy mistake since the Fed stubbornly maintained its tight monetary policy between 1929 and 1933 even as the international economy and financial system was collapsing.[9]

9 An alternative rule that a number of Monetarists, recognizing the instability of the demand for money, have come to embrace is to target nominal GNP (McCallum 1984). This rule has much to recommend it; however, in practice it would be very difficult to implement, since quarterly information on GNP is not available for up to a month after the end of the previous quarter. Moreover, revisions in GNP estimates are commonplace, so it would be very difficult to know how well the monetary authorities were performing and it would be difficult for the authorities to know on what information they should

A competitive monetary regime

WHY THE GOLD STANDARD IS NOT AN OPTION

Recognizing the shortcomings of a Monetarist rule as a device for achieving price stability, some economists, such as Arthur Laffer and Charles Kadlec (1981), Robert Mundell (1981), and Alan Reynolds (1983, 1984), and even some prominent conservative politicians have proposed restoring the gold standard. Supporters of the gold standard were influential enough with President Reagan and Congress to have brought about the appointment of a commission to study the role of gold in the U.S. monetary system (U.S. Gold Commission 1982). They also were able to insert a plank in the 1984 Republican platform urging that restoration of a gold standard be given serious consideration.

Its supporters argue that a gold standard has some important attractions. First, it is conceptually simple. A gold standard is established by maintaining convertibility between currency and a fixed weight of gold at a stipulated conversion rate. As long as convertibility is maintained, the gold standard is in operation. Second, gold has always had a mystique that generated support for the notion of making the dollar or pound or some other currency as good as gold. That mystique has undoubtedly eroded over the years, but its vestiges may still be present. An emotional attachment to a monetary standard would help to sustain public support for the short-term sacrifices that are occasionally needed to keep a monetary regime credible. Third, the gold standard has historically provided greater protection against inflation than managed paper currencies have provided. Finally, its supporters insist, a gold standard eliminates any need for monetary targeting while still imposing a constraint on the actions of the monetary authority.

Of these suggested advantages, only the first and possibly the second are both true and relevant. The contention that the gold standard provided greater price stability than we have had under managed paper currencies is certainly true if we don't count the Great Depression of 1929–33. But that episode is the most relevant one for us in considering whether to reestablish the gold standard because it shows the risks inherent in an attempt to reintroduce the gold standard after its abandonment for even a short time, much less a half century.

That episode also casts doubt on the fourth supposed advantage of the gold standard – that it would eliminate the need for monetary targeting while constraining the actions of the monetary authority. In fact, the Great Depression shows that discretionary management by the monetary authorities is as necessary under the gold standard as it is under a pure

base their decisions. That is why it is preferable to develop a system that provides some direct feedback to the monetary authority from the public through a kind of convertibility arrangement, as I propose in the next chapter.

fiat system. With the vast majority of the world's gold stocks in their hands, the world's central banks have the power, by their collective decisions, to make the value of gold just about whatever they choose. A true international gold standard, to be sure, would link all national currencies on the gold standard, but the common purchasing power of those currencies would be determined by the decisions of the various national monetary authorities. In particular, with much the largest holdings of gold, the U.S. monetary authorities would be able to control the world price level.

Advocates of the gold standard usually suggest that the dollar-gold parity be set at around $400 an ounce, which is near the current (as of December 1988) price of $420 an ounce. No one can predict how reestablishing a link between the dollar and gold would affect the world's demand for gold. So there is no guarantee that linking the dollar with gold at the current price would not have major repercussions on the general price level.

If the monetary authorities were willing to allow their gold stocks to increase or decrease indefinitely while maintaining the $400-an-ounce price, they could prevent any major changes in the price level from occurring. But that is precisely what they were unwilling to do in the past. For some reason, countries don't seem to be willing to allow substantial reductions in their gold reserves if that is what is needed to stabilize the gold market. By instead attempting to maintain their gold hoards, they force the public to begin bidding down the prices of everything else as people offer other goods in the market to acquire more gold. That is the deflationary scenario that unfolded so tragically in the Great Depression. And a similar inflationary scenario would also be possible, though probably less likely, if after convertibility had been reestablished there were a reduction in the international demand for gold.

As Keynes, Hawtrey, and Robertson recognized over sixty years ago, the huge quantities of gold reserves that accumulated in central bank coffers in the nineteenth century made the gold standard a managed system. Unless central banks properly managed their reserves of gold, the value of gold – and hence the value of money – was subject to enormous variation. The debacle of the Great Depression proved how right Keynes was in 1923. It is unfortunate that he never realized that he had diagnosed the cause of the depression six years before it took place. Had he done so, he need never have made his brilliantly muddled attempt to revolutionize economic theory.

Some advocates of the gold standard take it as a virtue of the system that it would build up enormous stocks of gold in the coffers of the various national monetary authorities (Lehrman 1985). Yet the resources engaged in extracting the otherwise useless reserves from the ground would be entirely wasted. Moreover, that monetary demand for gold would constitute an implicit subsidy to the two largest gold producers in the world, South Africa and the Soviet Union. Most disturbing of all, the further accumulation of indestructible, inextinguishable gold reserves would create an ever-larger overhang of gold that would constantly threaten to destabilize the world economy if those reserves were not properly managed by the monetary authorities that were holding them.

Some of the older advocates of the gold standard used to concede frankly that the gold standard could not possibly guarantee perfect price stability. Yet they believed that the risks of trusting a discretionary monetary authority to manage the currency were so great that it was safer to tolerate the vagaries of the gold market than the whims of the monetary authorities. Whether it was ever true that the value of gold was independent of the actions of the monetary authorities,[10] it was certainly no longer true by the beginning of the twentieth century. Until the gold standard broke down, there was a powerful argument for not trying to replace it with something new and untried. Even resurrecting it after the war might have worked had policy makers understood that with their enormous hoards of gold, it was they who had the responsibility for determining its value. It certainly was not gold that was determining the value of their currencies. Without such understanding, disaster could not be avoided.

But under the circumstances, the mistake, however tragic, was understandable. To contemplate repeating the same mistake again, when the task is not even one of restoring a gold standard that has lapsed for a few years, but one of recreating it after fifty years, would not be a mistake – it would be folly.

THE PROBLEM WITH A TOTALLY PRIVATE MONETARY REGIME

Since my argument throughout this book has been that the free market is a more efficient supplier of money than the government, it might be expected that I should follow F. A. Hayek and other advocates of completely free banking in proposing that the character of our monetary regime be left entirely to the choices of competing private suppliers. But for reasons I made clear in Chapter 8, I believe that there is an important, though narrowly circumscribed, role for the government to play in a

---

10 Evidently Ricardo did not think so in 1819, since he castigated the Bank of England for accumulating an excessive amount of gold when England restored the gold standard after the Napoleonic Wars and thereby driving up the price of gold. Now it may be that the large gold discoveries in the middle of the nineteenth century reduced the Bank of England's share of the gold market enough to have limited its subsequent influence on the value of gold, but eventually other countries, particularly the United States, accumulated so much gold that its value became a variable subject to central-bank control.

monetary system. The logic is simple. A private supplier of money would have an incentive to provide holders of its money with competitive interest. It could provide that interest no matter what path the price level expressed in terms of its money actually followed. Holders of money, therefore, would be indifferent about alternative paths of the price level because competitive interest payments would equalize the real returns under all possible paths.

But although money holders would be indifferent about alternative price-level paths, there are benefits that would accrue to all potential transactors if the future path of the price level could be pinned down in advance. Since the benefits from eliminating price-level uncertainty would not hinge on the size of cash holdings, private money suppliers would not have the appropriate incentive to choose fully predictable price-level paths. They would simply be committed to paying competitive interest on their moneys.

Thus private money suppliers would simply offer to create money denominated in an existing monetary unit, whatever it might be. And if governments ceased defining their own monetary units, banks would offer to create moneys denominated in terms of some real commodity – quite possibly gold. But as I have been arguing, there is little reason to expect that the value of gold would follow a highly predictable path over time. That is why there is a very powerful case for having the government commit itself to creating a monetary unit that would have a highly predictable future value in terms of which private money suppliers could freely create their own monetary instruments.

CONCLUSION

The tone of this chapter, I fear, has been highly critical, if not destructive. I began by explaining the limitations on the ability of an activist economic policy to improve economic performance. At the same time, I pointed out that the absence of a rule constraining an activist economic policy poses a conflict between illusory short-term benefits and the achievement of long-term stability. The absence of long-term stability implies a deterioration of economic performance as people undertake costly measures to cope with the potentially avoidable uncertainty imposed on them by monetary policy.

But what sort of constraint can we impose on monetary policy? I argued not only that the Monetarist rule for a constant rate of growth of some measure of the money stock is unrealizable in practice but that the very attempt to pursue it can be seriously destabilizing. I then considered an alternative rule for monetary policy – the gold standard – and argued that, given the size of the available monetary gold reserves, it would impose no effective constraint on the behavior of the monetary authorities. Moreover, the failure of monetary authorities to realize the extent of their control of the price level under a gold standard would create an unacceptable potential for instability.

So if activist, unconstrained monetary policy is costly and destabilizing and the most widely discussed rules for constraining monetary policy are also destabilizing, must we throw up our hands in despair? I think not. For as I argue in the next chapter, there is an approach, based on ideas developed early in this century, that can constrain the monetary authority, eliminate avoidable uncertainty, and provide a stable environment for productive economic activity.

I I

A proposal for monetary reform

Another plan is a convertible paper currency, the paper to be redeemable on demand, – not in any required weight or coin of gold,
but in a required purchasing power thereof. Under such a plan, the
paper money would be redeemed by as much gold as as would have
the required purchasing power. Thus, the amount of gold obtainable
for a paper dollar would vary inversely with its purchasing power per
ounce as compared with commodities, the total purchasing power of
the dollar always being the same. The fact that a paper dollar would
always be redeemable in terms of purchasing power would theoretically keep the level of prices invariable.

Irving Fisher, *The Purchasing Power of Money*

The goal of monetary reform based on free banking poses a dilemma.
On the one hand, the free market could provide us with a highly efficient,
low-cost medium of exchange. But on the other hand, purely free-market
moneys could not protect everyone from the costs of price-level uncertainty. Free-market moneys would minimize the costs of holding money,
but they would not necessarily minimize the more general costs of price-
level uncertainty. Those costs would still be borne by workers, employers, borrowers, lenders – indeed, by everyone who contemplates entering
into commitments for the future exchange of values expressed in nominal
terms.

In the previous chapter I argued that to eliminate price-level uncertainty, we need a monetary regime dedicated to that objective. I considered and concluded, on historical as well as theoretical grounds, that
the two best-known proposals for eliminating price-level uncertainty would
actually contribute to, not minimize, that uncertainty. In particular, both
would increase the dangers of a rapid decline in the price level (the most
dangerous form of price-level instability).

So it may be that all we can realistically hope to do is to create a
monetary regime in which the monetary authority would be legally obligated to keep the price level constant over time. That may not seem like

much of a change, since it is not obvious how such an obligation could be enforced. But the Federal Reserve Board and monetary authorities elsewhere are not now even instructed to pursue price-level stability as their primary objective. The monetary authorities are now understood to have, and are encouraged to exercise, discretion in their choice of targets as well as instruments. They are constrained only by their own views of what is best for the economy and the political pressures that can be brought to bear on their decisions. So prescribing a price-level target which the monetary authority would always be obligated to aim for, and to which all other targets would be subordinated, would be a considerable improvement over current arrangements. A commitment to stable prices in terms of which the monetary authority would be expected to explain and justify its choices of instruments would greatly reduce the uncertainty, if not the mystery, that now envelops the actions of the monetary authorities and the future path of the price level.

Although this is not the place to make the argument in detail, one could make a strong case that it was confusion about the objectives of monetary policy that helped cause the stock market crash of October 1987.[1] That confusion was caused by increasing fears in 1987 that the Fed, especially after the departure of Paul Volcker and his replacement by a prominent Republican economist, Alan Greenspan, might become more amenable to an inflationary policy calculated to improve Republican electoral chances by depressing the dollar in foreign-exchange markets, improving the United States' trade balance, and defusing protectionist pressures in Congress.[2] The fear of rising inflation was reflected not only in rising interest rates but in a steepening yield curve.

With inflationary expectations pushing up interest rates, Mr. Greenspan was caught in an uncomfortable position. To try to reduce interest rates by loosening monetary policy might simply confirm suspicions that he was seeking to depress the dollar even further. That would only push interest rates even higher. Yet to establish his antiinflationary credentials by tightening monetary policy might also raise short-term interest rates and jeopardize the economic expansion. Here we have a remarkable example of how a lack of constraint on monetary policy self-destructively drains the monetary authority of its ability to influence the real economy in a beneficial way.

Despite the unsettled state of financial markets, expectations of further economic growth and rising earnings fueled a continuing stock market

---

1 I owe much of the argument in the next several paragraphs about the causes of the crash of 1987 to Earl Thompson. In addition, much of the chapter has been inspired by his 1981 and 1986 papers advocating a labor standard.

2 Indeed, that is just what happened the last time a Republican president, Richard Nixon, appointed a Republican economist, Arthur F. Burns, as chairman of the Fed.

boom in early 1987. Yet the anomalous divergence between rapidly rising stock prices and falling bond prices in the first half of 1987 only added to financial instability. Those who attributed rising nominal interest rates not to inflationary expectations but to rising real rates (perhaps caused by a persistent budget deficit) must have regarded the surge in the market as unsustainable. And even some of those who correctly perceived the rise in interest rates as an indication of rising inflation expectations may have viewed the prospect of inflation as unfavorable to future earnings. Thus opinions about the direction of stock prices were diverging, not converging, in the months before the crash. That divergence created increasing volatility in prices and rising trading volumes.

When stock prices began to fall after peaking in August while trading volumes rose, technicians became increasingly bearish. Finally, the convergence in early October of evidence of a weakening Reagan presidency, an increasing likelihood of protectionist legislation owing to that weakness and to the persistent trade deficit, statements by Alan Greenspan welcoming a further 30 percent reduction in the dollar's exchange rate, Treasury Secretary James Baker's threat to allow the dollar to fall further if Germany did not relax its economic policy, and bad news from the Persian Gulf, sparked a sell-off that began on Wednesday, October 14, and culminated on Black Monday, October 19.

Unlike the crash of October 1929, this one was not produced by a deliberate policy of deflation by the Fed and other major central banks. Favorable underlying economic conditions and assurances by the Fed that it would provide adequate liquidity have therefore allowed the economic expansion to continue and the stock market to recover much of its losses. Nevertheless, the crash shows the dangers to which an inherently uncertain monetary environment exposes the entire economy.

As an increasingly competitive monetary system continues to blur the distinctions between monetary and nonmonetary instruments, the demand for currency is inevitably becoming more and more unstable. So even as the governors of the Federal Reserve Board monetary authorities seem on their own to be assigning more weight than they once did to keeping the price level stable (W. Angell 1987), they are finding it increasingly difficult to do so by traditional means. That makes it more urgent than ever for monetary theorists to devise a set of arrangements that will keep the price level stable automatically so that we no longer have to rely on the fallible judgment of the monetary authorities.

In contemplating this problem, monetary theorists would do well to revisit the discussions of price-level stability that took place early in this century. Those discussions produced a consensus of sorts among leading monetary theorists that price-level stabilization ought to be the overriding objective of monetary policy. Indeed, all through the 1920s, John

Maynard Keynes was an eloquent advocate of that objective for monetary policy. Unfortunately, that emerging consensus was undone by the Great Depression and the Keynesian revolution it ushered in. But whereas Keynes and most of the other advocates of price-level stabilization believed that the monetary authorities, properly guided by expert economic advice, could achieve that goal if it was their objective, Irving Fisher attempted to devise a plan that would automatically guarantee a stable price level.[3]

Ironically, after presenting the plan in two books (Fisher 1911/1985, 1920), Fisher was so impressed by the performance of the Federal Reserve Board in keeping prices stable throughout most of the 1920s that, by 1928, he concluded that his plan was no longer necessary. And also ironically, the effect of the Great Depression on Fisher, as on Keynes, was not to confirm his earlier support of a plan for maintaining stable prices but to lead him to propose an entirely new policy – 100 percent reserve banking (Fisher 1935). Yet Fisher's original proposal is worth contemplating. We ought to take it seriously not because it is an ideal plan but because it focuses on just the right issue, constructing a mechanism that will automatically achieve stable prices without having to rely on the discretionary judgment of the monetary authorities.

STABILIZING THE PRICE LEVEL VIA INDIRECT CONVERTIBILITY

There are only two ways of controlling the value of money. One is for the issuer to commit itself to redeem its money for a stipulated amount of some other valuable asset. Private issuers of money have no choice but to take that approach. That is why banks have always promised to redeem their moneys. Currently they promise redemption of their liabilities at par in government currency. But the principle is the same as when they promised redemption in gold or silver coins or in a stipulated weight of gold or silver. Governments, too, have used this method to control the value of their money – the gold standard being the most notable such example.

The other method of controlling the value of money is to control its nominal quantity without making the money redeemable for anything else. Only governments can take advantage of this approach. Without a commitment to redeem, a private issuer has no way of imparting value to its money. But owing to their ability to force a demand for their currencies on the public by legal restrictions and by making them acceptable in payment of taxes, governments can make their currencies substantially

---

3 Fisher, in turn, was probably influenced by a similar proposal made over a century ago by Simon Newcomb (1879).

more valuable than the materials of which they are made. How much more than their material value the currencies are worth depends on how many currency units the governments choose to create. So if the value of an inconvertible currency is to be kept stable, its quantity must be constantly adjusted to compensate for shifts in demand. But the more competitive the monetary environment becomes, the less likely it is that the monetary authority will be capable of making the quantity adjustments necessary to keep the price level stable. That is why pinning down the value of money, as Fisher proposed, by some variation of the redemption principle seems preferable to trying to stabilize the price level by discretionary changes in the quantity of currency.

The obvious problem with using the redemption principle to pin down the value of the monetary unit is that there is no asset – certainly not gold – with a reliably stable value in which to make the unit redeemable. But that problem need not be insuperable. For instead of making the currency unit redeemable for a specified amount of gold, we could make it redeemable for a constant purchasing power.

How could a currency unit be redeemable for a constant purchasing power? To get the principle down, let's look at an ideal case: If the value of the dollar were stabilized in terms of a market basket of commodities traded in organized commodities exchanges, the value of the ideal standard market basket at current prices could be continuously monitored. Stabilizing the value of the basket would mean that although the relative prices of individual commodities could fluctuate freely, the aggregate of commodities in the basket could always be purchased for a constant number of dollars.

The first step would be to compute the value of the market basket at current prices. Suppose the market basket was worth $1,000. One way to keep the value of the market basket at $1,000 would be to offer always to accept or to make delivery of the entire basket in exchange for $1,000. That commitment would be very costly since it would require the government and anyone who wanted to redeem dollars to deliver or to hold an unwieldy basket of commodities. But there would be a simpler way of redeeming dollars for the market basket than actually transferring the basket itself. That would be to redeem $1,000 into whatever quantity of gold had the same market value as the market basket.

Suppose that initially, when the basket was worth exactly $1,000, the market price of gold was $400 an ounce. Then, instead of cashing in $1,000 at the Treasury for the commodities in the standard market basket, one could simply exchange the $1,000 for 2 1/2 ounces of gold. Or, instead of delivering the basket to the Treasury for $1,000, one could simply deliver 2 1/2 ounces of gold.

Would such an arrangement really ensure that $1,000 could always be exchanged for the standard basket and vice versa? Consider what would happen if the value of the basket rose to $1,100. Anyone could then take $1,000 to the Treasury and demand to receive $1,100 worth of gold in return. At $400 an ounce, that would be 2 3/4 ounces of gold (an effective price of $363.36 an ounce). Seeking to profit from such arbitrage transactions, holders of commodities would liquidate their stocks in order to obtain the currency to turn in for redemption. Inventory liquidation and a currency drain would operate to force down the value of the standard basket. The process would continue until the value of the market basket had fallen to $1,000. The mechanism at work here is no different from the one which ensures that the value of the underlying basket of stocks equals the value of a stock index futures contract when the contract expires.

So if all we were trying to do was to stabilize the value of a basket of commodities traded in organized exchanges, it is easy to see that indirect convertibility would work splendidly. Continuous arbitrage would prevent the market value of the basket from deviating from its guaranteed target value. But stabilizing such an index is not really what we want to do if we are serious about stabilizing the value of our monetary unit. What we really want is to stabilize a much broader index of prices. The commodities that are traded in organized exchanges are too narrow a subset of commodities in general for us to assume that by stabilizing their value we should be stabilizing the value of money in a meaningful sense.

But stabilizing a comprehensive index of prices is far more difficult than stabilizing the value of a basket of publicly traded commodities. The commodities included in broad price indexes are not traded in organized exchanges, so their prices are not continuously reported. Finding out what they are requires a costly survey of buyers and sellers. Any comprehensive price index can thus only be reported intermittently. The most familiar of these broad indexes, the Consumer Price Index and the Producer Price Index, are reported only once a month. And the value of the index is not known until a week or two after the end of the month for which it is calculated.

That brings us to the critical question concerning the stabilization of a broad price index. If the index or the value of the underlying basket cannot be known at all times, can we devise an arbitrage mechanism that will ensure that the value of money is stabilized in terms of that index? Irving Fisher's plan for a compensated dollar was designed to create such a mechanism. But on close inspection, it becomes evident that his proposal would not have created the desired mechanism.

What Fisher proposed was to have the government set an official gold price at which it would redeem dollars. But in contrast to a conventional gold standard, Fisher's plan provided for adjusting the price of gold to

Table 4. *Adjustment of gold price under Fisher's compensated dollar plan*

Target	Actual index in February (reported in March)	Official price of gold in February ($)	Correctly anticipated price of gold in March ($)	Profitable strategy
100	100	400	400	Do nothing
100	101	400	396.04	Sell gold to Treasury
100	99	400	404.04	Buy gold from Treasury

compensate for movements in the price index. Suppose the price of gold were initially set at $400 an ounce. If the price index for any month exceeded its target of 100, reaching, say, 101, the official gold price would be reduced by 1 percent to $396.04. That reduction in the official price would, in effect, increase the gold content of the dollar, making it more valuable. The gold price would continue to be reduced each month that the index remained above its target. On the other hand, if the index fell below 100, dropping to, say, 99, the gold price would be raised by 1 percent to $404.04, reducing the gold content of the dollar and making it less valuable.

But it is plain that arbitrage is not operating here. A change in the index creates no profit opportunity for buying or selling gold that would force the index back to its target. Indeed, the only profitable exchanges would occur in anticipation of an official change in the gold price. Suppose everyone anticipated that the next official report of the index would show that it had risen from 100 to 101. That expectation would imply a corresponding expectation that the official gold price would be reduced to $396.04, so everyone would have an incentive to sell gold to the Treasury immediately. The gold sales would expand the currency supply and, at least temporarily, would add to inflationary pressure. Similarly, if the public expected the price index to fall, speculators would buy gold in anticipation of a future increase in the gold price. Those purchases would contract the stock of currency, adding, at least temporarily, to deflationary pressure (see Table 4).[4]

4 Fisher himself suggested that to reduce the incentive for speculation against itself, the monetary authority ought to impose a 1 percent charge on all purchases and sales of gold. The additional charge for buying gold from, or selling gold to, the monetary au-

The defect in Fisher's plan was that it failed to link the redemption price of money to its purchasing power at the time of redemption. Without that link, there was no arbitrage mechanism to ensure that money always maintained the stipulated purchasing power. To provide that link Earl Thompson (1981, 1986) has proposed a modified version of Fisher's plan. The difference is that under Thompson's plan, the government would not try to peg the price of gold. Instead, it would buy and sell gold at the prevailing market price but with a provision that, should the index for the month in which the transaction took place deviate from its target, a compensating adjustment in the price would be made.

An example may be helpful at this point. Suppose the index were targeted at 100. If the index for the current month turned out to be 101, it would mean money had lost 1 percent of its purchasing power during the month. Thus, to compensate for the reduced purchasing power, anyone who bought gold (redeemed currency) from the Treasury during the month would be entitled to a 1 percent rebate on what was paid. Conversely, anyone who had sold gold to the Treasury would have to return 1 percent of the amount received (see Table 5).

But if the index had fallen to 99, it would mean that money had gained purchasing power. Since money had appreciated, a compensating dilution of its purchasing power would be in order. Thus whatever the price at which people bought gold from or sold it to the Treasury would have to be increased accordingly. Anyone who had sold gold to the Treasury during the month would receive a bonus of 1 percent of the transaction. And anyone who had bought gold from the Treasury during the month would have to pay an additional 1 percent.

That was just the response that successfully stabilized the value of a market basket of commodities. When the value of the market basket rose 10 percent above its target to $1,100, one could cash in $1,000 for the $1,100 worth of gold at the current market price of gold. If the market price were $400 an ounce, then one would get 2 3/4 ounces for $1,000, paying $363.36 an ounce. But when we are trying to stabilize a comprehensive index that is reported only once a month, we can't know by how much to adjust the effective redemption price until after the index for the month is reported. That is why the price at which the government buys and sells gold cannot be settled until after the index for the month in which the transaction took place is calculated. Adjusting the price to compensate for any change in the price index ensures that money can always be redeemed for a constant purchasing power.

Since there would be no commitment to peg the price of gold at any

thority would make speculative transactions unprofitable for any likely monthly change in the index.

Table 5. *Adjustment of gold price under Thompson's alternative plan*

Target	Actual index in February (reported in March)	Market price of gold on February 28 ($)	Realized price of gold after adjustment ($)	Profitable strategy
100	100	400	400	Do nothing
100	100	390	390	Do nothing
100	100	410	410	Do nothing
100	101	400	396.04	Buy gold from Treasury
100	101	390	386.10	Buy gold from Treasury
100	101	410	405.94	Buy gold from Treasury
100	99	400	404.04	Sell gold to Treasury
100	99	390	393.93	Sell gold to Treasury
100	99	410	414.10	Sell gold to Treasury

particular level, gold would really have no special role in this system. The index could be stabilized with virtually any asset as the redemption medium.

The beauty of the Thompson plan is that it would ensure that speculators anticipating movements in the index would minimize deviations of the index from its target. Even more important, the average expectation would be that the index would stay on target. To see why, suppose someone anticipated that the index for the current month would turn out to exceed 100. His incentive would be to redeem currency at the Treasury for gold while selling gold in the open market. If the index turned out to be 101, he would receive a 1 percent rebate on whatever he paid into the Treasury. Because of the offsetting sale of gold at the market price, the rebate would be pure profit.

Recall that under the Fisher plan, someone who expected the index to rise would sell gold to the Treasury at the official price, anticipating a later reduction in the official price. That was the wrong incentive, since those transactions would increase the amount of currency when prices were expected to rise.

The Thompson plan, however, works in the right direction. A general expectation that the index was going to rise would start a drain of currency from the economy as speculators bought gold from the government. Holders of inventories would have an incentive to liquidate rather than to add to their stocks; speculators would seek to borrow funds, driving up interest rates and further encouraging the liquidation of stocks. These effects would all tend to depress prices. So a general expectation of rising prices would automatically create downward pressure on prices.

And under the Thompson plan, an expectation that the index would fall below its target would induce people to try to sell gold to the Treasury for currency while buying in the open market, in anticipation of a later bonus. A general expectation that the index would be less than its target would cause gold to flow into the Treasury in exchange for currency. The automatic injection of currency into the economy would drive up prices during the month.

So although the index could turn out to be different from its target, the consensus would tend to be that it would stay on target. Any consensus that it would be above or below its target would itself cause prices to move in the opposite direction.

Thus none of the compelling objections against restoring the gold standard in its old form apply to Thompson's plan, even if it were carried out with gold as the medium of redemption. Sharp self-reinforcing fluctuations in the price level arising from the inherent instability of a speculative gold market in which existing stocks far exceed the current demand for industrial, commercial, or ornamental uses would not be possible. The monetary system would be fully insulated against any upheaval in the gold market because the monetary authority would not be committed to maintaining any particular price of gold. And by the same token, the largest gold-producing countries in the world, South Africa and the Soviet Union, would have no power to destabilize the monetary system by manipulating the gold market.

Nor do any of the objections against a Monetarist rule for controlling the quantity of money or against discretionary control of the quantity of money apply to the Thompson plan. Indirect convertibility would ensure that the quantity of currency would fluctuate automatically as needed to preserve a constant price level. The economy would not be deprived of currency when a demand to hold more money threatened to precipitate a deflation, nor would it be up to the monetary authority to try to use its own discretion in deciding how much additional currency to provide the public.

WHICH INDEX SHOULD WE STABILIZE?

Having taken care of form, we must now look after substance. Now that we have seen how a comprehensive price index could be stabilized in a manner analogous to the way the value of a commodity basket could be, we have to ask ourselves which index ought to be stabilized. This was a central question in the discussions of stabilizing the price level early in this century. Most of the advocates of price stabilization, like Knut Wicksell, Gustav Cassel, John Maynard Keynes, and Irving Fisher, favored stabilizing output prices. The rationale for stabilizing output prices is straightforward. The theoretical concept of the purchasing power of money is equivalent to the inverse of the price level of final output. So if our aim is to stabilize the purchasing power of money, an index of output prices would seem to be an obvious candidate for stabilization.

But there were also stabilizers, especially Robertson (1926) and Hawtrey (1932, chap. 3), who believed the appropriate target for policy to be a stable wage level, not a stable output-price level.[5] Interestingly, Keynes in *The General Theory* (1936/1973, p. 269) offhandedly suggested that "the maintenance of a stable general level of money-wages is, on a balance of considerations, the most advisable policy." But the suggestion was an isolated comment directed against using cuts in the general level of wages to maintain employment in a depression. He never seriously proposed stabilizing the wage level as a policy rule.

That, however, is precisely what I want to propose. To support my proposal, I shall now offer four reasons in ascending order of importance for stabilizing the wage level rather than the price level. The first two reasons, which come from the original debates about price stabilization, concern how technical progress and rising productivity should be reflected in the structure of wages and prices. There is one basic difference between stabilizing wages and stabilizing prices. In an environment of technical progress and increasing productivity, stabilizing the level of output prices means that increases in productivity will be reflected in rising money wages, while stabilizing the level of wages means that rising productivity will be reflected in falling output prices. Either way, workers will receive rising real wages. So it might not seem that it matters whether wages or output prices are being stabilized. Certainly in a frictionless economy in which the pace of productivity growth was always foreseen, it would not matter. But if the pace of productivity growth is not foreseen, the unanticipated gains will accrue to entrepreneurs under output-price stability and to recipients of fixed incomes (including workers under long-term contract) under wage stability. Thus a policy of wage stability ensures a wider sharing in unanticipated gains in productivity than a policy of output-price stability.

5 There were also those like Hayek (1931/1966) who did not favor any particular index of prices or wages but felt that the appropriate policy was to stabilize total aggregate factor incomes in nominal terms. This proposal might be viewed as a precursor of rules targeting the rate of growth of nominal GNP.

This brings me to the second reason for favoring a policy of wage stability. Under output-price stability, the windfall profits and losses accruing to entrepreneurs from unanticipated fluctuations in productivity might lead to destabilizing fluctuations in investment.[6] Holding the wage level constant would not require the injection or withdrawal of currency to offset unanticipated fluctuations in productivity and would not cause profits and investment to fluctuate if productivity changed unexpectedly.

Although they might have some validity, neither of these reasons seems overly compelling. By themselves, they would not constitute a very strong case for preferring wage stability to output-price stability as the aim of monetary policy. Yet I think they are at least worth mentioning as subsidiary benefits that would accrue from adopting a policy of wage stabilization.

Perhaps a stronger reason for preferring a stable wage level (or, more precisely, for preferring the falling output-price level that would typically follow from such a policy) is suggested by the literature on the optimal quantity of money (Friedman 1969; Samuelson 1969). The upshot of that literature is that as long as nominal interest rates are positive, there is an inefficient tax on holding non-interest-bearing currency. Responding to this tax, people undertake a whole range of extra transactions, such as buying and selling bonds or holding interest-bearing accounts they wouldn't otherwise hold, to reduce their holdings of non-interest-bearing currency. Estimates of how costly the tax on holding currency is vary, but even at the lower end of the range it is not a trivial sum, and at the higher end it is substantial. So apart from the benefits of a stable wage level, there is also something to be said for the gently falling price level and very low nominal interest rates that would normally follow from a stable wage level.

But the crucial reason for preferring a stable wage level to a stable output-price level is that a stable wage level would avoid substantial fluctuations in employment that might occur with a stable output-price level.[7] Maintaining a stable wage level would ensure that the labor market was always in some reasonable balance. In particular, falling wages in one location, occupation, or industry would be offset by rising wages elsewhere. So falling wage offers would always be a signal to workers that they might find better opportunities elsewhere. In contrast, when the wage level is not stabilized, workers who face worsening employment pros-

6 This argument was emphasized particularly by Hayek (1931/1966), by Haberler (1931), and by other Austrian economists who opposed price-level stabilization. Robertson (1926, 1948) also made the argument, though in a more tentative way.
7 The argument here again draws on the work of Earl Thompson (1981, 1986) and his arguments for a labor standard. Some of Thompson's arguments for making wage stability the goal of monetary policy were foreshadowed by those of Hawtrey (1932, chap. 5; 1967).

pects cannot tell if their prospects are worsening only in certain sectors but improving in others or if prospects are worsening for all workers. If the latter is true, then it would be in the interest of all workers to accept lower real wages in order to minimize the loss of employment. But if the former is true, then it will pay many of the workers whose wage prospects are deteriorating to shift employment and accept a period of transitional unemployment while waiting or searching for better wages.

Cumulative contractions in employment similar to those Keynes was trying to shed light on in *The General Theory* (1936/1973) can arise when workers mistake a general deterioration in labor-market conditions for a partial or sectoral change (Leijonhufvud 1968). When that happens, instead of accepting the lower wages necessary to maintain employment, workers resist wage cuts and accept unemployment in the mistaken expectation of finding better employment elsewhere. Thus, under a policy that stabilized the output-price level, a shock, like the oil shocks of 1973–74 and 1979–80, that reduced real wages would imply a general fall in money wages. Because of the confusion between a general and a sectoral deterioration of employment opportunities that I just mentioned, a cumulative decline in employment would result. Now a commitment to a stable price level would prevent this decline in employment from getting out of control, but the decline could still be substantial.

For example, Robert Hall (1984) estimated that unemployment might have risen to 15 percent after the oil shocks of the 1970s if economic policy had aimed at keeping the output-price level constant. Keeping money wages constant and allowing an increase in output prices to depress real wages would imply a smaller increase in unemployment than would keeping output prices constant and forcing money wages to fall.

The only possible problem with stabilizing nominal wage rates is that a labor-supply shock might force up real wages and trigger a shock-amplifying deflation. If, to consider the most likely source of such a shock, unions imposed higher nominal wages in unionized sectors of the economy, then stabilizing the wage level would force down prices and wages in the nonunionized sector. Instead of being able to find employment in the nonunionized sector, workers laid off as a result of the increased wages in the unionized sector would face deteriorating prospects in the nonunion sector as well. Thus, instead of producing an inflation that would cushion the impact of the wage shock on employment, a stable money-wage level would force a deflation that would amplify the initial shock.

Although a labor-supply shock would be a problem if we were stabilizing the wage level, it is hard to see what might produce such a shock. For one to occur, there would first have to be a significant increase in the monopoly power of labor unions. Whatever monopoly power labor unions now exercise could not produce the shock because it is already reflected in the current wage structure. So for labor unions to force up wages substantially in unionized sectors, they first would have to strengthen their monopoly power. Yet international competition, the declining importance of manufacturing in our economy, and domestic deregulation have been eroding the monopoly power of unions for some time. Nor does a reversal of that trend, which is the consequence of basic changes in the economy, not of transient shifts in political preferences, seem likely.

A LABOR STANDARD

Using the scheme of indirect convertibility I have described in this chapter to stabilize an index of wages would, in effect, create a labor standard. A dollar would always be convertible into the amount of purchasing power that would buy a stipulated amount of labor power. Since wages are typically measured in dollars per hour, the wage index can be reported as a certain number of dollars per hour, not as a pure number the way output-price indexes are. Stabilizing the wage index at, say, $10 an hour would mean that a dollar was indirectly convertible into the equivalent of six minutes of labor services.

Let me now summarize what a labor standard would accomplish. Under the normal conditions of technological progress and increasing productivity, a labor standard would imply a gently falling output-price level and very low nominal interest rates. But although a falling price level would be the rule under a labor standard, whenever the economy was hit by a shock that depressed real wages, the labor standard would easily accommodate the shock through a temporary increase in output prices. Such episodes might cause a temporary increase in short-term interest rates. But only short-term interest rates would rise significantly. Long-term rates would continue to stay low, reflecting the confident expectation of secularly falling prices under a labor standard.

While a labor standard ensured price stability and cushioned against supply shocks, a competitive banking system would eliminate all purely monetary shocks by supplying as much (but only as much) money as the public wanted to hold. No longer would monetary disturbances be the source of fluctuations in output and employment as they have in the past. This is not to say that the business cycle would be eliminated. Fluctuations could still arise from real disturbances such as supply shocks or from the inevitable dislocations associated with waves of new inventions and innovations that make economic growth in real economics an uneven and possibly cyclical process. But a stable wage level would prevent these shocks from transforming a cyclical downturn into a vicious contractionary spiral.

A proposal for monetary reform

Free banking under a labor standard would approximate the ideal of neutral money that was the objective of the monetary reformers and price-level stabilizers of the early part of this century. Earl Thompson (1986) may have exaggerated only slightly when he characterized free banking under a labor standard as a perfect monetary system.

MONETARY REFORM IN AN INTERNATIONAL SETTING

I have so far in this chapter treated monetary reform strictly from a national perspective, without exploring any of its international ramifications. But no satisfactory discussion of monetary reform can fail to attend to those international ramifications. There is one key issue of international monetary reform, and that is whether and how to control or restrain movements in exchange rates between currencies. That question has been debated almost endlessly for decades, especially since Milton Friedman's celebrated plea for flexible exchange rates (1953b). But it is remarkable how little that debate has added to John Maynard Keynes's discussion of international monetary reform in his *Tract on Monetary Reform* (1923/1971). Keynes insisted that every country had inevitably to choose between stabilizing its internal price level and stabilizing the exchange rate between its currency and another currency. A country could always do one or the other, but it could not do both. But Keynes, as his famous quotation from Lenin demonstrates, would have been appalled at the notion that the monetary system ought not to be anchored to any price-level objective.

Keynes's choice, of course, was for stabilizing the domestic price level and not the exchange rate because he believed (at least in 1923) that a stable domestic price level would guarantee a stable domestic economy with full employment. After the breakdown of the Bretton Woods System in 1971, most countries stopped trying to maintain fixed exchange rates. Fewer and fewer people seem satisfied with the way floating exchange rates have worked out. But the reason floating rates haven't worked out as they were expected to is that we have lost sight of the objective for which both Keynes and Friedman originally advocated sacrificing fixed exchange rates: domestic price-level stability. To have abandoned fixed exchange rates to ensure price-level stability would have been one thing; to have abandoned them to allow all countries to pursue monetary policies unconstrained by a commitment to any price-level target was quite another.

But in truth generalized floating was not adopted because of theoretical arguments. The main reason is simply that fixed exchange rates proved to be incompatible with the activist monetary policies that almost all countries felt obliged to follow after World War II.

With a fixed exchange rate between two currencies, only one of the two countries can follow an independent monetary policy. So the general problem posed by fixed exchange rates is who gets to determine that independent monetary policy. Yet no sovereign government will willingly grant the monetary authority of another country the right to dictate without constraint what its monetary policy should be.

Although floating exchange rates did eliminate the inherent conflict between fixed exchange rates and monetary sovereignty, they have not worked out as Friedman and others insisted they would. They argued that floating rates would provide an automatic nondiscretionary way of harmonizing independent national monetary policies. In a world of unconstrained national monetary policies, however, major shifts in exchange rates seem to have become a disruptive force in the international economy.

Indeed, some of the early objections to proposals for floating exchange rates seem to have been confirmed. Fluctuations in exchange rates have often been large and sudden. Figure 5 shows the movements of the dollar-yen and the dollar-deutschmark exchange rates and the value of the trade-weighted dollar since 1973. Not infrequently, movements in exchange rates seem to have been dominated by speculation rather than economic fundamentals. Exporting and import-competing industries have alternately reaped windfall profits and suffered windfall losses from these extreme movements in exchange rates.

Some of the risks from exchange-rate fluctuations can be hedged against by forward-market transactions. But the risk that a shift in the exchange rate will render an entire investment project either profitable or unprofitable cannot be hedged against.

Under the gold standard, the pattern of international prices was constrained by the fixed currency parities in relation to gold. International arbitrage ensured that there was a close correspondence in the prices of similar goods in all countries. World trade adjusted itself to a stable pattern of prices that indicated which commodities the various countries had a comparative advantage in producing.

But now, with currency values unconstrained, there may be no such thing as an equilibrium exchange rate – certainly no such thing as a stable equilibrium rate (Karaken and Wallace 1981). Exchange rates can change for speculative reasons, and there is no underlying market pressure for them to return to their original levels. Instead, domestic prices adjust to the movement in exchange rates. The change in domestic prices is usually slower than the speculative change in exchange rates, however. Thus formerly profitable exporting or import-competing industries can be rendered unprofitable by a change in exchange rates when wages and other input prices adjust sluggishly to such a change. If nothing else, the

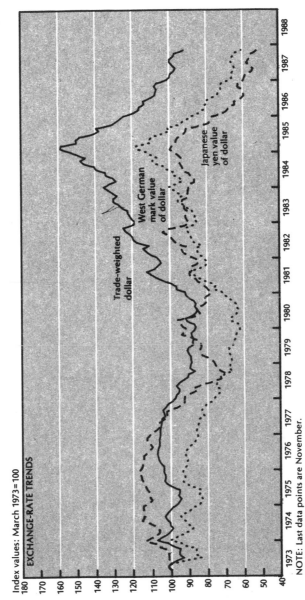

Figure 5. Exchange-rate movements since 1973
(*Source:* Federal Reserve Bank of Cleveland, *Economic Trends*, December 1987, p. 20)

added risk of producing in the tradable-goods sector is causing resources to be withdrawn from that sector and moved into domestic nontradable-goods production, which is less subject to the risk of adverse exchange-rate shifts.[8]

The added risk of investing in the tradable-goods sector is a deterrent to investment in exporting and import-competing industries. It is also an incentive for those who have already invested in import-competing industries to lobby for protectionist legislation and for those who have invested in export industries to lobby for export subsidies. Ad hoc quotas, so-called voluntary quota agreements, and international market-sharing agreements that clearly violate the letter if not the spirit of GATT (General Agreement on Tariffs and Trade) and often of domestic antitrust legislation have proliferated at a frightening pace in this decade. Even if a full-scale trade war is avoided, international economic integration and the international division of labor are being eroded. That erosion, of course, also undermines the foundation for continued growth of the world economy.

Dissatisfaction with floating exchange rates in general and a view that extreme instability of exchange rates is inconsistent with an open international trading system has led some to propose restoring fixed exchange rates or, at least, limiting the range within which exchange rates may fluctuate. However, aside from nearly meaningless incantations about the need for the coordination of national monetary policies, these proposals do not address the central question of who is going to determine the single monetary policy that can be followed by a group of countries with fixed exchange rates. Until they do, all such proposals are superficial, unrealistic, and misleading.

They are superficial because they presume that it is possible to control exchange rates without fundamentally changing the manner in which national monetary policies are carried out. No monetary authority can peg an exchange rate without also surrendering control over its domestic price level or any other domestic target it is trying to meet.

Proposals for fixed exchange rates are therefore unrealistic because they take it for granted that some countries will surrender the choice of their monetary policy to the unconstrained monetary authority of another country. But it was precisely the desire of other countries to reclaim that independence after U.S. monetary authorities shrugged off the mild constraints of the Bretton Woods System that led to the collapse of fixed exchange rates. A world with truly fixed exchange rates is a world with one currency. Advocates of fixed exchange rates simply ignore the inability of countries to agree on who should be allowed to conduct

8 I am indebted to Axel Leijonhufvud for making this point to me.

monetary policy on everyone else's behalf. Platitudes about limiting exchange-rate fluctuations and coordinating monetary policies only evade the central issue.

Proposals for fixed exchange rates are misleading because the threat to an open international trading system that has emerged in recent years under flexible exchange rates does not stem from flexible exchange rates. It stems from the absence of any constraint on the monetary policies of all major countries. Without a commitment by the monetary authorities to price stability that might anchor expectations, speculators pay little attention to anticipated changes in the future terms of trade between countries. Instead they guess about the monetary policies different countries will adopt and about the political developments that shape those policies. They may even guess about the guesses of other speculators about those monetary policies and political developments. The absence of any credible commitment to a price-level target leaves exchange rates free to wander about more or less at the whim of speculators.

The United States, therefore, would remove a major source of uncertainty in international currency markets by committing itself credibly to a policy of price-level stabilization. If other countries continued to pursue unconstrained monetary policies, speculation could still drive exchange rates, but people would have at least one stable currency as an alternative.

A commitment to stabilize the price level would therefore greatly increase the international demand for dollars. That would exert upward pressure on the dollar's exchange rate against other currencies. However, a free banking system under a labor standard (or any other form of price-level stabilization) would automatically supply the additional dollars demanded internationally. The additional quantity of dollars would prevent the additional demand for them from causing deflation and would moderate the appreciation of the dollar in foreign exchange markets.

Constant unpredictable changes in tastes and technology will always cause changes in the patterns of international trade and investment that must be reflected in changes in the pattern of international prices. Countries can choose whether to let these changes work themselves out in exchange rates or in their domestic price levels. The point of committing the monetary authority to a predictable course of behavior is to guarantee that changes in the pattern of international prices reflect only the unavoidable changes in the underlying terms of trade between countries and not arbitrary disturbances introduced by the actions of unconstrained national monetary authorities. We can't eliminate all uncertainty. But we can minimize uncertainty if monetary policy can be constrained in a predictable way.

Once the United States adopted a labor standard, other countries would be able to choose for themselves whether the benefits would be greater from a fixed exchange rate with the dollar or from a stable internal price level.[9] And the United States would have no reason to encourage countries to choose one or the other. But once U.S. monetary policy was con-

---

9 The discussion here is particulary relevant for the monetary problems faced by many less-developed countries (LDCs). LDCs chronically suffer from weak and supposedly overvalued currencies. When they seek financial assistance from international agencies such as the International Monetary Fund and the World Bank, the international agencies impose conditions calculated to improve the recipients' capacity for meeting their obligations.

Unfortunately, among those conditions is usually a requirement that a recipient LDC devalue its currency or allow it to float downward against other currencies. Floating or devaluation is supposed to improve the recipient's balance-of-payments position, increase its debt-paying capacity, and allow it to eliminate or relax foreign-exchange controls.

Yet floating and devaluation can be fatal policy mistakes for an LDC. Any government that issues an inconvertible currency has to find some substitute for convertibility to maintain a positive value. As a sovereign power, a government can, so to speak, force people to hold its currency by making it legal tender and by accepting it in payment of taxes. But the government's power to do so is not unlimited. So unless people have confidence in a government's stability and its future good behavior, they will correspondingly reduce the amount they hold of its currency.

Governments of developed countries with stable political institutions usually command enough public confidence to be able to keep their currencies from depreciating rapidly even without a legal commitment to make their currencies convertible into a valuable real asset or another stable currency. But LDCs are not only economically underdeveloped, they are also politically underdeveloped. They lack the political, legal, and governmental institutions that, under normal conditions, allow advanced countries to keep their currencies tolerably stable. Citizens of LDCs would not willingly hold the currencies issued by their governments if they were not forced to. They would prefer holding either dollars or some other major currency. But LDCs can't create dollars themselves; they can only acquire dollars by exchanging their own goods and services for them. That is, they would have to pay seignorage in the form of a foreign-trade surplus to acquire them.

Actually, LDCs could largely avoid the burden of seignorage if they would allow private banks – either foreign or domestic – to create the dollars, much as banks create them outside the United States in the Eurodollar market. But if LDCs insist on providing their own currencies, they must create the confidence necessary for their currencies to be generally held and used, in the same way that a private bank creates confidence in the money it creates. They must make their currencies convertible into the dollar or another major currency.

To recommend devaluation or floating to an LDC is to recommend that the country give up what may be the only means of building the confidence people must have in the country's currency if they are to be willing to accept and hold it. Devaluation or floating therefore deprives people in LDCs of a money in which they can have confidence. They seek to avoid holding the currency, driving its value down even further. A vicious cycle gets under way. Depreciation undermines confidence in the currency, loss of confidence intensifies the depreciation, and so on. There may well be no way of stopping such a depreciation as long as the currency remains unpegged to a stable currency.

Depriving a country of a useful money is no way to promote economic development. Too little money can be a major barrier to development. Too little money makes trading more costly because people have to rely on inefficient means of trading like barter. When the cost of trading is increased, fewer mutually beneficial transactions are made and resources are wastefully used up in those transactions that are undertaken. Since, as Adam Smith taught us, the division of labor is limited by the extent of the market,

strained in a predictable way, other countries would have far more incentive than they do now either to peg their currencies to the dollar or to adopt monetary regimes aimed at domestic price stability. Many countries might well choose to peg their currencies to the dollar, just as many countries pegged their currencies to sterling and gold in the nineteenth century. The gold standard in the late nineteenth century was not created by a deliberate international agreement; it was the product of a slow evolution. Another international monetary system based on fixed exchange rates will come about not because of any international agreement, but only because countries independently find it in their individual interest to peg their own currencies to some other currency. Few countries, of course, will be likely to peg their currencies to another currency whose value is not itself pinned down by some reliable commitment.

THE FUTURE OF MONETARY REFORM

I should not deny that unsolved problems in devising an ideal monetary regime for the United States and for the world economy still exist. But those unsolved problems need not deter us from beginning the process of monetary reform. For one thing, the evolution of a truly competitive monetary system, as I have tried to make clear, is proceeding so rapidly that existing instruments for maintaining macroeconomic stability are becoming increasingly inadequate.

As their inadequacy becomes more and more evident in the future, we shall have to seek new mechanisms for ensuring stability. As always, there will be those who will warn against the evils of the competitive innovations in our monetary and financial system and will advocate restoring the simpler and, in their view, safer world of the past. I doubt that reversing the trend of monetary evolution is possible; and even if it were, it would not be desirable.

In this chapter I have suggested how, by stabilizing a price index through a form of indirect convertibility, we could avoid macroeconomic instability emanating from monetary disturbances. Doing so would provide a stable monetary regime fully compatible with our evolving competitive monetary and financial system.

But besides avoiding instability caused by discretionary monetary policy, we also want to avoid instability caused by nonmonetary supply shocks that can also be the source of inefficient unemployment. To protect ourselves against such shocks, either we could allow for limited discretion in a monetary regime that stabilized output prices, or we could adopt a

anything that discourages trade is an obstacle to bringing about the transition from self-sufficiency and subsistence farming to specialization and production for the market that is a principal feature of economic development.

monetary regime with a labor standard. Since there are other good reasons to want the gently falling product prices and very low nominal interest rates that a constant wage index would generate in the absence of supply shocks, a labor standard seems to offer the best of all possible worlds – no discretion, optimal price-level behavior, and invulnerability to supply shocks.

We ought not to expect monetary reform to create a monetary system that all countries will adopt. What we can do is create conditions of monetary stability wherever we can. In an uncertain world, such anchors of stability would invite others to share in that stability. Some countries would devise monetary regimes such as I have suggested aimed at stabilizing some suitable index of prices. Other countries would then be able to pick one of these currencies to peg their own currencies to, just as countries in the nineteenth century could choose to link their currencies to the pound and gold or, for a time, to the French franc and silver. We are unlikely ever to see a world with one international currency, but it is possible that we shall have a world with a few major stable currencies stabilizing different price indexes. Exchange rates between the currencies would be flexible but quiescent. On the basis of their own unique circumstances, smaller countries would be able to choose one of the major currencies to peg their currencies to. After the monetary instability that has bedeviled the world for the past two or three decades – indeed, for most of this century – that is far from an unappealing prospect.

References

Abbott, Charles Cortez. 1937. *The New York Bond Market, 1920–1930*. Cambridge, MA: Harvard University Press.

Angell, James A. 1926. *The Theory of International Prices*. Cambridge, MA: Harvard University Press. Reprinted. New York: Augustus M. Kelley, 1965.

Angell, Wayne. 1987. "A Commodity Price Guide to Monetary Targeting." Paper presented to Lehrman Institute seminar, New York, December 10.

Auernheimer, Leonardo. 1974. "The Honest Government's Guide to the Revenue from the Creation of Money." *Journal of Political Economy* 82(3): 598–606.

Bagehot, Walter. 1915. *Lombard Street: A Description of the London Money Market*. London: Smith, Elder. Reprinted. New York: Arno Press, 1978.

Bailey, Martin J. 1956. "The Welfare Cost of Inflationary Finance." *Journal of Political Economy* 64(2): 93–110.

Barro, Robert J. 1979. "Money and the Price Level under the Gold Standard." *Economic Journal* 89(1): 13–33.

1983. "Inflationary Finance under Discretion and Rules." *Canadian Journal of Economics* 16(1): 1–16.

Batchelder, Ronald W. 1986. "The International Monetary Fund Agreement and Optimal International Debt Contracting." Manuscript, UCLA Department of Economics, November.

Benjamin, Daniel K., and Levis A. Kochin. 1979. "Searching for an Explanation of Unemployment in Interwar Britain." *Journal of Political Economy* 87(3): 441–78.

Benston, George J., Robert A. Eisenbas, Paul M. Horvitz, Edward J. Kane, and George G. Kaufman. 1986. *Perspectives on Safe and Sound Banking: Past, Present, and Future*. Cambridge, MA: MIT Press.

Black, Fischer. 1970. "Banking and Interest Rates in a World without Money: The Effects of Uncontrolled Banking." *Journal of Bank Research* 1 (Autumn): 9–20. Reprinted in Fischer Black, *Equilibrium and Business Cycles*, pp. 1–20. New York: Basil Blackwell, 1987.

1972. "Active and Passive Monetary Policy in a Neoclassical Model." *Journal of Finance* 27(4): 801–14. Reprinted in Fischer Black, *Equilibrium and Business Cycles*, pp. 21–39. New York: Basil Blackwell, 1987.

1974. "Uniqueness of the Price Level in Monetary Growth Models with Rational Expectations." *Journal of Economic Theory* 7(1): 53–65. Reprinted

References

in Fischer Black, *Equilibrium and Business Cycles*, pp. 60–73. New York: Basil Blackwell, 1987.

1987. "A Gold Standard with Double Feedback and Near Zero Reserves." In Fischer Black, *Equilibrium and Business Cycles*, pp. 115–20. New York: Basil Blackwell.

Blackstone William. 1773. *Commentaries on the Laws of England*. London. Reprinted. Chicago: University of Chicago Press, 1979.

Blaug, Mark. 1985. *Economic Theory in Retrospect*. 4th edition. Cambridge: Cambridge University Press.

Blinder, Alan. 1984. Commentary on "Credibility and Monetary Policy" by Bennett T. McCallum. In *Price Stability and Public Policy: A Symposium Sponsored by the Federal Reserve Bank of Kansas City*, pp. 129–35. Kansas City, MO: Federal Reserve Bank of Kansas City.

Bloomfield, Arthur I. 1959. *Monetary Policy under the International Gold Standard*. New York: Federal Reserve Bank of New York.

Bordo, Michael D. 1975. "John Cairnes on the Effects of the Australian Gold Discoveries, 1851–72: An Early Application of the Methodology of Positive Economics." *History of Political Economy* 7(3): 337–59.

1986. "Money, Deflation and Seigniorage in the Fifteenth Century: A Review Essay." *Journal of Monetary Economics* 18(3): 337–46.

Boyd, Walter. 1801. *A Letter to the Right Honourable William Pitt, on the Influence of the Stoppage of Issues in Specie at the Bank of England; on the Prices of Provisions, and Other Commodities*. London: J. Wright.

Burns, Arthur R. 1927. *Money and Monetary Policy in Early Times*. New York: Alfred A. Knopf. Reprinted. New York: Augustus M. Kelley, 1969.

Cairnes, John E. 1873. *Essays in Political Economy*. London: Macmillan. Reprinted. New York: Augustus M. Kelley, 1965.

Cameron, Rondo, with the collaboration of Olga Crisp, Hugh T. Patrick, and Richard Tilly. 1967. *Banking in the Early Stages of Industrialization*. New York: Oxford University Press.

Cannan, Edwin. 1925. *The Paper Pound of 1797–1821: The Bullion Report*. 2nd edition. London: P. S. King. Reprinted. New York: Augustus M. Kelley, 1969.

1930. "The Problem of Unemployment." *Economic Journal* 40(1): 45–55.

Checkland, S. G. 1975. *Scottish Banking: A History, 1695–1973*. Glasgow: Collins.

Churchill, Winston. 1930. "The Dole." *Saturday Evening Post*, March 29, 6–7.

Clark, Truman A. 1984. "Violations of the Gold Points, 1890–1908." *Journal of Political Economy* 92(5): 791–823.

Cooper, S. Kerry, and Donald R. Fraser. 1984. *Banking Deregulation and the New Competition in the Financial Services Industry*. Cambridge, MA: Ballinger Press.

de Cecco, Marcello. 1985. "Monetary Theory and Roman History." *Journal of Economic History* 45(4): 809–22.

de Roover, Raymond. 1944. "What Is Dry Exchange?" *Journal of Political Economy* 52(3): 250–66. Reprinted in Raymond de Roover, *Business, Banking, and Economic Thought in Late Medieval and Early Modern Europe*, pp. 183–99. Chicago: University of Chicago Press, 1976.

1948. *Money, Credit, and Banking in Mediaeval Bruges*. Cambridge: The Mediaeval Academy.

1954. "New Interpretations in Banking History." *Journal of World History*

References

(2): 38–76. Reprinted in Raymond de Roover, *Business, Banking, and Economic Thought in Late Medieval and Early Modern Europe*, pp. 200–38. Chicago: University of Chicago Press, 1976.

1956. "The Development of Accounting prior to Luca Pacioli according to the Account Books of Medieval Merchants." In *Studies in the History of Accounting*, edited by A. C. Littleton and B. S. Yamey. London: Sweet and Maxwell. Reprinted in Raymond de Roover, *Business, Banking, and Economic Thought in Late Medieval and Early Modern Europe*, pp. 49–79. Chicago: University of Chicago Press, 1976.

1963. *The Rise and Fall of the Medici Bank*. Cambridge, MA: Harvard University Press.

Despres, Émile, Charles Kindleberger, and Walter S. Salant. 1966. "The Dollar and World Liquidity: A Monetary View." *The Economist* 218 (February 5): 526–29. Reprinted in Charles Kindleberger, *International Money: A Collection of Essays*, pp. 42–52. London: George Allen and Unwin, 1981.

Diamond, Douglas W., and Phillip H. Dybvig. 1983. "Bank Runs, Deposit Insurance and Liquidity." *Journal of Political Economy* 91(3): 401–19.

Dowd, Kevin. 1987. "Option Clauses and the Stability of a Laisser Faire Monetary System." Discussion Paper 87.5, Money and Finance Project, School of Management and Economic Studies, University of Sheffield.

1989. *The State and the Monetary System*. Oxford: Philip Alan.

Durant, Will. 1939. *The Life of Greece*. New York: Simon and Schuster.

1942. *Caesar and Christ*. New York: Simon and Schuster.

Dwyer, Gerald P., and Thomas R. Saving. 1986. "Government Revenue from Money Creation with Government and Private Money." *Journal of Monetary Economics* 17(2): 239–49.

Einaudi, Luigi. 1953. "The Theory of Imaginary Money from Charlemagne to the French Revolution." In *Enterprise and Secular Change: Readings in Economic History*, edited by Frederic C. Lane and Jelle C. Riemersma, pp. 229–61. Homewood, IL: Irwin.

England, Catherine. 1985. "Private Deposit Insurance." *Cato Policy Analysis*, No. 54, June 21.

Fama, Eugene. 1980. "Banking in the Theory of Finance." *Journal of Monetary Economics* 6(1): 39–57.

1983. "Financial Intermediation and Price-Level Control." *Journal of Monetary Economics* 12(1): 7–28.

Feavearyear, Arthur. 1963. *The Pound Sterling*. Revised edition. Oxford: Oxford University Press.

Fetter, Frank W. 1965. *The Development of British Monetary Orthodoxy, 1797–1873*. Cambridge, MA: Harvard University Press.

Finley Moses I. 1973. *The Ancient Economy*. Berkeley: University of California Press.

Fischer, Stanley. 1981. "Towards an Understanding of the Costs of Inflation: II." *Carnegie-Rochester Conference Series on Public Policy* 15 (Autumn): 5–42.

Fischer, Stanley, and Franco Modigliani. 1978. "Towards an Understanding of the Real Effects and Costs of Inflation." *Weltwirschaftliches Archiv* 114(4): 810–33.

Fisher, Irving. 1911. *The Purchasing Power of Money*. New York: Macmillan. Revised edition 1913. Reprinted. New York: Augustus M. Kelley, 1985.

1920. *Stabilizing the Dollar*. New York: Macmillan.

1935. *100% Money*. New York: Adelphi.

References

Fratianni, Michele, and Franco Spinelli. 1984. "Italy in the Gold Standard Period, 1861–1914." In *A Retrospective on the Classical Gold Standard, 1821–1931*, edited by Michael D. Bordo and Anna J. Schwartz, pp. 405–41. Chicago: University of Chicago Press.

Fremling, Gertrude. 1983. "Monetary Policy under a Gold Standard: How Effective Is It?" Unpublished doctoral dissertation, University of California at Los Angeles.

⸻ 1985. "Did the United States Transmit the Great Depression to the Rest of the World?" *American Economic Review* 75(5): 1181–85.

Friedman, Milton. 1953a. "Discussion of the Inflationary Gap." In Milton Friedman, *Essays in Positive Economics*, pp. 251–62. Chicago: University of Chicago Press.

⸻ 1953b. "The Case of Flexible Exchange Rates." In Milton Friedman, *Essays in Positive Economics*, pp. 157–203. Chicago: University of Chicago Press.

⸻ 1954. "Why the American Economy Is Depression-Proof." In *Nationalekonomiska Foreningens Fordhandlingar*. Reprinted in Milton Friedman, *Dollars and Deficits*, pp. 72–96. Englewood Cliffs, NJ: Prentice-Hall.

⸻ 1960. *A Program for Monetary Stability*. New York: Fordham University Press.

⸻ 1962. *Capitalism and Freedom*. Chicago: University of Chicago Press.

⸻ 1968. "The Role of Monetary Policy." *American Economic Review* 58(1): 1–17. Reprinted in *The Optimum Quantity of Money and Other Essays*, pp. 95–110. Chicago: Aldine Publishing Co., 1969.

⸻ 1969. "The Optimum Quantity of Money." In Milton Friedman, *The Optimum Quantity of Money and Other Essays*, pp. 1–50. Chicago: Aldine Publishing Co.

Friedman, Milton, and Anna J. Schwartz. 1963. *A Monetary History of the United States, 1867–1960*. Princeton: Princeton University Press.

⸻ 1982. *Monetary Trends in the United States and the United Kingdom: Their Relation to Income, Prices, and Interest Rates, 1867–1975*. Chicago: University of Chicago Press.

⸻ 1986. "Has Government Any Role in Money?" *Journal of Monetary Economics* 17(1): 37–62.

Fullarton, J. 1845. *On the Regulation of Currencies*. 2nd edition. London: John Murray. Reprinted. New York: Augustus M. Kelley, 1969.

Girton, Lance, and Don Roper. 1978. "J. Laurence Laughlin and the Quantity Theory of Money." *Journal of Political Economy* 88(4): 599–625.

Glasner, David. 1985a. "A Reinterpretation of Classical Monetary Theory." *Southern Economic Journal* 52(1): 46–67.

⸻ 1985b. *Politics, Prices, and Petroleum*. Cambridge, MA: Ballinger Press.

⸻ 1986. "Why Free Banking Is Anti-Inflationary." Manuscript, author's files, Washington, D.C.

⸻ 1988. "Where Keynes Went Wrong." *Encounter* 71(5): 57–65.

⸻ 1989. "On Some Classical Monetary Controversies." *History of Political Economy* 21(2).

Goodhart, Charles A. E. 1984. *Monetary Theory and Practice: The U.K. Experience*. London: Macmillan.

⸻ 1987a. *The Evolution of Central Banks*. Cambridge, MA: MIT Press.

⸻ 1987b. "Why Banks Need a Central Bank." *Oxford Economic Papers* 39(1): 75–89.

Gorton, Gary. 1985a. "Bank Suspensions of Convertibility." *Journal of Monetary Economics* 15(2): 177–93.

References

1985b. "Clearinghouses and the Origin of Central Banking in the United States." *Journal of Economic History* 45(1): 277–83.

Greenfield, Robert L., and Leland Yeager. 1983. "A Laissez-Faire Approach to Monetary Stability." *Journal of Money, Credit, and Banking* 15(3): 302–15.

Gurley, John G., and Edward S. Shaw. 1959. *Money in a Theory of Finance.* Washington, D.C.: Brookings Institution.

Haberler, Gottfried. 1931. *The Different Meanings Attached to the Term "Fluctuations in the Purchasing Power of Gold" and the Best Instrument or Instruments for Measuring Such Fluctuations.* Geneva: League of Nations, March.

Hall, Robert. 1981. "The Government and the Monetary Unit." Manuscript, Stanford University Economics Department.

1984. "Monetary Policy with an Elastic Price Standard." In *Price Stability and Public Policy: A Symposium Sponsored by the Federal Reserve Bank of Kansas City,* pp. 137–59. Kansas City, MO: Federal Reserve Bank of Kansas City.

Hawtrey, Ralph G. 1932. *The Art of Central Banking.* London: Longmans Green.

1947. *The Gold Standard in Theory and Practice.* 5th edition. London: Longmans Green.

1967. *Incomes and Money.* New York: Barnes and Noble.

Hayek, F. A. 1929. *Geldtheorie und Konjunkturtheorie.* Translated and printed in English as *Monetary Theory and the Trade Cycle.* London: Jonathan Cape, 1933. Reprinted. New York: Augustus M. Kelley, 1966.

1931. *Prices and Production.* London: Routledge. 2nd (1935) edition reprinted. New York: Augustus M. Kelley, 1966.

1939. Introduction to W. H. Thornton, *Paper Credit of Great Britain.* London: George Allen and Unwin. Reprinted. New York: Augustus M. Kelley, 1969.

1976. *Choice in Currency: A Way to Stop Inflation.* London: Institute of Economic Affairs.

1978. *Denationalization of Money: An Analysis of the Theory and Practice of Concurrent Currencies.* 2nd edition. London: Institute of Economic Affairs.

Hicks, John R. 1969. *A Theory of Economic History.* New York: Oxford University Press.

Hollander, Samuel. 1979. *The Economics of David Ricardo.* Toronto: University of Toronto Press.

Huertas, Thomas. 1986. "Safety First, Stability Last? The Case Against 100% Deposit Insurance." Paper presented at the Liberty Fund/Manhattan Institute Conference on Competitive Monetary Regimes, New York.

Hughes, J. R. T. 1984. "Stagnation without 'Flation: The 1930s Again." In *Money in Crisis,* edited by Barry N. Siegel, pp. 137–56. Cambridge, MA: Ballinger Press.

Hume, David. 1752a. "Of Money." In David Hume, *Essays Moral, Political, and Literary.* Reprinted in David Hume, *Writings on Economics,* edited and introduction by E. Rotwein, pp. 33–46. Madison: University of Wisconsin Press, 1955.

1752b. "Of the Balance of Trade." In David Hume, *Essays Moral, Political, and Literary.* Reprinted in David Hume, *Writings on Economics,* edited and introduction by E. Rotwein, pp. 60–77. Madison: University of Wisconsin Press, 1955.

References

Humphrey, Thomas M. 1981. "Adam Smith and the Monetary Approach to the Balance of Payments." *Federal Reserve Bank of Richmond Economic Review* 67 (November/December): 3–10.

Jevons, William Stanley. 1875. *Money and the Mechanism of Exchange.* London: H. S. King.

    1884. *Investigations in Currency and Finance.* Edited by H. S. Foxwell. London: Macmillan.

Johnson, Harry G. 1971. "The Keynesian Revolution and the Monetarist Counterrevolution." *American Economic Review* 61(2): 1–14. Reprinted in Harry G. Johnson, *Further Essays in Monetary Economics,* pp. 50–64. London: George Allen and Unwin, 1972.

    1972a. *Inflation and the Monetarist Controversy.* Amsterdam: North Holland.

    1972b. "Political Economy Aspects of International Monetary Reform." *Journal of International Economics* 2(4): 401–23.

Johnson, Harry G., and Elizabeth L. Johnson. 1976. *The Shadow of Keynes.* Chicago: University of Chicago Press.

Johnston, R. B. 1982. *The Economics of the Euro-Market: History, Theory, and Policy.* London: Macmillan.

Jonung, Lars. 1987. "The Economics of Private Money: The Experience of Private Notes in Sweden, 1831–1902." Manuscript, University of Lund Economics Department.

Joplin, Thomas. 1823. *Outlines of a System of Political Economy.* Reprinted. New York: Augustus M. Kelley, 1970.

Kahn, Richard F. 1931. "The Relation of Home Investment to Unemployment." *Economic Journal* 41(2): 173–98.

Kaldor, Nicholas. 1982. *The Scourge of Monetarism.* Oxford: Oxford University Press.

Kane, Edward J. 1985. *The Gathering Crisis in Federal Deposit Insurance.* Cambridge, MA: MIT Press.

Karaken, John. 1983a. "The First Step in Bank Deregulation: What about FDIC?" *American Economic Review* 73(2): 198–203.

    1983b. "Deposit Insurance Reform, or Deregulation Is the Cart Not the Horse." *Federal Reserve Bank of Minneapolis Quarterly Review,* Spring, pp. 1–9.

Karaken, John, and Neil Wallace. 1981. "On the Indeterminacy of Equilibrium Exchange Rates." *Quarterly Journal of Economics* 96(2): 207–22.

Keynes, John Maynard. 1919. *The Economic Consequences of the Peace.* London. Reprinted in *The Collected Writings of John Maynard Keynes,* Vol. II. London: Royal Economic Society, 1971.

    1923. *A Tract on Monetary Reform.* London: Macmillan. Reprinted in *The Collected Writings of John Maynard Keynes,* Vol. IV. London: Royal Economic Society, 1971.

    1925. *The Economic Consequences of Mr. Churchill.* Reprinted in *The Collected Writings of John Maynard Keynes,* Vol. IX, pp. 207–30. London: Royal Economic Society, 1972.

    1930. *A Treatise on Money.* London: Macmillan. Reprinted in *The Collected Writings of John Maynard Keynes,* Vols. V–VI. London: Royal Economic Society, 1971.

    1931a. *Essays in Persuasion.* London: Macmillan. Reprinted in *The Collected Writings of John Maynard Keynes,* Vol. IX. London: Royal Economic Society, 1972.

    1931b. "Economic Notes on Free Trade II: A Revenue Tariff and the Cost of

References

Living." *New Statesman and Nation,* April 4. Reprinted in *The Collected Writings of John Maynard Keynes,* Vol. XX, pp. 498–505. London: Royal Economic Society, 1981.

1936. *The General Theory of Employment, Interest and Money.* London: Macmillan. Reprinted in *The Collected Writings of John Maynard Keynes,* Vol. XII. London: Royal Economic Society, 1973.

Kindleberger, Charles. 1984. *A Financial History of Western Europe.* London: George Allen and Unwin.

King, Robert G. 1983. "The Economics of Private Currencies." *Journal of Monetary Economics* 12(1): 127–58.

Klein, Benjamin. 1974. "The Competitive Supply of Money." *Journal of Money, Credit, and Banking* 6(4): 423–53.

1976. "The Social Costs of the Recent Inflation: The Mirage of Steady 'Anticipated' Inflation." *Carnegie-Rochester Series on Public Policy* 3: 185–212.

Knapp, Georg F. 1905. *Die Staatliche Theorie des Geeldes.* Abridged edition, translated and printed in English as *The State Theory of Money.* London: Macmillan,, 1924.

Kraay, C. M. 1964. "Hoards, Small Change, and the Origin of Coinage." *Journal of Hellenic Studies* 84: 76–91.

Kydland, Finn E., and Edward C. Prescott. 1977. "Rules Rather Than Discretion: The Inconsistency of Optimal Plans." *Journal of Political Economy* 85(3): 473–92.

Laffer, Arthur, and Charles Kadlec. 1981. "The Point of Linking the Dollar to Gold." *Wall Street Journal,* October 13.

Laidler, David. 1981. "Adam Smith as a Monetary Economist." *Canadian Journal of Economics* 14(2): 185–200.

1987. "Thornton, Henry." In, *The New Palgrave,* edited by John Eatwell, Murray Milgate, and Peter Newman, Vol IV, pp. 633–36. New York: Stockton.

Lane, Frederic C. 1937. "Venetian Bankers, 1496–1533: A Study in the Early Stages of Deposit Banking." *Journal of Political Economy* 45(2): 187–206.

Lange, Oskar. 1942. "Say's Law: A Restatement and Criticism." In *Studies in Mathematical Economics and Econometrics,* edited by O. Lange, F. McIntyre, and T. O. Yntema, pp. 49–68. Chicago: University of Chicago Press.

Lehrman, Lewis. 1985. "Protectionism, Inflation, or Monetary Reform: The Case for Fixed Exchange Rates and a Modernized Gold Standard." Memorandum for Morgan Stanley Investment Research, New York.

Leijonhufvud, Axel. 1968. *On Keynesian Economics and the Economics of Keynes.* New York: Oxford University Press.

1975. "Costs and Consequences of Inflation." In *The Microeconomic Foundations of Macroeconomics,* edited by G. C. Harcourt. London: Macmillan. Reprinted in Axel Leijohufvud, *Inflation and Coordination,* pp. 227–69. New York: Oxford University Press, 1981.

1987. "Constitutional Constraints on the Monetary Powers of Government." In *The Search for Stable Money: Essays on Monetary Reform,* edited by James A. Dorn and Anna J. Schwartz, pp. 129–43. Chicago: University of Chicago Press.

Litan, Robert. 1987. *What Should Banks Do?* Washington, D.C.: Brookings Institution.

Longfield, Samuel Mountifort. 1840. "Banking and Currency" (Parts I–IV). *Dublin University Magazine* 15: 3–15, 218–33; 16: 371–89, 611–20.

References

Lucas, Robert E. 1976. "Econometric Policy Evaluations: A Critique." In *The Phillips Curve and Labor Markets,* edited by Karl Brunner and Allan Meltzer, pp. 19–46. Amsterdam: North Holland. Reprinted in Robert E. Lucas, *Studies in Business-Cycle Theory,* pp. 104–30. Cambridge, MA: MIT Press, 1981.

Macaulay, Thomas B. 1914. *The History of England.* London: Macmillan.

McCallum, Bennett T. 1984. "Credibility and Monetary Policy." In *Price Stability and Public Policy: A Symposium Sponsored by the Federal Reserve Bank of Kansas City,* pp. 105–28. Kansas City, MO: Federal Reserve Bank of Kansas City.

McCloskey, Donald N. 1983. "The Rhetoric of Economics." *Journal of Economic Literature* 21(2): 381–417.

   1985. *The Rhetoric of Economics.* Madison: WI: University of Wisconsin Press.

McCloskey, Donald N., and J. Richard Zecher. 1976. "How the Gold Standard Worked, 1880–1913." In *The Monetary Approach to the Balance of Payments,* edited by J. A. Frenkel and H. G. Johnson, pp. 357–85. Toronto: University of Toronto Press.

McCulloch, J. R. 1831. *Historical Sketch of the Bank of England: With an Examination of the Question as to the Prolongation of the Exclusive Privileges of That Establishment.* London: Longmans.

Machlup, Fritz. 1970. "Euro-Dollar Creation: A Mystery Story." *Banca Nazionale del Lavoro Quarterly Review* 23(94): 219–60.

Maitland, Frederic W. 1908. *The Constitutional History of England.* Cambridge: Cambridge University Press.

Meltzer, Allan H. 1981. "Comments on 'Monetarist Interpretations of the Great Depression.'" In *The Great Depression Revisited,* edited by Karl Brunner, pp. 148–64. Boston: Martinus Nijhoff.

Menger, Carl. 1871. *Grundsatze der Volkwirtschaftslehre.* Translated and printed in English as *Principles of Economics.* New York: New York University Press, 1981.

   1892. "On the Origin of Money." *Economics Journal* 2(2): 239–55.

Mints, Lloyd. 1945. *A History of Banking Theory.* Chicago: University of Chicago Press.

Mises, Ludwig von. 1912. *Theories des Geldes und der Umlaufsmittel.* Translated and printed in English as *The Theory of Money and Credit.* London: Jonathan Cape, 1934. Reprinted. Indianapolis: Liberty Press, 1979.

Miskimin, Harry A. 1984. *Money and Power in Fifteenth Century France.* New Haven: Yale University Press.

Mommsen, Theodore. 1860. *Geschichte des Romische Munzwesen.* Leipzig, 1860.

Mundell, Robert. 1981. "Gold Would Serve into the 21st Century." *Wall Street Journal,* September 30.

Newcomb, Simon. 1879. "The Standard of Value." *North American Review* 129:233–37.

Niehans, Jurg. 1984. *International Monetary Theory.* Baltimore: Johns Hopkins University Press.

Nurkse, Ragnar. 1944. *International Currency Experience.* Geneva: League of Nations.

O'Brien, Denis P. 1975. *The Classical Economists.* Oxford: Clarendon Press.

Officer, Lawrence. 1986. "The Efficiency of the Dollar-Sterling Gold Standard, 1890–1908." *Journal of Political Economy* 94(5): 1038–73.

Palyi, Melchior. 1972. *The Twilight of Gold.* Chicago: Henry Regnery.

Patinkin, Don. 1961. "Financial Intermediaries and the Logical Structure of

References

Monetary Theory." *American Economic Review* 51(1): 95–116. Reprinted in Don Patinkin, *Studies in Monetary Theory*, pp. 31–54. New York: Harper and Row, 1972.

1965. *Money, Interest and Prices*. 2nd edition. New York: Harper and Row.

Peltzman, S. 1965. "Entry in Commercial Banking." *Journal of Law and Economics*. 8:11–50.

Pennington, James. 1826. "First Memorandum to Huskisson: Observations on the Private Banking Establishments of the Metropolis." In *The Economic Writings of James Pennington*, edited and introduction by R. S. Sayers, pp. xlv–li. London: London School of Economics, 1963.

Phelps, Edmund S. 1972. *Inflation Policy and Unemployment Theory*. New York: W. W. Norton.

Phillips, A. W. 1958. "The Relation between Unemployment and the Rate of Change in Money Wage Rates in the United Kingdom, 1861–1957." *Economica* 25(4): 283–99.

Radford, R. A. 1945. "The Economic Organization of a P.O.W. Camp." *Economica*, n.s. 12 (November): 189–201.

Reynolds, Alan. 1983. "Why Gold?" *Cato Journal* 3(1): 211–32.

———. 1984. "Gold and Economic Boom: Five Case Studies, 1792–1926." In *Money in Crisis*, edited by Barry N. Siegel, pp. 249–68. Cambridge, MA: Ballinger Press.

Reynolds, Robert L. 1938. "A Business Affair in Genoa in the Year 1200: Banking, Bookkeeping, a Broker, and a Lawsuit." In *Studi di storia e diritto in onore di Enrico Besta*, edited by A. Giuffrè, Vol. II, pp. 165–81. Milan.

Ricardo, David. 1809. "The Price of Gold: Three Contributions to the *Morning Chronicle*." Reprinted in *The Works and Correspondence of David Ricardo*, edited by Piero Sraffa, Vol. III, pp. 13–46. Cambridge: Cambridge University Press, 1951.

———. 1810–11. *The High Price of Bullion*. London: John Murray. Reprinted in *The Works and Correspondence of David Ricardo*, edited by Piero Sraffa, Vol. III, pp. 47–127. Cambridge: Cambridge University Press, 1951.

———. 1952a. *The Works and Correspondence of David Ricardo*, edited by Piero Sraffa, Vol. VI. Cambridge: Cambridge University Press.

———. 1952b. *The Works and Correspondence of David Ricardo*, edited by Piero Sraffa, Vol. IX. Cambridge: Cambridge University Press.

Richards, Richard D. 1929. *The Early History of Banking in England*. London: P. S. King. Reprinted. New York: Augustus M. Kelley, 1965.

Robbins, Lionel C. 1934. *The Great Depression*. London: Macmillan.

Robertson, Dennis H. 1926. *Banking Policy and the Price Level*. London: P. S. King.

———. 1931. "Mr. Keynes' Theory of Money." *Economic Journal* 4(3): 395–411.

———. 1948. *Money*. 4th edition. New York: Pittman.

Rockoff, Hugh. 1975. *The Free Banking Era: A Reconsideration*. New York: Arno Press.

———. 1984. "Some Evidence on the Real Price of Gold, Its Costs of Production, and Commodity Prices." In *A Retrospective on the Classical Gold Standard, 1821–1931*, edited by Michael D. Bordo and Anna J. Schwartz, pp. 613–44. Chicago: University of Chicago Press.

Rolnick, Arthur J., and Warren E. Weber. 1983. "New Evidence on the Free Banking Era." *American Economic Review* 73(5): 1080–91.

References

1984. "The Causes of Free Bank Failures: A Detailed Examination." *Journal of Monetary Economics* 14(3): 267–91.

1986. "Gresham's Law or Gresham's Fallacy?" *Journal of Political Economy* 94(2): 186–201.

1988. "Explaining the Demand for Free Bank Notes." *Journal of Monetary Economics* 21(1): 47–71.

Rothbard, Murray. 1963. *America's Great Depression.* Princeton: Van Nostrand.

Rueff, Jacques. 1925. "Les Variations du chomage en Angleterre." *Revue Politique et Parliamentaire* 125 (December 10): 425–36.

1931. "L'Assurance chomage cause du chomage permanent." *Revue Economique Politique* 45 (March/April): 211–41.

1947. "The Fallacies of Lord Keynes' General Theory." *Quarterly Journal of Economics* 51(2): 343–67.

Samuelson, Paul A. 1969. "The Non-Optimality of Money Holding under Laissez-Faire." *Canadian Journal of Economics* 2(2): 303–08.

Samuelson, Paul A., and Robert M. Solow. 1960. "Analytical Aspects of Anti-Inflation Policy." *American Economic Review* 50(2): 177–94.

Sargent, Thomas J. 1986. *Rational Expectations and Inflation.* New York: Harper and Row.

Sargent, Thomas J., and Neil Wallace. 1976. "Rational Expectations and the Theory of Economic Policy." *Journal of Monetary Economics* 2(2): 169–83.

Say, J. B. 1880. *A Treatise on Political Economy.* 4th edition. Philadelphia. Reprinted. New York: Augustus M. Kelley, 1971.

Schumpeter, Joseph. 1954. *The History of Economic Analysis.* New York: Oxford University Press.

Scott, Kenneth. 1987. "The Defective Design of Federal Deposit Insurance." *Contemporary Policy Issues* 5(1): 92–99.

Selgin, George. 1988. *The Theory of Free Banking.* Totowa, NJ: Rowman and Littlefield.

Selgin, George, and L. H. White. 1987. "The Evolution of a Free Banking System." *Economic Inquiry.* 25(3): 439–58.

Shackle, G. L. S. 1967. *The Years of High Theory.* Cambridge: Cambridge University Press.

Shearer, Ronald A., and Carolyn Clark. 1984. "Canada and the Interwar Gold Standard, 1920–35: Monetary Policy without a Central Bank." In *A Retrospective on the Classical Gold Standard, 1821–1931*, edited by Michael D. Bordo and Anna J. Schwartz, pp. 277–308. Chicago: University of Chicago Press.

Short, Eugenie D., and Gerald P. O'Driscoll. 1983. "Deregulation and Deposit Insurance." *Federal Reserve Bank of Dallas Economic Review,* September, pp. 11–22.

Smith, Adam. 1776. *The Wealth of Nations.* Reprinted. New York: Modern Library, 1937.

Smith, Vera C. 1936. *The Rationale of Central Banking.* London: P. S. King.

Sowell, Thomas. 1972. *Say's Law: An Historical Analysis.* Princeton: Princeton University Press.

Strange, Susan. 1986. *Casino Capitalism.* New York: Basil Blackwell.

Taussig, Frank W. 1927. *International Trade.* New York: Macmillan.

References

Temin, Peter. 1976. *Did Monetary Forces Cause the Great Depression?* New York: W. W. Norton.

Thompson, Earl A. 1974a. "The Theory of Money and Income Consistent with Orthodox Value Theory." In *Trade, Stability and Macroeconomics*, edited by G. Horwich and P. A. Samuelson, pp. 427–53. New York: Academic Press.

1974b. "Taxation and National Defense." *Journal of Political Economy* 82(4): 755–82.

1978. "A Reformulation of Macroeconomic Theory." Manuscript, UCLA Economics Department.

1979. "An Economic Basis for the 'National Defense' Argument for Aiding Certain Industries." *Journal of Political Economy* 87(1): 1–36.

1981. "Free Banking under a Labor Standard." Prepared for the U.S. Gold Commission. Manuscript, UCLA Economics Department.

1986. "A Perfect Monetary System." Paper presented at the Liberty Fund/ Manhattan Institute Conference on Competitive Monetary Regimes, New York.

Thornton, Henry. 1802. *An Enquiry into the Nature and Effects of the Paper Credit of Great Britain.* Reprinted with an introduction by F. A. Hayek. London: George Allen and Unwin, 1939. Reprinted. New York: Augustus M. Kelley, 1969.

Timberlake, Richard H. 1984. "The Central Banking Role of Clearinghouse Associations." *Journal of Money, Credit, and Banking* 16(1): 1–15.

Tobin, James. 1948. "The Fallacies of Lord Keynes' *General Theory:* Comment." *Quarterly Journal of Economics* 62(4): 763–70.

1963. "Commercial Banks as Creators of Money." In *Banking and Monetary Studies*, edited by D. Carson, pp. 408–19. Homewood, IL: Irwin.

1980. "Discussion." In *Models of Monetary Economics*, edited by John H. Karaken and Neil Wallace, pp. 83–90. Minneapolis: Federal Reserve Bank of Minneapolis.

1982. Discussion of a paper by Alan Blinder. In *Monetary Policy in the 1980s*, pp. 41–46. Kansas City, MO: Federal Reserve Bank of Kansas City.

Tooke, Thomas, and William Newmarch. 1857. *A History of Prices and of the State of the Circulation from 1792 to 1856.* Vol. VI. London.

Torrens, Robert. 1837. *Letter to the Right Honourable Lord Viscount Melbourne.* London.

Triffin, Robert. 1958. *Gold and the Dollar Crisis.* New Haven: Yale University Press.

United Kingdom. Parliament. 1918. *First Interim Report of the Committee on Currency and Foreign Exchanges after the War.* Cmnd. 9182. Reprinted. New York: Arno Press, 1979.

United States Gold Commission. 1982. *Report to the Congress of the Commission on the Role of Gold in the Domestic and International Monetary Systems.* Washington, DC: The Commission.

Ure, P. N. 1922. *The Origin of Tyranny.* Cambridge: Cambridge University Press.

Usher, Abbot P. 1943. *The Early History of Deposit Banking in Mediterranean Europe.* Cambridge, MA: Harvard University Press.

Vilar, Pierre. 1969. *A History of Gold and Money, 1450–1920.* London: Verso. New edition, 1984.

References

Viner, Jacob. 1937a. *Studies in the Theory of International Trade.* New York: Harper and Brothers. Reprinted. New York: Augustus M. Kelley, 1965.

    1937b. "Mr. Keynes on the Causes of Unemployment." *Quarterly Journal of Economics* 51: 147–67.

Wallace, Neil. 1983. "A Legal Restrictions Theory of the Demand for 'Money' and the Role of Monetary Policy." *Federal Reserve Bank of Minneapolis Quarterly Review* 7(1): 1–7.

Wanniski, Jude. 1978. *The Way the World Works.* New York: Basic Books.

Whale, P. Barret. 1937. "The Workings of the Pre-War Gold Standard." *Economica* n.s. 4(1): 18–32.

Wheatley, John. 1807, 1822. *An Essay on the Theory of Money and Principles of Commerce.* Vols. I and II. London.

White, Lawrence H. 1984. *Free Banking in Britain: Theory, Experience, Debate, 1800–1845.* Cambridge: Cambridge University Press.

Yeager, Leland B. 1968. "Essential Properties of a Medium of Exchange." *Kyklos* 21(1): 45–69.

    1978. "What Are Banks?" *Atlantic Economic Journal* 6(4): 1–14.

    1984. "The Image of the Gold Standard." In *A Retrospective on the Classical Gold Standard, 1821–1931,* edited by Michael D. Bordo and Anna J. Schwartz, pp. 651–69. Chicago: University of Chicago Press.

Index

abstract monetary unit(s), 9, 161
accounting, 22
Act of Union, 37
activist monetary policy: and exchange
   rates, 241–42; undesirability of, 206,
   207–09, 213–14, 225–26
Addison, Joseph, 35
Alaska, 99
Amsterdam, 33
antitrust legislation, 244
arbitrage, 100, 112, 232; international,
   242; mechanism(s) for, 232–33, 234
Aridor, Yoram, 31–32
Aristotle, 4
asset portfolios, 78n8, 107, 196; risky,
   184
assets (bank), 13, 21, 32, 65–66, 90, 111,
   164, 188–89; book value/market value,
   186, 201–02; composition of, 103; illiquid, 197, 198; liquidation of, 15–16;
   risky, 182; value of, 189
assets (economic): unproductive use of,
   211–12
Australia: gold discoveries, 85, 86–89, 98
Austria: collapse of banking system, 138;
   see also Credit Anstalt
Austria-Hungary, 42, 99, 110
Austrian School, 128–29, 131, 132

Bagehot, Walter, 74; *Lombard Street,* 84,
   106
Baker, James, 229
balance of payments, 94, 158
balance of trade, 24–25, 74, 100
balance sheets (bank), 14–15, 15f, 18–19,
   201–02
balanced budgets, 43, 147
Bank Charter Act (England), x, 37, 41,
   64, 71, 79, 81–84, 85, 89, 90, 101,

155, 178, 214, 217; permission for
   Bank of England to violate, 106–07
bank charters (U.S.), 36–37, 156–57
bank failures, 126, 157, 205; and deposit
   insurance, 185–87, 188–89, 191–92,
   193; England, 77; in Great Depression,
   128, 129, 130–31
bank holidays, 126
bank money, 22, 34, 70, 182; amount of,
   adjusts to demand for, 70; currency distinct from, 174–75, 176–77; Middle
   Ages, 25
Bank of Amsterdam, 33
Bank of Deposit, 32–33
Bank of England, 41, 64, 71, 77–78, 81,
   97, 115, 119, 138; and Bullionist Controversies, 74–75; establishment of,
   34–36; gold devices, 104n6; gold drain,
   71–72; gold reserves, 76–77, 78, 79–
   80, 97, 101, 106, 224n10; interventions
   by, 93; as lender of last resort, 84,
   106–07; monopoly privileges of, 37,
   79, 90; note issues, 96, 101, 217; reor-
   ganization of, 82–84; responsibility for
   banking system stability, 73, 78, 80;
   and restoration of convertibility, 76–
   77; suspension of convertibility, 125–
   26
Bank of France, 115, 119, 120, 121, 123,
   136; gold reserves, 127
Bank of Italy, 37
bank runs, 101, 190, 201, 203; contagious, 189, 191, 194, 199–201; deposit
   insurance and prevention of, 195
banking: economies of scale in, 13; emergence of, 8–13, 44; entry into, 156–57,
   183, 184; evolution of, 1–26; medieval,
   9, 22–25; and state monopoly over
   money, 32–34, 36; suppression of, 32–
   33; unregulated, 36–37; *see also* com-

Index

convertibility (cont.)
price level through indirect, 230–36, 240, 247; suspension of, 34, 107, 110, 200, 201; suspension of, in England, 42, 71–80, 125–26; and value of money, 52, 53
copper, 7; coins, 95
corporate takeovers, 212
cost/price relation, 53
costs: of banking, 13, 17, 20, 22, 23; of borrowing, 65; of holding commodities, 6, 7; of holding money, 9, 10, 26, 49–50; of inflation, 210; of money production, 7, 12, 27–28, 44; of participating in political process, 211; of price-level uncertainty, 227; of producing gold, 85; production, 53; of regulation, 183; of reserve requirements, 169; of trading, 6, 7, 8–9, 26
counterfeiting, 31, 77
country banks (England), 71n2, 77, 78–79, 80, 81, 82, 90
credit, 77–78, 106, 220; inflationary expansion of, 34, 128–29; with money changers, 10; transferable, 9n5, 10, 11
Credit Anstalt, 125
credit cards, 167, 168
Croesus, 30
Cromwell, Oliver, 34
Cunliffe Committee: *Interim Report,* 115–16, 131
currency(ies), 28, 94, 157; bank denominated, 176; confidence in, 42–43, 246n9; demand for, 155, 190, 199–200, 205, 216, 229–30; distinct from bank money, 174–75; inelastic, 107; and monetary stability, 80–81; multiple, 9; non-interest-bearing, 238; overvalued (LDCs), 246n9; stable, 245, 248; transfers, 93; value of, 230–31, 242–44; *see also* debasement (currency); international currency; national currencies
currency parities: fixed, 242
Currency Principle, 80–81
currency reform of 1717 (England), 97
Currency School, 81, 82, 83, 89, 90, 155, 178

Darmstadter Bank, 125
Davanzatti, Bernardo, 4n2
de Cecco, Marcello, 41n6
de Roover, Raymond, 10n6
debasement (currency), 31, 32, 38–39, 41–42, 50, 54; anticipation of, 38–39; restorations of, 43, 76, 97

default(s), 165, 189; risk of, 25, 196, 197
deflation, 67, 68, 99, 114, 116, 128, 136, 147, 175, 245; in bank runs, 200, 201; and bankruptcy, 190; deposit insurance and, 195; effect on wages and employment, 150; in England, 76–77, 116–17, 118–19, 135, 138, 139; expectations of, 124–25, 126; and full employment, 140; gold movements and, 122; gold prices and, 127; gold standard and, 105; in Great Depression, 223; in 1920–21, 113, 116, 117, 135; policies causing rapid, 68; U.S. responsibility for, 122, 130
demand: aggregate, 148, 149, 173, 174
demand deposits: Eurodollars held as, 163; non-interest-bearing, 167–68; prohibition of interest on, 156, 182
demand for currency, 155, 205, 216; in bank runs, 190, 199–200; instability of, 229–30; *see* demand for high-powered money
demand for gold, 67–68, 113, 114, 115, 122, 223–24; and Great Depression, 127–28, 129–30; in international financial collapse, 124; and World War I inflation, 110–11, 112
demand for high-powered money, 166, 169–70; *see* demand for currency
demand for liquidity, 124, 125, 217, 218, 219
demand for money, 55, 67, 89, 205, 216; banking system adjusts to, 62–63; and gold reserves, 67–68, 126; interest rate equates with supply, 171, 172–74 (*see also* spread[s]); and Monetarist rule, 217; and money supply, 143–45, 148; shifts between notes and deposits in, 104–06, 107
democratization, 41, 44
deposit creation, x, 28, 44, 173; under competition, 56, 57, 58, 155–56; costless, 17–18, 19, 20, 21; obligation created by, 188–89; unrestricted, 163–64; for wartime revenue, 34
deposit insurance, *see* federal deposit insurance
depository institutions, 202; competitive pressures on, 170–71; financial instruments offered by, 167–68; market value of, 187
Depository Institutions Deregulation and Monetary Control Act (DIDMCA) (U.S.), 170
Depository Institutions Deregulation Committee (U.S.), 170–71